Folk Visions & Voices

EST. 75 1938
YEARS
THE UNIVERSITY OF GEORGIA PRESS 2013

Folk Visions & Voices

TRADITIONAL MUSIC AND SONG IN NORTH GEORGIA

Field collecting, text, drawings and paintings by Art Rosenbaum.

Photographs by Margo Newmark Rosenbaum. Musical transcriptions by Béla Foltin, Jr.

Foreword by Pete Seeger.

The University of Georgia Press   Athens

The original publication of this book was made possible in part by a grant from the University of Georgia Research Foundation. Their assistance is gratefully acknowledged. Publication of this reprint edition was supported in part by the Kenneth Coleman Series in Georgia History and Culture.

Paperback edition, 2013
© 1983 by the University of Georgia Press
Athens, Georgia 30602
www.ugapress.org
All rights reserved
Designed by Sandra Strother Hudson
Set in Century Old Style with Windsor Old Style display
Printed and bound by Thomson-Shore

The paper in this book meets the guidelines for permanence and durability of the Committee on Production Guidelines for Book Longevity of the Council on Library Resources.

Printed in the United States of America
17   16   15   14   13   P   5   4   3   2   1

The Library of Congress has cataloged the hardcover edition of this book as follows:

Folk visions & voices : traditional music and song in North Georgia / field collecting, text, drawings, and paintings by Art Rosenbaum; photographs by Margo N. Rosenbaum; musical transcriptions by Béla Folton, Jr.; foreword by Pete Seeger.
   xv p., 240 p. of music, [4] p. of plates; illus. (some col.) 22 × 27 cm.
   Principally melodies with chord symbols, in part with banjo or guitar tablature; includes fiddle tunes.
   Includes bibliography.
   1. Folk music—Georgia. 2. Folk-songs, English—Georgia. 3. Fiddle tunes.
4. Georgia—Songs and music. I. Rosenbaum, Art.
M1629.7.G4F64 1983   83-6473

Paperback ISBN-13: 978-0-8203-4613-7
ISBN-10: 0-8203-4613-6

Frontispiece: *Dilmus Hall with His Devil and Drunkards Sculpture, Athens.* (Charcoal, 22" × 30", 1980. Collection of John and Gail Enns.)

Contents

Foreword

WHAT WILL HAPPEN to this fine collection of old songs remembered in the northern counties of the State of Georgia U.S.A.? Will it gather dust on library shelves? No. *Folk Visions and Voices* reads like a good historical novel. One gets immersed in the "collecting," in the people and their families, and in their lives. It's an invitation to learn more about north Georgia through music and song.

Some folklorists have dug up dead bones from one graveyard to bury them in another. But if the good people of Georgia take this book off the shelf from time to time—and I'm sure they will—they'll have many a wonderful evening leafing through it. They will learn how their forefathers and foremothers lived and thought. If they are fortunate enough to know someone who can read music notation they'll learn some beautiful melodies, rhythms, and instrumental accompaniments. Who knows? Some of these old songs and stories may become popular favorites again in your home, as they once were popular favorites with others.

Popular favorites? Yes. Not in the sense of a "top forty" record which is heard for a few days and then (mercifully) never heard of again, but in the life of each person or each family or group that likes to make their own entertainment. These are *real* popular favorites, often known only to those who sing and play them. Then, as people travel and families move apart, they carry their good memories with them across the land or the ocean. Years later, these songs or stories inspire someone else. And maybe in a future century some talented and dedicated folklorists like the Rosenbaums will collect them all over again—perhaps on microtape for the solar system's central library.

A future century? Who knows if we will be able to put the nuclear genie back in the bottle? Who knows if we can teach technocrats that before novel chemistry poisons us all we must discipline the inventors and the manufacturers, as well as the users, of dangerous inventions?

This book can help in the struggle. "Think globally, act locally." Some of the songs may be dangerous, too. Who is to decide? You. The reader, the singer, the storyteller, the fiddler or banjo picker. If we do our job right, there *will* be people in future centuries. They will carry on traditions of homemade music. When we are pushing up the daisies, our children's children's children, playing among those daisies, will be singing some of these songs.

PETE SEEGER

Beacon, New York
December 1982

Acknowledgments

I MUST START by crediting my wife and collaborator, Margo N. Rosenbaum, with the overall conception of *Folk Visions and Voices:* the combining in exhibition and ultimately in book form a photographic, audio, graphic, and painted presentation of the sounds, faces, and stories of the people who were carrying on the musical traditions of north Georgia in the late 1970s and early 1980s.

Special thanks to my colleague Ed Lambert in the Department of Art, University of Georgia, for making it possible for us to mount the first presentation of *Folk Visions and Voices* at the off-campus Image Gallery, which he directed. Doc Barnes and the Gospel Chorus were guests at the opening in 1978. Doc was surprised to see the old cotton warehouse, where he had loaded cotton many a time for a dollar a day, converted into an art gallery—he sang a little and talked about how we should help each other inch a little higher. Later, the great American painter Philip Guston came to the show. At the time I had completed numerous drawings, but there were only three paintings in the presentation, and Guston told me I "had a lot of painting to do."

Thanks to Frank Ruzicka, head of the Department of Art, University of Georgia, for continued encouragement and for support in the form of two summer faculty research grants. Special appreciation to my colleague Robert Clements, for helping to bring this work to the attention of the National Endowment for the Arts, and to the Folk Arts Division of NEA, especially its director, Bess Lomax Hawes, for the support of the ongoing fieldwork and presentation of the material in 1978–80.

The culminating exhibition of *Folk Visions and Voices* took place at Nexus, Incorporated, Third Floor Gallery, in late 1980. Thanks to the director, Janie Geiser, for arranging the show, and to her succes-sor, Michael Gaston, for seeing it through, as well as to Pat Dowdy and the rest of the gallery staff, and the Atlanta Department of Cultural Affairs, whose support was invaluable.

Professor Harry Oster of the University of Iowa and Professor John Cohen of the State University of New York at Purchase visited us in Georgia as consultants on the project. Their encouragement and suggestions, particularly Harry's on fieldwork and John's on the complex questions of developing a synergy of folkloristic and artistic concerns, were essential to the development of the fieldwork and new presentation modes.

Thanks to our two research assistants, Fred Hay from Toccoa in northeast Georgia and Joel Cordle from Summerville in northwest Georgia, for their contacts, leads, spadework, and information about their home areas. We are especially appreciative of Joel's discovery of W. Guy Bruce in Trion, and of Fred's introducing us to his old friend Jake Staggers in Toccoa.

Special thanks to my close associate in the Georgia Folklore Society, its present president, George Mitchell, for sharing generously of his vast experience in doing fieldwork in Georgia; for encouraging many of our "finds" by bringing them to a wider audience at the Georgia Grassroots Festival and its successor, the Georgia Folklife Festival; and for his helpful suggestions on questions of fieldwork, photography, and presentation.

Professor John Garst of the University of Georgia provided detailed and helpful information in the area of white spirituals and shape-note hymns, as did Professor Gene Wiggins of North Georgia College in questions relating to early commercial recording in Georgia.

Special thanks go to our colleague, Béla Foltin, Jr., ethnomusicologist and head of the Fine Arts and Media Division, University of Georgia Libraries, for his accurate and singable transcriptions of the musical performances from our field tapes; he also devoted countless hours to the music autography for this book. And our work, and Béla Foltin's, was aided immeasurably by the work of Randy Camp of the Media Division of the University of Georgia Libraries, in indexing the field recordings and in tape preparation and duplication. And thanks to Neil Rosenbaum for helping with the sound recording on numerous field trips.

At this writing two LPs of our north Georgia recordings have been released: the Flyright Company of Sussex, England, issued *Goin' to Georgia: The Eller Brothers and Ross Brown* (Flyright 546); and Folkways Records issued *Down Yonder: Old-Time String Band Music from Georgia with Gordon Tanner, Joe Miller, and John Patterson* (Folkways FTS 31089). We thank Bruce Bastin of Flyright and Moe Asch of Folkways for their interest in these performers. The chapters on the Eller and the Tanner circles of musicians were expanded from my annotations of these records. Thanks to all those, too numerous to list, who, knowing our interest, have suggested, and continue to suggest, that we look up such and such a fiddler, such and such a gospel singer.

And finally, the greatest appreciation must go to the traditional singers and musicians of north Georgia who worked with us on this project. We met them as interested strangers, but we were welcomed into their homes, churches, and social gatherings. They shared some of their most precious traditions with us, and in many cases we grew to be close friends. Black and white, sacred and secular musicians, they all combine together in the patchwork quilt that is *Folk Visions and Voices*. In a real sense this is their book.

Introduction

NORTH GEORGIA begins at the edge of the old rolling cotton-belt plantation country, along a line running roughly east and west through Atlanta; it extends up through the red clay hills, piney woods, and textile-mill towns of the Piedmont, into the Blue Ridge Mountains up to the borders of North Carolina and Tennessee. This varied landscape has given rise to and nurtured a variety of impressive musical traditions, emblematic of southern folk music, and well-springs of later American music. Among these are the stirring antebellum spirituals and lined-out hymns of black country churches, the old-time black frolic tunes and bottleneck blues, the bitter hammer-and-pick songs that helped build the railroads and highways, the ebullient dance music of the Piedmont fiddle bands, the mournful and tragic unaccompanied mountain ballads, the raucous backwoods banjo tunes and songs. Since the early part of this century, when these forms, though in flux and transition, were flourishing, great changes in communications and in the social and economic order have transformed their physical and human settings. One might wonder, as we did when we began field collecting in north Georgia in 1977, whether the sounds of these traditions might still be widely heard in mountain cabins, old-fashioned churches, and back-country dance halls; or whether they had been obliterated or changed beyond recognition as distinctive regional forms by the interstate highways that have sliced through the ridges and valleys of northwest Georgia, by the sprawl of shopping-center and condominium development out of Atlanta up into the mountains, and by the pervasive influence of gospel, pop, and country music via radio and television. We learned that these older folk styles had by no means vanished, although, with a few exceptions such as some traditional church practices, they were no longer central to community life. Indeed, we found exceptional examples of all the important older forms, and at times these seemed to have grown in strength and beauty in the struggle for survival. The people who have chosen to remember and continue to perform them emerge as extraordinary folk, usually older, individualistic and at times even eccentric, possessed of keen memories, authentic and exemplary performing styles, and a commitment to the "old-time way," not out of antiquarianism or nostalgia, but for reasons of personal and artistic choice.

Folk Visions and Voices was produced over several years of collecting this music across north Georgia, of interviewing the singers and musicians in order to learn about their lives and the part these traditions played in them over the years, and of developing a documentation in drawings, paintings, and photographs, of the people and their environments. The original mode of presentation was a traveling exhibition of the visual work, with a tape-recorded anthology of selections from the field recordings playing in the gallery. When possible, live performances were given by the people we had come to regard as our artistic collaborators rather than merely sources or informants. The culminating exhibition of the project at Nexus Incorporated's Third Floor Gallery in Atlanta in 1980 was opened with a two-day festival of the singing, playing, and dancing of most of the tradition bearers the reader will meet in this book.

Growing out of our field collecting and the exhibition, this book continues the original intentions of the project. A broad and diverse collection of north Georgia folk songs, ballads, instrumental music, and religious songs is presented in accurate transcriptions of melody

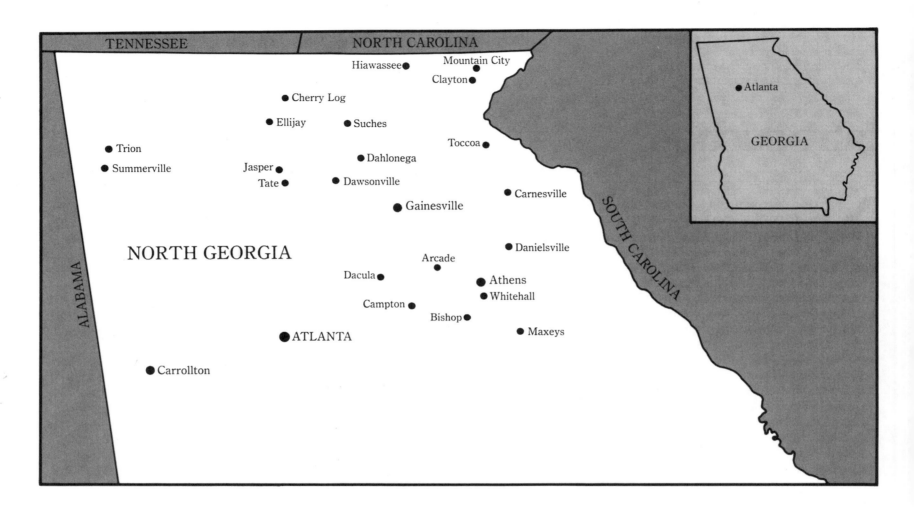

and text from field tapes. These examples are placed at the ends of chapters that center on a family, a performing group, an individual, or several individuals representing a given tradition. The drawings, paintings, and photographs complete the presentation.

We have emphasized the folk and their stories because we feel it is important to reveal in some depth the lives and attitudes of some of the exceptional people who have carried the older forms of folk music and culture into the last decades of the twentieth century. They provide this picture in their own words as much as possible, although the author is present as a first-person participant in the conversations. We feel it is a distortion to edit an interview, with its leading questions and interplay of two personalities, into a long monologue. Of necessity we have done some condensing and at times collating as we developed extensive interviews into biographical chapters; yet we have tried to preserve the flow and style of each person's way of expressing himself or herself, retaining the elements of dialect, emphasis, and even repetition to keep the characteristic flavor and style of the speech and thought of these diverse, highly articulate, and colorful people. We are writing in 1982, and we frame our observations in this present and recent past; yet we are well aware that time passes and circumstances change.

The musical examples were chosen from about two thousand items on our north Georgia field tapes. Because this book is intended to be a useful, even singable, introduction to the range of folk-music styles in the area, we have balanced a number of typical and familiar songs—variants of "John Henry," "Cindy," "Down Yonder," "Barbara Allen," "Goin' Down the Road Feelin' Bad"—with rarer pieces like "The Battle of the Boyne," "No Room at the Hotel," "Five to My Five," and others. A few recent compositions that show the vitality of song making have been included. This book is introductory and presentational rather than specialized and scholarly. Its depth should grow out of the richness of the intertwining of lives, songs, and images; we offer no sweeping new theses about such familiar categories as Anglo-American balladry, country blues, and traditional spirituals. Those wishing to explore the recorded material more deeply can study the indexed tape collection in the archives of the Georgia Folklore Society in the University of Georgia Libraries.

After the song title we give the Child designation if the song belongs to Francis Child's select number of traditional British ballads; we give the Laws number if the song was catalogued by G. Malcolm Laws as either an American ballad from British broadsides or a native American ballad. The headnotes give the performer, the location, and the date of the principal field recording from which the printed tune and text were transcribed. In a few cases additional verses from other recordings of the item by the same performer were used to make a more complete piece and to fulfill what would have been the intention of the informant; in no case were texts from more than one performer collated.

In addition the headnotes provide information about the informants' sources, when possible, and brief musicological comments, observations about style of performance, function of the piece in its context, and other remarks that will be helpful in understanding the material. The biographical and discographical references are limited;

they are intended to serve as touchstones to the major published versions of the items (with an emphasis on collections from nearby areas, such as the Brown collection from North Carolina) and to significant commercial and field sound recordings, both as sources and as interesting comparative material from the region. When at some time in the future a complete and definitive study of Georgia folk song and music is prepared, including published and unpublished collected material and all commercial and field recordings, the bibliographical and discographical references should follow the example of thoroughness set in a scholarly work such as Norm Cohen's study of American railroad songs, *Long Steel Rail* (1981). In his discussion of "Reuben's Train" (see "Seventy-four" and "Five Hundred Miles" in the present collection), Cohen includes 30 references to published and unpublished written examples, and a discography with 282 entries! This exemplary exhaustiveness is beyond the scope of the present collection.

It should be stressed again that this book is a presentation of traditional performers and their material as we found them in the late seventies and early eighties. If the past figures most importantly in the performers' biographies and our comments, it is because past generations and lifetimes have led up to what we heard in the Piedmont and mountains of Georgia when we were doing our fieldwork; but in no case was a song transcribed from an old record, an earlier collection, or even an old manuscript or sound recording in the possession of an informant. It is Ray Knight's place in the chain of tradition in 1982 that we offer here; it would have been possible to print transcriptions of Ray's tapes of his source for much of his material, the late fiddler L. D. Snipes, or of Snipes's source for some of his songs, the early recording artist of Fannin County, Fiddlin' John Carson. But these earlier pieces in the complex mosaic of tradition will have to be put in place in a future comprehensive study.

In our fieldwork we concentrated on the older Anglo-American and Afro-American traditions because we value them highly and feel an urgent need to recover them while it is still possible. We are aware of industrial and urban folklore and the folklore of newly arrived ethnic groups in Georgia, such as the Spanish-Americans and the Asians. We realize as well that folk music evolves constantly; that today's bluegrass, modern gospel, and urban blues developed from the country string band, the early spiritual, and the rural blues traditions; and that the older forms had even earlier precedents in the unrolling fabric of the tradition. Yet the coming of radio in the twenties marked a decisive turning point: while initially the popular "hillbilly" and "race" recordings and the activity of local groups in the early days of radio both documented and proliferated authentic regional folk music, nationally popular performers and styles progressively eroded local styles. Georgia was an important musical center in the early twenties: performers like Fiddlin' John Carson and the Skillet Lickers were making their pioneer country recordings; blues recording artists like Peg-Leg Howell and, later, Blind Willie McTell and Charlie Lincoln were emerging; and gospel and country groups were beginning to perform on the radio. Many of the contributors to the present collection either played an active role in or were influenced by the record and radio industries in the transitional period. The Dacula fiddler Gordon Tanner remembered the time in the early twenties when his father, Gid Tanner, was asked to record commercially the fiddle tunes he had grown up with in the rural Piedmont. Gid's records attained great popularity beyond the region, and when Gordon himself led his father's Skillet Lickers in "Down Yonder" and "Back Up and Push," these successful recordings went on to influence the playing and repertoire of virtually every fiddler from Maine to California. In turn, the music of performers like Jimmie Rodgers of Mississippi and the Carter Family of Virginia was finding its way to Georgia on the airwaves and on discs. Of course, books and printed music had played a part in disseminating and preserving some of the oldest British-American ballads over the centuries; and the nineteenth-century tent and minstrel shows drew upon, transformed, and renourished folk traditions across America. Yet radio, television, and recordings enormously accelerated the process of change, and, while one is always cautious about claiming to have gathered the last blossoms of a tradition, there will not be many more years when one will be able to meet active tradition bearers, inheritors of family and local styles, whose memories reach back before the wrenching changes wrought by modern communications. As much as we would wish the contrary, we cannot imagine that we shall meet many more mountain ballad singers like Maude Thacker or black banjo pickers like Jake Staggers. It is a testimony to the tenacity of the north Georgia traditions that it has been possible even at this late date to assemble a rich, varied, and representative collection of the folk music of the region. Though important scattered fieldwork had been done and much invaluable material was preserved on commercial recordings, it is regrettable that no such collection was made when the work would have been easier.

As artists as well as field collectors, we hope that the interpretive visual work complements and enriches the more straightforward biographical material and musical examples. It is the singer, not the song, depicted in our work, and the folk have been willing and encouraging, if at times perplexed or amused, models; they have accepted unfamiliar artistic and photographic conventions and styles, and the occasional exercise of artistic license, with the wise understanding that our art, like theirs, must have some elbow room. The making of sketches and occasionally painting from life in the people's home environments intensified the rapport and productivity in field situations. Equally important, we have benefited from the visual-aesthetic attitudes of the folk, ranging from the awareness of expressive and communicative gesture, movement, and stance of old-time church singers; through the sense of color and form that many mountain people put into their quilts, their buildings, and changes in their natural surroundings; to the more idiosyncratic and deliberate visions in Howard Finster's paintings, assemblages, and environmental art. The photographs necessarily function as more factual witnesses of time and place; yet we have tried to produce works that can stand as revealing and provocative images.

Bessie Jones, the great Afro-American singer from the coast of Georgia, has said: "These songs I sing are antiques. *I'm* an antique. But it's all right to be an antique if you're a *good* antique!" And when Hiawassee fiddler Ross Brown says, "I don't care *nothin'* about up-to-date," he does not mean he wants to return to the past—rather he is refusing to accept a Nashville- or Hollywood-imposed definition of his experience or his music. It is our feeling that the people who shared their traditions with us concur in the perception that old-time music, like all good art, can speak to us across boundaries of time and space. And a growing sense of the value of the traditions, the new opportunities for performance offered by events like the Georgia Folklife Festival, and the occasional but significant instances of the younger generation learning the older styles, may assure some continuity to the folk music of north Georgia.

Transcriber's Comments

THE TRANSCRIPTIONS in this anthology were produced with performance in mind. It is hoped that they reproduce the nuances and ornamentation of the original without making them useless for performance. In the language of ethnomusicology, these transcriptions contain elements of both descriptive and prescriptive notation.

In reading these transcriptions it should be kept in mind that in the performance of folk music there is usually considerable variation present both in the pitch and in the durational values of notes, as well as in the tempo of performances. The most apparent of these variations were indicated in the transcription by the symbols listed below. To have indicated all variations, again, would have made the transcriptions meaningless for the use intended.

Instrumental accompaniments or solo sections were transcribed whenever they were made up of new musical material; that is, they were not simply doublings or reiterations of the vocal line. Otherwise, banjo and guitar accompaniments are given in the form of chord symbols with the solo instrument written in staff notation.

The songs that have instrumental accompaniments usually contain alternating instrumental and vocal sections. In the transcriptions the instrumental introduction, and the instrumental interlude when different from the introduction, are given only once. It should be understood that some variation of it is played between verses or sections of the song.

For the convenience of instrumentalists, a few banjo and guitar tunes or breaks have been transcribed in tablature as well as musical notation. In tablature the parallel lines do not represent the lines of the musical staff but rather the strings of the instrument, with the top line corresponding to the first string, and so on. The notes to which the strings are tuned appear next to the lines at the beginning of the tab notation. Numbers on the lines denote the frets at which the string is to be stopped, and an *O* indicates that the string remains open. Time values are indicated with sticks and flags, as in music notation. Directly under each note or chord are letters showing how the string or strings are sounded: *I* for index finger, *T* for thumb, *M* for middle finger, *B* for downward brush. *H* shows that the note is a hammer-on; *P*, a pull-off. Tunes in banjo tablature are played twice as fast as the notes indicate; that is, a quarter note in the tablature should be played as an eighth note.

The following symbols are used in transcriptions:

 Scoop up to or down from a note; beginning or termination of scoop, respectively, is not clear.

 Grace notes sliding to or from another note; they may lead up or down.

 A note of uncertain pitch; usually indicates spoken notes on or about the pitch indicated by the *X*.

 Indicates pitch variation of varying degrees from the note indicated.

 Half flat.

♯ Half sharp.

Goin' to Georgia

THE ELLER FAMILY AND ROSS BROWN:
MUSIC MAKERS OF TOWNS COUNTY

A SMALL ROAD turns north off the highway between Hiawassee and Clayton in the Blue Ridge Mountains at the northernmost edge of Georgia. Pavement gives way to dirt as you head up into increasingly beautiful country. The place is known as Upper Hightower, because Hightower Creek arises here, and the mountain called Hightower Bald dominates the landscape. Lawrence Eller also calls it "the garden spot of the world," and there is far more affection than irony in his tone as he considers the creek-bottom, ridge, and mountain country where his family has lived, labored, and made music for over four generations. He and his brother Vaughn have lived on the family land all their lives, with the exception of Lawrence's few stints doing industrial work in the North and Vaughn's hitch in the navy during World War II. Most of the time they survived on subsistence farming, keeping bees, and doing work for others in Towns County—clearing land, construction, "work rougher 'n anyone else would do." Now they live with their wives in houses about a quarter-mile apart on the road; their mother, Leatha, a spry, diminutive woman in her eighties, still able to sing old-fashioned gospel songs and songs of her own composition to her rolling piano accompaniment, stays in a third house between them with another of her sons, L. P., who can neither hear nor speak but has been a fine traditional chair maker. Leatha's sister Berthie Rogers lives in neighboring Rabun County, as did Leatha's daughter Paralee McCloud, until her death in the summer of 1981. A visit in 1980 by Paralee, her husband, and her aunt to Leatha's home was the occasion for the recollecting of old ballads and for the two octogenarian sisters to sing old-time gospel songs around the piano. Leatha recited the poems she had written to hold fast to memories of earlier times.

Lawrence and Vaughn, with their old friend Ross Brown, were the main string band, the most called-upon music makers in the county in the thirties. They have recently been getting some satisfaction in seeing a revived interest in their music, close to home at the Georgia Mountain Fair and at the Georgia Grassroots Festival in Atlanta. After an LP we produced of their music was released on the British label Flyright, they were invited to perform at the Smithsonian Festival of American Folklife and the National Folk Festival. Their rough, honest, and intensely emotional mountain music can cut like a Barlow knife through audiences accustomed to Nashville pop-country groups and the pyrotechnics of the young bluegrassers. The brothers, who thought that musical tastes had passed them by, now feel vindicated by renewed interest and appreciation. Yet their musical expression is still rooted in the rich experiences of their formative years: memories of their mother singing old love songs and ballads at the spinning wheel, of the lonesome sound of their grandfather's fife or song bow, and of the music they themselves learned and played during their courting years. Recently Lawrence was looking up past the near ridges, up toward the peak of Hightower Bald. "Used to be full of houses there," he said. "I could take you up there, show you rock chimleys yet. And ever' Easter Sunday, back yander when I commenced to pickin' the banjo, we'd go to the bald fields up there, a bunch of us, and they'd run a reel in that old field. And the whole field would be covered up, with young people. I'd pick the banjer and Vaughn'd play guitar, and they'd run a reel in that old field. That was in our best days."

The Eller family settled in Towns County before the Civil War, having come down from Buncombe County, North Carolina. Family tradition recalls a hard, simple life of clearing the land, building log

Lawrence Eller in His Farmyard. (Upper Hightower, 1978.)

houses, plowing steers, and raising corn on the hillsides to be hauled off on the old-fashioned sleds that Lawrence remembers how to make. There was little enthusiasm for the Confederate cause in many mountain areas of Georgia during the Civil War, and Lawrence and Vaughn's grandfather Uncle Alf Eller hid out from conscription by the Rebel cavalry in the brush along Hall Creek. Vaughn still treasures his grandfather's Civil War–era fife and can sing a verse of an old war song, a variant of "Fare You Well, My Darling," that Alf played on it.

See how she wrings her lily-white hands and mournfully does cry,
He's going to the army, and in the war he'll die.

Uncle Alf lived until 1934 and was a strong musical influence on Vaughn, especially, who lived with him for a time. "Barbara Allen" was one of the old ballads Vaughn remembers his grandfather singing.

Grady Eller, Lawrence and Vaughn's father, died in 1975 at the age of eighty, having passed on to his sons the traditional arts of log construction, shingle making, and other skills necessary in an age of self-sufficiency. He was also a fine old-time singer and played the organ for family gatherings. He also taught Vaughn how to fashion and play the mouth bow, or "song bow." Leatha taught her boys and Paralee several of the old songs and ballads, and gave them a sense of the exuberance of mountain music. She still remembers a certain neighbor who would often ride back up the road from town at midnight, pretty well drunk, stop and wake her up, and ask her to play "Little Brown Jug" on the organ. "And he'd dance 'er," recalls Vaughn.

Lawrence Eller was born in 1916 and Vaughn in 1918, into a large family: Grady and Leatha Eller raised six children. There was more hard work than schooling in their childhoods, but this was relieved by family and neighborhood gatherings at which music played an important part. "People back then used to visit each other more than they do now," Lawrence remembers. "They'd come in, and there'd be a houseful. They'd set and tell jokes. . . . They'd sing. I've heard my mother's brothers coming out there, and they'd sing, most of the night, them old songs."

In this musical atmosphere it was not surprising that the boys took up music making at an early age. Lawrence began playing the banjo at about eight or nine. "I got ahold of one, had an old catskin head on it, a home-made banjer, didn't have no frets, but I could note hit, make it say the words plainer than this one here," Lawrence told me, between picking tunes on the solid Bacon instrument he has played for the last thirty years. His first piece, which he worked out for himself in the evenings on the front porch of the family home, was the railroad song "Count the Days I'm Gone." Soon thereafter he started to get some pointers from a neighbor named Will Ogles, who had moved into Towns County from around Fontana, North Carolina. Ogles was a chair maker by trade, and word had it that he had been in some kind of trouble in his home state. He sang many of the old songs associated with the rowdy mountain banjo pickers, "Ground Hog," "Poor Ellen Smith," and others, and played in the typical thumb-and-finger style of western North Carolina. Lawrence remembers that Ogles double-noted, that is, brought the thumb over to play extra notes on the inside strings; but Lawrence never learned this. He did develop a serviceable and distinctive personal approach, with an emphasis on melody, and embellished by chokes, slides, and work high up on the neck.

Vaughn began playing the guitar when he was ten or eleven, and his start was, like his brother's, typical for that time. He ordered a Sears Roebuck mail-order guitar and "set around and beat around on it, beat around on it." Soon Vaughn and Lawrence were playing together, and by the time they were in their early teens, they were making music not only for neighborhood dances but for the people who would converge on the county seat on court day. People in Hiawassee still remember the two teenagers picking and singing for the crowds that would gather under the big oak trees on the square when the court recessed at noon. "I heard them talkin' the other day," Lawrence told me, "that they would long for Saturday to come, so they could come down and hear us." Usually it was not possible to catch a ride, as cars were few on the dirt mountain roads, so the boys would walk the twelve miles to Hiawassee and back with their guitar and banjo. They were also called on to play in the new Holiness churches that were coming into the country, because they could set the people on fire at revivals with fast gospel pieces like "Shouting on the Hills of Glory" and "Honey in Rock." The old-fashioned Baptist church the boys were brought up to attend would not have accepted this kind of music in their services.

Vaughn Eller Playing the Song Bow. (Upper Hightower, 1977.)

In the early thirties Lawrence and Vaughn started ordering large numbers of records from the hillbilly catalogs, and what they learned from this source greatly expanded their repertoire and influenced their way of performing many of the songs they had learned from family and local tradition. They learned the tight-harmony style of "brother" teams like the Callahan Brothers and the Monroe Brothers; the Carter Family and Mainer's Mountaineers were other favorites.

The boys married in their early twenties, Lawrence to Ruby Hunter, Vaughn to Louise Allen. Lawrence and Ruby have no children; Vaughn and Louise, one daughter. Through the hard times of the depression they continued to make music for Saturday-night dances, sometimes joined by fiddler Ross Brown from Hiawassee. The dances would be held in people's homes up and down the creek, and there would usually be a caller who could call an eight-handed or sixteen-handed reel. If there was no caller, "they'd just get out and flat-foot 'er"; that is, individuals would tear loose in their own sorts of buck dance. There was little drinking and no trouble at these neighborhood dances, in contrast to their counterparts in other areas, where there was often heavy drinking and fighting. When Vaughn was off in the navy during World War II, Lawrence would often play all night for dances by himself.

Community dances and music sessions declined after the war. People were moving away in search of work, and the influence of mass-produced entertainment made inroads on the tradition. Vaughn pretty much neglected his music for thirty years after his return from the navy, though Lawrence continued to play for his own satisfaction. In recent years, stimulated by the interest in old-time music that was emerging locally and away from home, they have been working up their old numbers again, getting used to each other's "time." Now their voices and instruments blend into their old sound.

WHEN ROSS BROWN PLAYED for dances with the Eller Brothers back in the thirties, they would generally stick to a small number of tried and true breakdowns. Recently they have added the fiddle to a larger number of tunes and songs as they rehearse to perform the old pieces. Ross was born in Towns County in 1909, of a family that, like the Ellers, had migrated to Georgia from North Carolina in the early 1800s. A peach farmer and nurseryman most of his life, he still tends a small orchard next to the comfortable brick home he and his wife, Gertrude, a retired schoolteacher, live in outside Hiawassee. Ross also worked for years as a plumber. He is a comical man, a great jokester with a wild imagination, a skillful harmonica and banjo player as well as a fiddler, and a good flat-footed buck dancer. He serves as the spokesman for the group in public performances and will introduce a song by telling the audience that the group was presented a brick house, down "in Gainesville, Georgia, for playin' this one tune—a brick at a time. Run us completely out of town." He vows that the talent in his family for music making never went beyond his great-grandfather's knocking out his front teeth in an attempt to play the jew's-harp. He claims that his chief early inspiration in music came from an old sow who used to run under the floor of his family's house out in the country when he was a kid. "She went to rubbin' her back against a splinter hangin' down from the floor board, and played a tune that was somewhere between 'Amazing Grace' and 'Weeping Willow.' " Ross will tell you that he has just about achieved his lifelong ambition to play music like that.

He did begin playing the fiddle at thirteen. He is left-handed but started to play bowing right-handed; he accomplished the feat of relearning with the violin restrung for left-handed playing after three years. Ross learned old fiddle tunes like "Snowbird" from Uncle Joe Swanson, a local blind fiddler who stayed with his family periodically. He started playing the banjo on a borrowed fretless instrument; he now plays a fretted banjo upside down, double-noting with thumb lead to achieve the characteristic regional style. Two of his best tunes are "Coal Creek March" and "Weeping Willow." In his younger days he would travel through the mountains on his Harley-Davidson motorcycle and was known to cut up a bit when "feeling good" at a dance, playing the fiddle over his head, behind his back, and the like. Nowadays he is a bit more sedate, but he still has a great time making music and will take any occasion to play, whether it be on the stage of the Georgia Mountain Fair on a show emceed by his brother-in-law, Fiddling Howard Cunningham, with Jim Southern's bluegrass gospel group, with whom he cut an LP, or in a rustic building called the Log Cabin on Highway 76, where he hosts jam sessions open to the public. Ross's musical relationship with the Eller Brothers has its ups and downs: he is not above criticizing Lawrence for picking too hard, a habit Lawrence acquired when he started wearing a thumb pick and metal finger pick to make himself heard at dances before the day of microphones and amplifiers. Lawrence in his turn will comment that Ross doesn't bear down enough on the bow; but the driving banjo line, backed by Ross's thoughtful and moody fiddle and Vaughn's tightly melodic guitar bass, forms the special sound of their band. Their admirers would not want it to be different.

Vaughn Eller is a quiet and reflective man who can put tremendous energy into his music, despite some recent poor health. He has composed several lyric and Jimmie Rodgers "blue yodel"–style songs of his own. I asked him about the unique quality of mountain music, and he said, "It has a special atmosphere about it. It rings clearer here than it does in the flatlands." Lawrence is a more outgoing and demonstrative person, equally passionate about mountain music. He loves to jam with other string musicians but resents flashy bluegrass pickers who try to upstage him—with little success, incidentally. "I tell them they have their style, and I have my old-time style." There is little doubt about which he prefers. He will play alone for hours, for his own satisfaction. "I love that old mountain music," he told me. "There's some times, I'm at the house, I'll kindly take the blues, and get on that porch there, and I just pick the fire out of that thing. Lots of 'em hear me a-singin', down the creek. I really get the blues, that's when I shear down on that thing. That man ain't livin' that loves it more than I do. That man never picked it that enjoys it more than I."

Goin' to Georgia

Sung by the Eller family: Lawrence Eller, Leatha Eller, Paralee McCloud, and Berthie Rogers, with piano by Berthie Rogers; Upper

Hightower, Towns County, August 21, 1980. This mountain lyric song, related to "On Top of Old Smoky" and "I'm Troubled in Mind," is traditional in the Eller family; there is, however, some variation in the verses sung within the family, and when Lawrence sings it to his own banjo accompaniment, the rhythm is quicker and more regular than the stop-and-go performance to piano accompaniment (compare Lawrence's version with Ross Brown and Vaughn Eller, Flyright LP 546). See Brown, 3:527, no. 449, as a Negro song; also, Henry, p. 236; Sharp, 2:14. It was recorded commercially by Riley Puckett.

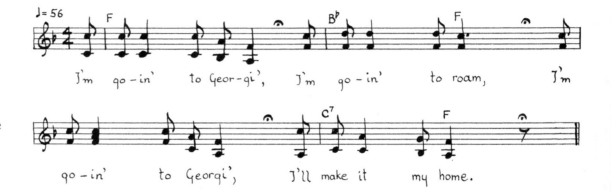

1. I'm goin' to Georgi', I'm goin' to roam.
   I'm goin' to Georgi', I'll make it
   my home.

2. I once loved a young man and I loved
   him for my life,
   He ofttimes did promise for to make me
   his wife.

3. Well he fulfilled his promise, and he
   made me his wife,
   You can see what I come to by being
   his wife.

4. My baby is cryin', a-cryin' for bread;
   My husband is a-gamblin', Lord, I wish
   I was dead.

5. Come all you young ladies, take warning by me,
   Never place your affections on a green
   growing tree.

6. They'll hug you, they'll kiss you, they'll
   tell you more lies
   Than the cross-ties on the railroad or
   the stars in the skies.

7. A thief he will rob you and take what
   you have,
   But a false-hearted lover will lead you
   to the grave.

8. Your grave will decay you and turn you
   to dust,
   Not a-one out of ten thousand that a
   poor girl can trust.

9. I'm going to Georgi', I'm going to roam,
   I'm a-going to Georgi' for to make it
   my home.

10. Goin' to build me a little cabin on the
    mountain so high,
    Where the wild beasts and the snow-
    birds can hear my sad cry.

11. I'm goin' to Georgi', I'm a-goin' to roam,
    I'm goin' to Georgi', to make it
    my home.

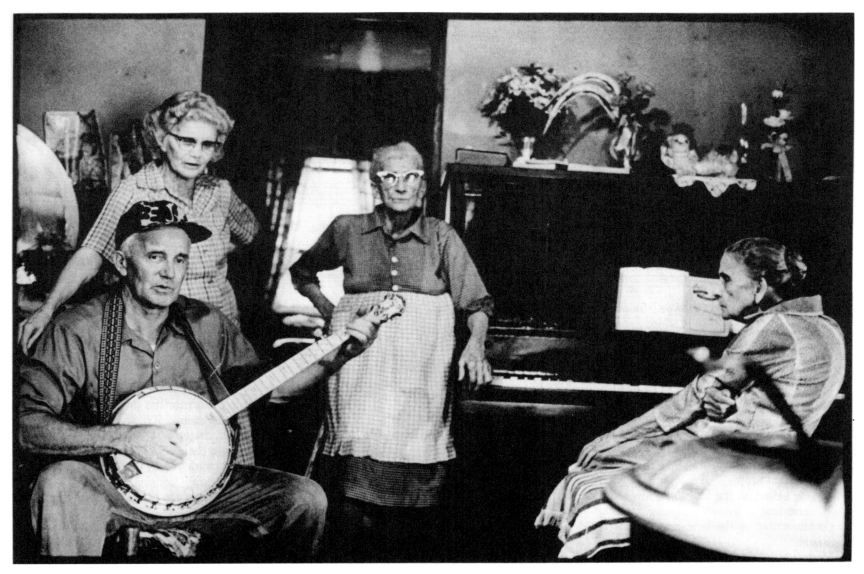

"Goin' to Georgia." *The Eller Family: Lawrence, Paralee, Leatha, and Berthie.*
(Upper Hightower, 1980.)

The Little Ship

("The Golden Vanity," Child, no. 286)

Sung by Paralee McCloud of Mountain City,
Rabun County; Upper Hightower, Towns

County, July 12, 1981. Mrs. McCloud learned
this ballad from her father, Grady Eller, who
"single-noted" it on the organ, that is, played
the melody in unison with his singing. The
use of the first person in the fourth verse lends
a special immediacy to this text. The Carter
Family recorded this ballad commercially, and
there is an interesting Kentucky performance
to banjo by Justus Begley on Library of Congress L7. See Child, 5:136–42; Belden, p. 97;
Brown, 2:191; Cox I, p. 64; Cox II, p. 196;
Lomax I, p. 191; Morris, p. 326; Randolph,
1:195; Riddle, p. 143.

1. There was a little ship went sailing o'er
   the sea,
   And the name of the ship was the Merry
   Golden Ship,
   As she sailed on the lonesome low-
   and-low,
   As she sailed on the lonesome sea.

2. Hadn't been on board but about three
   weeks,
   Till he came in sight of the Reva-
   trukalee,
   As they sailed on the lonesome low-
   and-low,
   As she sailed on the lonesome sea.

3. Says, "I have money and plenty to eat,
   And I have a loving daughter I will give
   unto thee
   If you sink 'em in the lonesome low-
   and-low,
   If you sink 'em in the lonesome sea.

4. Had a little tool all for the use,
   And I bored nine holes in the old hull
   at once,
   And I sunk 'em in the lonesome low-
   and-low,
   And I sunk 'em in the lonesome sea.

5. "Captain, oh captain, take me on board,
   For if you don't you have falsified
   your word,
   For I'm sinking in the lonesome low-
   and-low,
   For I'm sinking in the lonesome sea.

6. "If it wasn't for the love I had for
   your men
   I would do unto you as I done
   unto them,
   I would sink you in the lonesome low-
   and-low,
   I would sink you in the lonesome sea."

7. There was a little ship and she sailed
   o'er the sea,
   And the name of the ship was the Merry
   Golden Ship,
   But they sunk her in the lonesome low-
   and-low,
   They sunk her in the lonesome sea.

My Home's in Charlotte, North Carolina

Sung by Lawrence Eller; Upper Hightower, Towns County, 1977. Lawrence remembers his mother singing this lyric song in the evenings, when he was a small child, as she worked at her spinning wheel, spinning the yarn she used to knit socks and sweaters. Lawrence's unaccompanied performance is free and rubato, and owes much to his mother's singing; when he sings it to banjo (Flyright LP 546), the rhythm is more regular. This song frequently has been recorded as "My Home's Across the Blue Ridge Mountains," and Brown (3:326) prints a North Carolina version from Bascom Lamar Lunsford, "My Home's Across the Smoky Mountains." Roberts (p. 105) gives a Kentucky variant, "Icy Mountain."

1. My home's in Charlotte, North Caro-
      lina, my true love,   *(three times)*
   For I never expect to see you any more.

2. Where's that golden ring I gave you,
      my true love? *(three times)*
   For I never expect to see you any more.

3. I can't keep from cryin', my true love,
      (three times)
   For I never expect to see you any more.

4. Come lay your little arms around me,
      my true love,   *(three times)*
   For I never expect to see you any more.

5. My home's across the Blue Ridge
      Mountains, my true love,
      (three times)
   For I never expect to see you any more.

Cindy in the Summertime

Sung by Lawrence Eller, with mouth bow by Vaughn Eller; Hiawassee, Towns County, December 1977. A wooden bow strung with one string and plucked, using one's cheek and head for resonance and overtones, is a widespread primitive instrument, played by Australian Aborigines, African Pigmy hunters, and others. It has been known to blacks in Georgia (compare Jake Staggers's description of a mouth bow, p. 76) and elsewhere in the South, and has been played by whites in the Appalachians and Ozarks. Its current popularity in the folk revival derives from Jimmie Driftwood's discovery of the Stone County, Arkansas, player Charlie Everidge. (For a

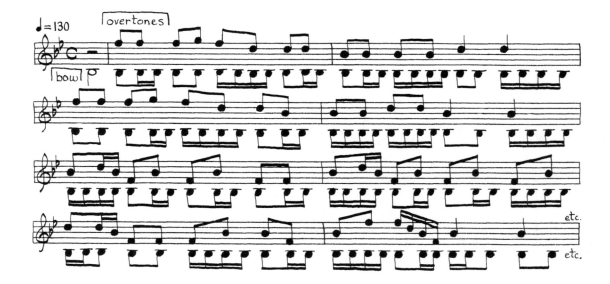

discussion of the Appalachian song bow by George Reynolds with Boyd Queen, see Foxfire, vol. 6, pp. 84–92.) Vaughn learned to make the "song bow" from his father, and he played it as a boy in the quiet of evening "down across the creek" for the pleasure of his family, sitting on the front porch. He carves it from a locust tree branch, gently tapered, a slightly rounded triangle in cross-section (unlike the flat Ozark bow), and sounds it with the handle of his pocket knife. In the transcription, the bottom line gives the rhythm of the picking and the pitch of the drone; the top line, transposed down, gives the overtones produced by the player's mouth. Lawrence, who only recently tried singing to the bow, also plays this well-known frolic tune on the banjo. See Brown, 3:527 (North Carolina); Henry, p. 434 (Tennessee); Lunsford, pp. 42–43; Randolph, 3:376; Roberts, p. 166 (Kentucky); White, p. 161. The Ellers perform this on Flyright LP 546.

1. Cindy in the summertime, Cindy in the fall,
   Can't have Cindy all the time, don't want Cindy at all.

   Chorus:
   Get along home, get along home,
   Get along home, Cindy, fare you well!

2. You ought to see my Cindy, she lives away down South,
   She's so sweet the honey bees all swarm around her mouth.   (*Chorus*)

3. Wish I had a needle as fine as it could sew,
   I'd sew that gal to my coat-tail, and down the road I'd go!   (*Chorus*)

4. Went upon the mountain, give my horn a blow,
   Hollered back to Cindy, oh yander she go.   (*Chorus*)

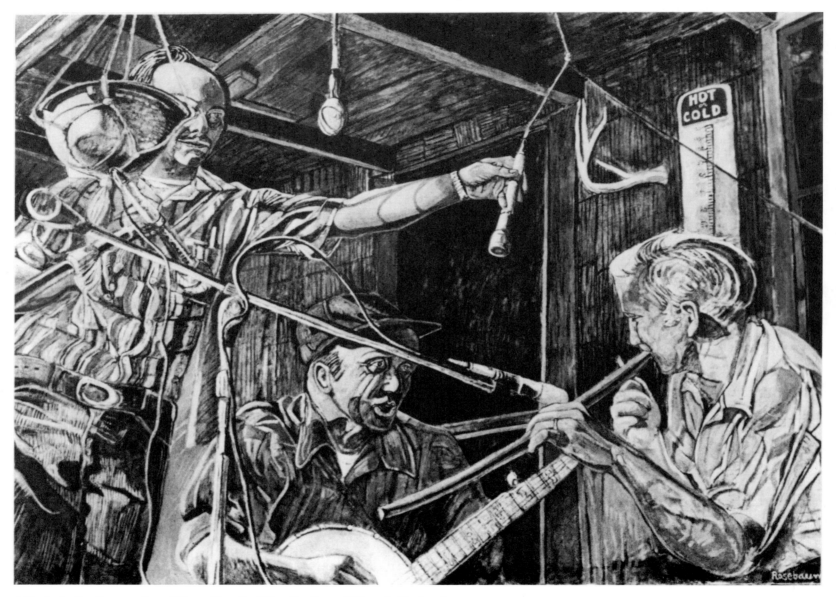

"Cindy in the Summertime." Recording the Eller Brothers. (Oil and alkyd resin on canvas, 48" × 66", 1978.)

Don't Go Ridin' Down That Old Texas Trail

Sung by Lawrence Eller with five-string banjo, with fiddle by Ross Brown and guitar by Vaughn Eller; Hiawassee, Towns County, May 8, 1978. Lawrence learned this previously unreported song, which seems to be related to "Roll On, Buddy, Roll On," from Glynn Ledford, a singer, banjo picker, and spoons player who was one of the musicians who occasionally joined Lawrence and Vaughn when they played under the old oak trees on court day in Hiawassee. It is a typical mountain banjo song, and the western references are apparently thrown in for romantic color. This performance can be heard on Flyright LP 546.

Chorus:
Don't go ridin' down that old Texas trail,
Don't go ridin' down that old Texas trail,
Oh my darling, stay at home, don't go out alone,
Don't go ridin' down that old Texas trail.

1. Oh the nights they are gettin' mighty long,
   Oh the nights they are gettin' mighty long,
   Oh the nights are gettin' long, and I'm singin' you this song,
   Don't go ridin' down that old Texas trail. *(Chorus)*

2. Oh my darling, you done me wrong,
   Oh my darling, you done me wrong,
   Oh you done me wrong, I'm singing you this song,
   Don't go ridin' down that old Texas trail. *(Chorus)*

What You Gonna Name That Pretty Baby?

Sung by Leatha Eller with piano; Upper Hightower, Towns County, May 6, 1978. Leatha Eller has sung traditional ballads and songs all her long life; she played the organ as a young woman but turned to the piano after breaking her hip in the 1950s. In recent years she has begun to compose songs and poems. A recurring theme is old age, and in writing about an old church that was torn down, she used the first person:

> *How old am I, does anybody know?*
> *I've been here ever since a long time ago.*
> *People are all gone that stood by me,*
>   *I know,*
> *My body's getting feeble, my props*
>   *bending low,*
> *And soon beated down to dust I will go.*

Another poem she recites decries today's lack of concern for the very young and the very old:

> *As the days comes and as they go,*
> *Old people and babies ain't wanted any more;*
> *They're tossed about like a ship on the shore:*
> *Swim or drown, we don't want you no more.*
>
> *On come an old lady with a cane in her hand,*
> *Creepin' along, doin' the best she can;*
> *She walked and she walked till her strength*
>   *give out,*
> *And through the burning hot sand her feet*
>   *give out.*

Here she commented, "Just study about it, see if it ain't so!"

What you gonna name that pretty baby? Gonna call it Jesus of Naza-ree, borned in a stall, laid him in a manger, cattle all lowing, and the birds all sing-in', go shout it loud on each high mountain, go tell it a-broad on land and sea, that Jesus is born, so the bright star told us, Jesus, Man of Cal-va-ry.

On she walked with tear-dimmed eyes,
On come some ladies just a-skippin' by.
And some of the heads a-hangin' low and
*   some's h'isted high.*

I went a little fu'ther with tear-dimmed eye,
And said to myself, they have to die as well
*   as I.*

In a lighter vein she reflected on an incident of
her childhood:

I was raised in the Blue Ridge Mountains
Where the water run so full and free,
Out between them big old rock cliffs
The water was as cold as it could be.

We made our corn and rye by the bushels,
Everything there were to eat,
We did not go hungry, we was on our feet.

We set down under an old log tree
With the sweat a-runnin' down our back;
We set and rested a minute or two,
Then we had to get up and go to makin' tracks.

We went to those rock cliffs late of an evenin'
To get our dewberries and our raspberries.
An old rattlesnake give us a warnin'
Not to take another step.

So they sung their songs high and low,
I think the key they sung it in was G,
And that meant for us to go!

"It was so," she added. "We left them to sing
their song by theirself!"
"A few Christmases ago," Leatha made up
this fine gospel-style Christmas song.

---

1. What you gonna name that pretty baby?
   Gonna call it Jesus of Nazaree,
   Borned in a stall, laid him in a manger,
   Cattle all lowing, and the birds all
       singin',

   Chorus:
   Go shout it loud on each high mountain,
   Go tell it abroad on land and sea,
   That Jesus is born, so the bright star
       told us,
   Jesus, Man of Calvary.

2. Joseph and Mary went on a long
       journey,
   Till they came to the Bethlehem stall.
   There Jesus was born by the
       Virgin Mary,
   The King of Kings and Lord of
       all. *(Chorus)*

3. Angels rejoicing in the heavens above,
   And the wise men brought their gifts
       of love.
   The star in the East was the guiding
       light,
   To show the good shepherds to the Baby
       that night. *(Chorus)*

Written by Leatha Eller. © 1983, Leatha Eller.

Leatha Eller and Her Son Lawrence.
(Upper Hightower, 1979.)

Ellen Smith

(Laws F2)

Sung by Lawrence Eller with five-string banjo; Upper Hightower, Towns County, October 23, 1978. Lawrence learned this murder ballad from Will Ogles, who had brought it down to Georgia from North Carolina, its state of origin. Ogles's version is very close to the one recorded by Bascom Lamar Lunsford, though he learned it well before he could have heard the recording. It was recorded for Brunswick by Dykes Magic City Trio in the thirties, and by Mrs. Texas Gladden on Disc in the forties. See Laws II; and Brown, 3:326; Fuson, p. 132; NLCR, p. 159; and Roberts, p. 118.

Oh, it's poor lit-tle El-len, pretty as a dove, oh, where did she ram — ble, and who did she love?

1. Oh it's poor little Ellen, pretty as a dove,
   Oh, where did she ramble, and who did she love?

2. It was a cloudy day, the rain was falling down,
   A ball from my pistol knocked Ellen on the ground.

3. It's I stobbed her to the heart, she fell upon her breast,
   The bloodhounds and officers they gave me no rest.

4. They picked up their rifles, they hunted me down,
   They found me a-loafin' all around that old town.

5. Oh pretty little Ellen, pretty as a rose,
   How I love little Ellen nobody knows.

6. It's I got a letter yesterday, I read it today,
   Saying the flowers on Ellen's grave was fading away.

7. If I could go home and stay when I go,
   Round sweet Ellen's grave pretty flowers I would sow.

Dance All Night with a
Bottle in Your Hand

Sung by Lawrence Eller with five-string banjo, fiddle by Ross Brown; Upper Hightower, Towns County, October 24, 1978. The 1926 recording of this song by Gid Tanner and His Skillet Lickers (Co. 15200) was very popular in Georgia, and the instrumental performance by the Ellers and Ross Brown (Flyright 546) is derived from this. Lawrence, however, sings and plays an older version traditional in his family. Its refrain and reference to Jeff Davis identify this as a Civil War song; the fact that it is Jeff Davis and not, as in some related songs, John Brown to be hanged from the sour apple tree, bespeaks the Unionist sympathies in the mountains of north Georgia.

1. Dance all night with a bottle in your
     hand,
     Bottle in your hand, bottle in your
     hand,
   Dance all night with a bottle in your
     hand,
     As we go marching along.

Dance all night with a bottle in your hand, bottle in your hand, bottle in your hand,

dance all night with a bottle in your hand, as we go marching a-long.

2. We'll hang Jeff Davis from a sour
     apple tree,
     Sour apple tree, sour apple tree,
   Hang Jeff Davis from a sour apple tree,
     As we go marching along.

3. Old Aunt Peggy, won't you fill 'em up
     again,
     Fill 'em up again, fill 'em up again,
   Old Aunt Peggy, won't you fill 'em up
     again,
     As we go marching along.

A Towns County String Band. Vaughn Eller, Lawrence Eller, and Ross Brown.
(Upper Hightower, 1979.)

Snowbird

Played by Ross Brown on fiddle; Hiawassee, Towns County, 1978. There are several old Appalachian fiddle tunes variously called "Snowbird" and "Snowbird in the Ash Bank"; Ross learned this distinctive piece from Uncle Joe Swanson, the blind Towns County fiddler whom he knew as a youngster. Uncle John Patterson plays a very interesting and highly syncopated version of "Snowbird in the Ash Bank" on Arhoolie 5018.

My Number Will Be Changed

DOC AND LUCY BARNES, FAMILY AND FRIENDS, AND THE LIVING SPIRITUAL IN ATHENS

DOC AND LUCY BARNES live in a small house on a rise of ground up a red-clay road from the junction of South Lumpkin Street and the Macon Highway on the south side of Athens. Theirs and a few other houses are all that is left of a once extensive black community there; now condominiums and apartment complexes for University of Georgia students surround the neighborhood of houses, sheds, and gardens, an evocative holdover of an earlier time. The builder of one of the encroaching apartment buildings was looking for a name for his development and came up the road to ask the wiry septuagenarian what the hill was called. When Doc replied that it had no name, the man asked him his, then misheard Doc's answer; now the Bond Hill Apartments are called after a remarkable singer, guitar player, and prodigious source of folklore and oral history, a man who deserves a better tribute.

One day I had been recording part of the Barneses' vast repertoire—Doc has a notebook with the hand-written titles of 529 sacred pieces, and this is not their whole store of songs—and I asked him why he prefers the older songs and styles. "Well, I tell you," he answered, "if you play old-time music, you can get more out of it than you can this-here late stuff. *I* can. That's the way *that* run. I can get more out of it, more *meanin'* out of it. . . . You get up there singin' these-here fancy jumped-up songs, well somebody don't know what you talk—singin' about! If you get back in that old style, well, somebody know somethin' about it. But if you try to keep up with every record, people don't know what you . . . tryin' to sing." This belief in communication carries a religious imperative: Doc and Lucy sing the old spiritual with the lines:

You better mind how you sing, you better know what you
    singin' about,
You better give an account at the Judgment, you better mind.

Doc recently told me why the modest house he and Lucy had built with their own hands—"and never missed a day of work"—has been called "Holy Ghost Headquarters" by Henry Terrell, a good friend and longtime singing partner: "I have mo' singin' at my house than they do at lots of different churches! There's no other church in the state of Georgia or nowhere else that have mo' singin' than I do at my house! That's right." On any Saturday afternoon Doc will be rehearsing the Gospel Chorus, a small group of older singers from the Greater Macedonia Baptist Church, where he is a deacon, and any number of other people are likely to come by. He laughs: "I don't know who's comin', 'cause that's the Holy Ghost Headquarters! We was . . . rehearsin' Saturday evenin', I didn't know there was people comin' from New York there. I didn't know there's nobody comin' from North Carolina; I didn't know nobody comin' from Easley, South Carolina! They jus' go agin us all at once, fo'teen at one time! That was Saturday evenin' gone." And almost any other day of the week Doc and Lucy are singing for visitors who drop by, or just for themselves, sometimes until after midnight.

The songs they sing at home or in churches all over Athens and the surrounding countryside are woven into a fabric of memory and experience that Doc is anxious to share. This is part of what he means when he says his Bible teaches him it is better to give than to receive. Besides teaching the old songs to his nephew and his nephew's children, Doc feels he has to tell them what it was like to work

Doc and Lucy Barnes. (Athens, 1977.)

all day, sunup to sundown, from "can to cain't," and have three dollars to show for it at the end of the week. His father had earned that same amount for a month's work when he was hired out as a boy to do farm work, so there was some slow progress in a tough world. Still, his nephew Mickey "laughed till he cried" when Doc first told him about working for three dollars a week. Doc says, "You take these teenagers, they don't want to work for three dollars an hour! And I said, 'What you talkin about? I seen times if I's makin' three dollars an hour nobody showed me a red apple on a mast post fo' thousand feet high!' Down in Whitehall, colored women used to work in the white people's house, cook and wash, for a dollar and a half. A dollar and a half a week. Not a day, a week. . . . You do it or perish. And I know a set of people, I can carry you down to their door . . . they used to haul clothin' in a two-horse wagon, just stacked high . . . and how they could tell one white person's bundle from the other, I don't know, but they load 'em jus' as long as they could get them to stay up there—fifty cents a bundle! Four or five in the family, fifty cents a bundle, they'll tell you that their own selves."

We were sitting in Doc and Lucy's living room, trying to get at the meaning of the old songs. I suggested that they are about hard experience.

"Hard work," Lucy said.

"Like I said," Doc added, "so many millions and millions and millions of people in the world now, don't know the first beginning. They don't."

Lucy said, "They never been told."

Doc continued, "It's just like the song says, 'The half ain't never been told.' " And to me, "Just like you been sayin' about puttin' some of these things in the [University of Georgia] library, well, that'll give 'em somethin' to go *from,* but other than that, if somebody like me don't set down and tell them that, they might never know."

What Doc can tell about, besides the hard times his people went through, is his impressive store of oral lore, music, and skills ranging from barbecuing hogs the old-time way and making homemade rubboards, to fashioning and playing the ancient "quills," or pan-pipes—a complex body of traditionally learned abilities and expressive arts that have recently been termed "folklife." These were acquired over a lifetime of hard work, close family and community ties, and sustaining religious practice and belief.

Brady "Doc" Barnes was born May 1, 1908, in the country near Arnoldsville, in Oglethorpe County, east of Athens; he was one of four boys in a family of twelve children. His mother, Savannah, was a church member; his father, Jim Barnes, a hard-working sharecropper, was not, and was a gambler, besides. Doc knew both of his grandmothers, who were born in slavery times. He even knew his great-grandmother on his father's side, Leanna, who, he says, lived to the age of 121! He remembers them saying, " 'Son, you better be glad you didn't come along in slavery times. We would be out, and be in the field when the sun rise. Then, back in those days and times, [we] wo' one dress all week, and then on a Saturday night [we] pull that dress off . . . and wash it, and get it ready for Sunday.' Now I heard my great-grandmother say it, and I heard my grandmother say it. They worked till black dark on Saturday night. And then they would pull off those garments they had and get them ready for Sunday to go to church." Doc continued, talking about his father: "He said he used to work from Christmas to Christmas, and if he got five dollars for it [his parents kept most of his meager wages], he was well pleased. He was a wage-hand, as you call it. But after he started and raised a family, he's a 'cropper, then. He worked on shares then, and lots of times when Christmas come, they might got five dollars out of the whole crop, and they might not."

Doc started working along with his father, when he was "real young. Otherwise, I started to learn how to plow a mule . . . when I was about eleven years old. And my daddy said, 'I believe I got me another hand,' just like that. I said, 'Can't I plow good, papa?' He said, 'Yes . . . you gonna be one of my main men, plowin'.' That made me feel good, like I weighed three hundred, you know. You *had* to plow, then . . . , get out and make something, try to live off, you know." Doc remembers that as he grew up, cotton farming "commenced to gettin' a little bit better . . . until the boll weevil hit. When the boll weevils hit this country, to my memory, when they got rough [was] in 1924. And then that's when my daddy quit croppin' and we moved to Athens." Doc's dad worked for a man named Tylus Rivers, a landlord who drove a horse and buggy around to collect his rents. "Daddy did all he could for us. We fared pretty good, but some black people had it harder than we did. I'm not pattin' myself on the head. I had my share, but I know some peoples had it worse. . . . I knew one family, they would take hoecake patties, they would take that

*Singing at Doc and Lucy's. Doc and Lucy Barnes, with Mavis Moon and Kenny, Jackie, and
"Little Lucy" Gilmore. (Athens, 1977.)*

and break it and fill that up with lard like you put butter in bread, and eat that. I seen that in my lifetime."

Uncle Nat Marvers was an old root doctor Doc knew in those years. I asked him what a root doctor is, for anybody who didn't know.

"What is a root doctor for anybody didn't know? Well, there is a lot of sickness an American doctor couldn't do nothin' with. . . . I have been there to his [Marvers's] house. People from New York, Chicago, different foreign places, come there. I've seen people come there couldn't walk, leave there walkin'. I seen a person come there once, I thought he was 'hydrophobe,' y'know, bit by a mad dog, he's just slobberin', and the tongue done come out of his mouth, had to put cotton in his mouth, to keep him from eatin' his mouth up. . . . When he come there, hit was three mens had him in the back of a car, holdin' him down, and one of the men, the driver, went in to see the doctor, the old colored doctor, and said, 'We got so-and-so.' [The doctor] said, 'I knowed you was comin' fo' you got here. Bring him on here.' Had other patients, had to wait. Had a man out there plumb wild, said bring him in here. When he got him off of whatever it was, he just come to, you might say, just like a live man. . . . When he leave, he was just as normal as you and me. Talk."

Doc worked for Marvers. "Otherwise, when I was small, whenever his workman, his servant, couldn't be there, he'd get me to go with him to the woods, get his herbs. Medicine he made, he got from herbs." Doc remembers that his main herb was "John-the-conquer-root, would conquer most anything. He had some other ingredients he put with it. But that was his main root! John the Conquerer!" (Muddy Waters sings, "I got John the Conqueroo, I'm gonna mess with you" in his blues "Hoochie Coochie Man," implying that the herb had aphrodisiac power.) "I used to he'p him right smart. I was too young to work on a public job. When I's around he'd give me somethin' to do. If he give me a quarter a day, that was money then. He was a good doctor and his history reached I don't know how far. . . . He was one of the most famous root doctors there was in the South."

Doc remembers black soldiers boarding a train to go off to World War I: "They would be cryin', just like little children. Grown men would be cryin'. . . and those men just boo-hooed, and the train was packed—and I didn't know what it was about. . . . I'd just hear 'em say they was goin' to the war. I didn't know if the war was good or bad, or about them gettin' killed, 'cause I wasn't big enough. Some of them had red handkerchiefs. Used to have a blue cap, with a long bill on it, like people worked on the railroad, and 'most every colored person you'd see, want to be a railroad man, but them that didn't be a railroad man, they'd buy 'em. . . . And the ones you'd see on that train, that's how they was dressed. And packed like you walk in a chicken house."

From an early age Doc was keenly interested in singing and music. "Get me to the church, they'd be carryin' on with a meetin' . . . and it just get to sound so good, I couldn't get there quick enough. Light off and *run* to the church!" He did not commit himself to sacred music until much later in life, however, and he taught himself to play blues and dance pieces on the organ at the age of fourteen. Before long he was playing for "hot suppers, breakdowns, frolics" from "just about sundown Saturday till eight o'clock Sunday mornin'." These were held in people's homes around Athens and other communities, though Doc's mother "didn't never have nothin' like that at our house. . . . A man used to come by my daddy's house and get me many times, to play at the frolic. And my dad said, 'I want you to bring him back safe and sound just like you carried him away.' Said, 'I sho' will.' Well he did, sometimes a little late." Doc played and sang alone, and at times earned five dollars, "a mountain, then."

About this time Doc heard a man in his eighties named Joe Peelin play the "quills," the form of pan-pipe that was the main instrument of the slaves on Georgia's antebellum plantations but is now virtually extinct. "He'd talk what he's gonna blow on those quills, then he'd talk and sing it, then turn around and blow it. If he was gonna blow 'Jesus, Keep Me Near the Cross,' he'd sing it first, then turn around, get them things lined up there, and walk from one end to the other, do-diddle-do, ha, ha, ha!"

"You said that was on Broad Street?" I asked.

"On East Broad, right downtown there."

"And he attracted a big crowd?"

"Oooee! Sometimes the cops had to go up there and make the people scatter. Had the sidewalks blocked."

Doc figured out how to make and blow the quills himself. He copied Peelin's way of cutting reeds, notching them, and tuning them with wood plugs. Peelin had seven or eight reeds, and Doc

Interior, "Holy Ghost Headquarters." (Oil and alkyd resin on canvas, 56¼" × 56¼", 1979.)

"could get four or five. And I'd have every one of them tuned like you'd tune a guitar." He played for himself and for other children, " 'cause they couldn't do it."

At the age of seventeen Doc went to work at Oconee Manufacturing in the mill town of Whitehall. Three years later he met Lucy Jackson, a native of Wilkes County, at choir practice at the Macedonia Baptist Church; soon afterward they married. In 1933 Doc bought his first guitar at the Chick Piano Company, and he taught himself to play. "I seen other people, I believe I can do that too." At the time he was plowing "on Mr. Rob White's place," and told what that was like: "I used to go to that barn [in the morning] where he kept his mule, y'know, be so dark, I'd go in there feelin' for him, sometimes ketch his tail, switch it in my face, dark like that, you couldn't see the mule, jus' hear him." He would plow until after eight at night and would have "two big quarters, for fourteen hours' work, or fifteen. I had to work for that. If I didn't . . . I didn't get none, and nobody wasn't givin' nothin', not at that time. As the old sayin' said, you'd 'root, hog, or die poor.' So I made many a day fifty cents for sixteen hours' work. So they took us from that, they had a large woodyard, we used to furnish Athens, wood! They made from three to five trips every day in the year, 'cep' Sunday—and Saturday, that was the busiest day there was. And if you got off, that was [late] Saturday night."

I wondered when he had time for playing his new guitar.

"I'd stay up all day on Sunday, from the time I turned that mule loose, y'know. I'd get that guitar and hammer on it. I kep' it about ninety days. And I lose so much sleep, y'know, I'd try to work, I couldn't hardly keep my eyes open. I'd rather go without the guitar than go hungry! I'm gonna get rid of this guitar." Doc sold the guitar but felt bad about it. As soon as he could afford to, he bought another, and he has never been without a guitar since.

Among the "worldly," or secular, pieces that Doc learned back in his early days of guitar picking were "John Henry," bottleneck style—"I could *talk* John Henry"—and an old-time talking blues:

Down in the wildwood, sittin' on a log,
Finger on the trigger and eye on the hog.
Pulled that trigger, the gun said bip,
Jumped on that hog with all of my grip,

Such a-scrapin', pullin' hair, eatin' hog eye,
  Love chitt'lins too.

Down in the wildwood the other night,
Awful dark and didn't have no light,
Scramplin' around there, got ahold t' the goose,
White folks say you better turn 'em loose,
  Jumped in the gully, rolled bushes too!

And from Aunt Jane, an old neighbor lady, he learned a version of one of the earliest blues, "Careless Love":

Oh, what a foolish girl I was,
Love somebody and they don't love me . . .

In the thirties and forties, long before he became a church member, Doc was playing guitar and singing with jubilee quartets and quintets. This style required impeccable rhythm and skill at part singing, and Doc feels his "standard bunch," the Gospel Pilgrims, was one of the best. "We used to go to Atlanta, WOK broadcast station, and 'round Atlanta there, out to Lithonia, Augusta, Florida, South Carolina." Doc's rocking guitar backup to "Lord Guide My Feet" made it one of their most-requested numbers: "I'm not braggin' on myself, not braggin' on the group too much, and I don't like to pat myself on the head, but everywhere we went, people heard it once, they had to hear that—'Lord guide my feet while I run this race.' Now we had a baritone and tenor, they knowed exactly what's what." E. J. Johnson, Richard Johnson, Bell Thomas, Henry Grady Terrell, and Doc made up the original group.

When he finally became a church member, Doc stopped playing secular music in public. "As the old song say," he explains, " 'I'm on my way to heaven, not gonna turn around.' " However, he will oblige a request for "John Henry," or "Raise a Ruckus Tonight" around home. I asked him what he felt about the church's strictures against such songs.

"To the best of my knowledge, it's in the people, it's not in what you do. Now I listened to different preachers. Some—'I wouldn't have a TV in my house.' Well . . . if you got religion, a TV can't take it away! And that's just like a song some people sing: 'God gave it to me, and you can't take it away.' I remember once, way back years

*W. B. Thomas Gospel Chorus. Doc Barnes, Andrew Ferrell, Annie Will Jewell, Clyde Gilmore,
Mavis Moon, Little Babe Griffin, Lucy Barnes, Naomi Bradford, and Children. (Athens, 1977.)*

ago, Big Boy Terrell could tell you that, we had a program in —— Church. I had a guitar, and I heard some people say preacher don't like a guitar in a church. And so I went up there. Preacher was standin' in the pulpit, and he took it on himself to meet us, come on down, and oh, Lord God, 'You own this thing?' 'Yeah.' 'Well I don't 'low no guitar in my church.' 'Why?' 'I just don't like a guitar.' He [Terrell] said, 'Rev, just step right here to the do' a minute.' You know, back out of the company. And said, 'Look, you mean to tell me you don't like a guitar?' 'No.' He said, 'Well listen, it say you can have string music in heaven. If it don't my Bible is wrong.' And, 'Uh, yes, but I just don't like it.' Says, 'Well look, you ever looked in the back of a piano?' 'Yeah.' 'That guitar got strings on it like that piano has.' So Big Boy Terrell took him up, looked in the back of that piano. 'What's the difference in them?' And he convinced that preacher. . . . We showed him right in his church. We straightened him out right then and there."

Doc has no doubts about the appropriateness of putting his old-fashioned guitar playing as well as his singing to the service of his faith, and he has taught his two-finger picking technique to many young musicians, "white and black," most of whom have moved on to more modern styles. Since his retirement from his longtime job at Thomas Textiles, Doc and Lucy have been active as a duo, or with the Gospel Chorus, or with their blind friends, the Reverend Nathaniel and Sister Fleta Mitchell. They have appeared on several occasions at the University of Georgia and at city-sponsored events, as well as at innumerable church services, singings, and singing conventions. Their performances carry a sacred trust for them, and Doc says, "I put what God put into me to put into it. I don't get up for no show." Lucy feels much the same: "I ain't gonna get up and *play* with no singin'. I won't play with God." When she gets the spirit, she will "shout," get into the ecstatic movements that go along with singing and reach back to the African origins of the black American tradition. "When I start to singin', I just can't stand it, to save my life. I just get so full, I'm *pleased* to sing. I just can't help from singin'." When she was little, Lucy's father, Charlie Jackson—Doc remembers him as "the singingest black man around"—rehearsed the family choir every Wednesday night; the children had to stay seated until they were ready to sing. "And I wanted to sing," Lucy says.

Doc and Lucy Barnes exemplify the vitality of black sacred singing in the South. A combination of their own inner expressive and religious fervor, and ample opportunities to perform for appreciative audiences in both the black and white communities, continues to sustain this live tradition in them. The songs that follow are taken not only from the Barneses' performances but from those of other singers in their church, family, and social circles, and should give a varied if incomplete picture of this rich and living music.

Walk with Me

Sung by Brady "Doc" Barnes and Lucy Barnes; Athens, Clarke County, March 24, 1982. This beautiful spiritual is a prayer in song: as Doc put it, the singer is "askin' God for what he want throughout the song." The Barneses learned it years ago from Deacon Olsby in Madison, Georgia. "This old tedjious journey" is one of the finest metaphors for a life full of tribulations in the old spiritual tradition.

1. I'm your child, Lord, I'm your child,
   I'm your child, Lord, I'm your child,
   Whilst I'm on this old tedjious journey,
   I'm your child, Lord, I'm your child.

2. Walk with me, Lord, walk with me,
   Walk with me, Lord, walk with me,
   Whilst I'm on this old tedjious journey,
   Walk with me, Lord, walk with me.

3. Hear my prayer, Lord, hear my prayer,
   Hear my prayer, Lord, hear my prayer,
   Whilst I'm on this old tedjious journey,
   Hear my prayer, Lord, hear my prayer.

4. Try to sing, Lord, try to sing.
   Try to sing, Lord, try to sing,
   Whilst I'm on this old tedjious journey,
   Try to sing, Lord, try to sing.

Dead and Gone

Sung by Brady "Doc" Barnes with guitar; Athens, Clarke County, December 7, 1977. Doc learned this old spiritual from his grandmothers, both of whom were born in slavery—his father's mother, 'Nervy Barnes, and his mother's mother, Hannah Collins. He is proud of his contribution to the song's performance, a bottleneck-style guitar accompaniment that acts as a second voice to the vocal line. The melody is similar to that of the well-known spiritual "Every Time I Feel the Spirit." Perdue (p. 75) found a text titled "My Mother Died A-Shouting" in the WPA Georgia manuscripts. Courlander, p. 45, gives an Alabama version of this song as "Dear and Gone," sung by Dock Reed and Vera Hall. "Shouting" refers not to vocal exclamations, but to the West African sort of dancelike motions practiced at times of religious fervor to singing and rhythmic clapping and other percussive sounds.

Dead and gone, Lord, dead and gone, Lord, all the friends I have, dead and gone. My poor

mo-ther died a shout-ing, all the friends I have, dead and gone.

Dead and gone, Lord, dead and gone,
All the friends I have, dead and gone.

My poor mother died a-shouting,
All the friends I have, dead and gone.

Dead and gone, dead and gone,
All the friends I have, dead and gone.

Doc and Jim. (Charcoal, 22" × 30", 1977.)

My Number Will Be Changed

Sung by the Gospel Chorus of the Greater Macedonia Baptist Church, led by Sister Naomi Bradford; Athens, Clarke County, December 3, 1977. Sister Naomi Bradford was leading the Gospel Chorus and singing well into her early nineties— her voice could soar like the

Oh, don't you know my number it will be changed,

number will be changed, number will be

don't you know my number it will be changed --

changed, number will be changed, number will be

flight of a swallow over the background rhythms set down by the other old singers. Doc Barnes says he taught her this song, but it seems that she combined his version with one she had

known before. It is a proud statement of transcending the trials of this world—a song born in slavery. Sister Bradford died in the

summer of 1981, and her large and loving family and many friends believe that the promise of this song has been fulfilled.

Don't you know my number will be
    changed, it will be changed,
You know my number will be changed, it
    will be changed—
Soon as my feet strike Zion, I'm gonna lay
    down my heavy burden,
I'm gonna put on my robe in glory,
I'm gonna shout, sing, and tell the story,
My number will be changed, my number
    will be changed.
I heard the voice of Jesus say, "Come unto
    Me and rest,
Lay down, you weary wand'rer, your head
    upon My breast."

Soon, One Mornin'

Sung by the Reverend Willie Gresham with the congregation of the Greater Macedonia Baptist Church; Athens, Clarke County, December 3, 1977. A typical service in a traditional black church like the Greater Macedonia will begin with one of the old lined-out hymns. Then one or more of the deacons or members come to the front and kneel to pray in a half-sung, half-declaimed pentatonic statement, deeply emotional. Another hymn may follow, or someone may "raise" one of the older spirituals. Then the

choir, or rather, the one of the church's several choirs scheduled to sing that day, will offer a song. After the choir sings, the preacher will take over, leading a song himself and giving his sermon, itself a long and partly sung declamation, building up to a crescendo of feeling. This song was the Reverend Gresham's favorite, and he almost invariably sang it before he preached; the congregation knew it well and joined in on the repeated phrases. This is one of the finest of the old spirituals, with its intimate personification of death, and its affirmation of the singer's spirit and his faith. Gresham learned the song from his father, about whom Doc Barnes made the predictable comment: "If you think Willie Gresham can sing, you ought t've heard his dad!"

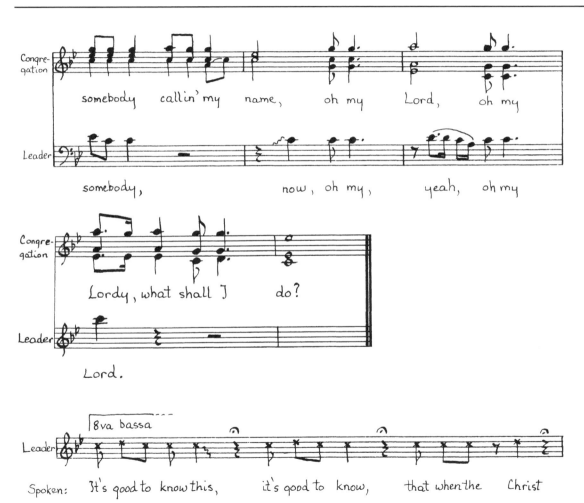

1. Hush and listen, somebody's callin' my name,
   Yes, hush and listen, somebody callin' my name (sound like Jesus, now),
   Hush and listen, there is somebody callin' my name, now,
   Oh my Lord, oh my Lordy, what shall I do?

2. You know that I'm, I'm so glad, church, that I got my religion in time,
   Hallelujah, I'm so glad, church, that I got my religion in time, thank you, Jesus,
   I'm so glad I got my religion in time,
   Oh my Lord, oh my Lordy, what shall I do?

3. I've got my ticket, and I know I have a right to ride (You ought to say that, church!),
   I've got my ticket, and I know I have a right to ride, hallelujah,
   I've got my ticket, and I know I have a right to ride,
   Oh my Lord, oh my Lordy, what shall I do?

Leader: was hung on the Cross, and when they buried Him in Joseph's

Leader: new tomb, when He rose up Sunday mornin', looked back at the grave,

Leader: took the victo-ry from the grave, took the sting out of Death.

Leader: If you been born a-gain, you can tell Death these words:

It's good to know this, that when the Christ was hung on the cross, and when they buried Him in Joseph's new tomb, when He rose up Sunday mornin', looked back at the grave, took the victory from the grave, took the sting out of Death. If you been born again, you can tell Death these words:

6. "Oh, Death, you can't do me no harm!
  Oh, Death, oh you can't do me no harm, hallelujah,
  Oh, Death, you can't do me no harm."
    Oh my Lord, oh my Lordy, what shall I do?

7. Hush and listen, there is somebody callin' my name,
  Hush and listen, there is somebody callin' my name, sounds like Jesus, now,
  Hush and listen, somebody callin' my name,
    Now oh my Lord, oh my Lordy, what shall I do?

Spoken:
Amen!

4. I died one time, and I ain't gonna die no more, hallelujah,
  I died one time, and I ain't gonna die no more, thank you, Jesus,
  I died one time, and I ain't gonna die no more, now,
    Oh my Lord, oh my Lordy, what shall I do?

5. Oh soon, one mornin', old man Death came in my room,
  Soon, oh soon one mornin', old man Death came in my room,
  Yes, soon, soon one mornin', old man Death came in my room,
    Oh my Lord, oh my Lordy, what shall I do?

"Soon, One Morning." The Reverend Willie Gresham, Preaching and Singing. (Charcoal, 22" × 30", 1977. Collection of Gisèle Pommier.)

Walk Together, Little Children

Sung by Brady "Doc" Barnes, with guitar, and Lucy Barnes; Athens, Clarke County, July 1978. As a young boy, Doc learned this song, *a version of the old spiritual "Great Camp Meeting in the Promised Land," from the Reverend Jim Williams, the pastor of Arnold's Grove Baptist Church; Williams sang it*

Oh, let us walk to-ge-ther, li'l children, little child-ren

don't, don't you get wor - ried, walk to-ge - ther, li'l

li'l child-ren, now, don't

child-ren, don't you get wor - ried,

walk to-ge - ther, li'l children little children, don't

don't you get

specifically to the children in Sunday School as a didactic piece. It is a favorite of Doc's sister Clyde Gilmore, who also learned it as a child.

I recorded a fragmentary version sung by the great early blues guitarist Scrapper Blackwell in Indianapolis in 1958; he had learned it from his father, a "lead violinist." Blackwell's version had the refrain "Oh, Lord, gre't God, ham camp meetin' in the Promised Land." See also Work, p. 143.

1. Oh, let us walk together, li'l children,
   little children, don't you get
   worried,
   Walk together, li'l children, li'l children,
   now, don't get worried,
   Walk together, li'l children, li'l children,
   don't you get worried,

   Chorus:
   Comin' up, oh, oh, Lord is
   Comin' up, oh, oh, oh, oop, my Lord you
   know there's a
   Great camp meeting in the Promised
   Land!

2. Oh, let us sing together, little
   children, *etc.*

3. Oh, let us shout together, little
   children, *etc.*

4. Oh, let us pray together, little
   children, *etc.*

Brother, You Oughtta Been There

Sung by the Reverend Nathaniel Mitchell, Sister Fleta Mitchell with piano, Brady "Doc" Barnes with guitar, and Lucy Barnes; Athens, Clarke County, September 29, 1979. Like Doc and Lucy Barnes, the Reverend Nate and Sister Fleta Mitchell are an Athens couple who have devoted their long married lives

together to furthering their faith through their musical talents. Both born blind, Nate in 1910 in Wilkes County and Fleta in Laurens County in 1913, their childhood memories recall hard work, despite their handicap, and music. Fleta washed dishes and shelled peas; she also learned to sing and play piano from her mother, and she joined in a family quartet after the work was done. Nate came from a family of sharecroppers who moved from place to place, and he picked cotton and shelled corn on a machine—and, unlike Fleta, he learned music alone, playing blues on a harp (harmonica).

Nate and Fleta met as teenagers at the Georgia School for the Blind in Macon, and began their courtship in what they remember as very happy days. (One of their schoolmates was Blind Willie McTell, who was to become one of the greatest blues recording artists as a singer and virtuoso on the twelve-string guitar. Besides his musical talents, Fleta recalls, "he was good in plays. They had me for Red Riding Hood, and he was the woodcutter, saved me from the wolf! He was apt.") Both Fleta and Nate studied music with John Allen

Oh, Brother, y'oughtta been there, Brother, y'oughtta been there, oh,

Brother, y'oughtta been there when the love come tricklin' down.

Seek, seek, seek, seek, and you shall find, knock, knock, knock and the do' shall be opened,

ask, ask, ask, and it shall be given when the love come trick-lin' down.

Williams at school, learning spirituals in the somewhat cultivated manner of the Fisk Jubilee Singers; but Nate credits Fleta with being his first real music teacher and training his powerful baritone voice. He got the call to preach in those years and convinced Fleta to quit playing worldly music: before their marriage in 1936, she had been playing blues for dances every night of the week, around Warrenton, Georgia. But she thought "it would be foolish, he gettin' up in the pulpit, and his wife out playin' the blues. So I asked the Lord to fix me up so I could make a minister a good wife." She did stop playing the blues, and never thought about them any more. "That [the blues] just leaves you, cut off, just like a washing machine, automatically be gone," as Fleta puts it.

In the early years of their marriage they traveled much of the time, doing revivals all over the South and as far north as Boston. They remember packing their bags at one in the morning, catching the Seaboard Coast Line train, and by sunup they'd "be somewhere!"

These days they work at their trade of chair caning but continue to be active in singing and playing at revivals, at the Holiness church where they are members, and at many other meetings and singings. Fleta is much in demand as an accompanist. Their music is a wonderful blend of the joyful jubilee style, the old spiritual style (which, as Fleta says, "puts you to thinking, gives you more of a powerful attitude") and the more formal vocal and instrumental music that they learned at school. Longtime friends of the Barneses', they often combine their voices, as in this catchy jubilee.

1. Oh, Brother, you oughtta been there,
   Brother, you oughtta been there,
   Brother, you oughtta been there
   When the love come tricklin' down.

   Chorus:
   Seek, seek, seek, seek, and you
        shall find,
   Knock, knock, knock, and the do' shall
        be opened,
   Ask, ask, ask, and it shall be given
   When the love come tricklin' down.

Similarly mother, sister, father, *etc.*

The Reverend Nathaniel Mitchell and Sister Fleta Mitchell. (Athens, 1979.)

Alone and Motherless

Sung by Lucy Barnes, guitar by Brady "Doc" Barnes; Athens, Clarke County, October 25, 1979. Lucy learned this song as a girl from her father, Charlie Jackson, in Wilkes County. *Structurally, it is a twelve-bar blues, and the guitar runs that Doc puts in the "holes" of the melody are in the blues style; Doc and Lucy acknowledge these points but feel that the references to mother and heaven place the song* squarely on the right side of the secular-sacred dichotomy. *They do claim that the popular group, the Staple Singers, heard them perform it in Athens years ago, and "made it into a blues," which Doc and Lucy resent.*

1. I'm alone and motherless ever since I
      was a child.
   Ah, lone an' motherless, ever since I
      was a child.
   Goin' home to your mother, be here
      after a while.

2. Ever since my mother was livin', I had
      the whole round world to please,
   Ever since my mother was livin', I had
      the whole round world to please.
   Mother she gone on to glory, eeeeeooo.

3. Jesus, sometime I wonder, did I, did I
      treat my mother right,
   Ooooooh, I wonder sometimes, did I,
      did I treat my mother right,
   Mother, she restin' in glory, eeeoooo.

Little Sally Walker

Sung by Brady "Doc" Barnes and Lucy Barnes; Athens, Clarke County, October 16, 1980. Although this has been one of the most widely known children's circle-game songs in America, Doc said he doubts that "ary kid in twenty different states can sing it, 'less some older head

♩ = 120

Lit -tle Sal -ly Wal — ker, sit -ting in the sau — cer,

cry - in' and a- weep-in' what she have done.

Rise, Sal-ly, rise, wipe your weepin' eyes,

turn to the eas', fly to the wes',

have taught them." He explained that "you get in a ring, and one in the middle." The rest of the play can be inferred from the text. A typical performance can be heard on Library of Congress LP L9. There is a good description of Bessie Jones's south Georgia version in her book Step It Down (p. 107), and Perdue (p. 28) has a version from Marietta, Georgia, called "Little Sally Saucer." See also Arnold, p. 147; Courlander, p. 75; and Newell, p. 70.

fly to the ve-ry one that you love the bes'. Put yo'

han' on yo' hip, let yo' back-bone slip, gonna

shake it to the eas', gonna shake it to the wes', gonna

shake it to the very one you love the bes',

Little Sally Walker, sitting in the saucer,
Cryin' and a-weepin' what she have done.

Rise, Sally, rise, wipe your weepin' eyes,
Turn to the eas', fly to the wes',
Fly to the very one that you love the bes'.

Put yo' han' on yo' hip, let yo' backbone slip,
Gonna shake it to the eas', gonna shake it
    to the west,
Gonna shake it to the very one you love
    the bes'.

We're Marching Round the Level

Sung by Mae Wills and Jim Wills; Athens, Clarke County, March 24, 1982. Jim and Mae Wills were old friends of Doc and Lucy Barnes. Jim and Doc worked together in the textile mills of Whitehall. The Willses were white and the Barneses black; during and after the days of segregation custom and society kept their church and other affiliations separate, but this did not prevent them from maintaining an exceptionally close personal and musical friendship over the years. Jim at one time was an excellent fiddler and banjo picker, and also played the mandolin and autoharp. The two couples exchanged visits frequently to play and sing, and on one such visit, only four months before Jim Wills's death, the Barneses were talking about the singing games they had played as children, and the Willses recalled one, "Marching Round the Level." Mae Wills added, after singing this song: "Kids don't do that no more. They got TV, they don't take time to sing no more, like we did. That's all we had to look forward to, get out and play games. We'd play by moonlight." "Marching Round the Level" is usually known as "Marching Round the Levee." See Killen, p. 220, for a Georgia version with the same title. Jones, pp. 76–77, gives a south Georgia version of the more familiar form of this song, "Go In and Out the Window." Newell gives a New York City variant, "Go Round and Round the Valley," pp. 128–29, as well as "Walking on the Levee," pp. 229–30.

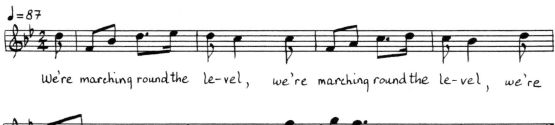

1. We're marching round the level,
   We're marching round the level,
   We're marching round the level
   For we have gained the day.

2. Stand forth and face your lover, *etc.*

3. I kneel because I love you, *etc.*

4. One kiss before I leave you, *etc.*

The Willses and the Barneses. (Athens, 1982.)

Free, Go Lily

Sung by Brady "Doc" Barnes and Lucy Barnes; Athens, Clarke County, October 16, 1980. This is another singing game Doc and Lucy remember from their childhoods. See Jones, "Way, Go Lily," for another Georgia version; also Brewer, p. 370.

Free, go li-ly, sometime, come skippin' through the window, sometime, gonna

h'ist my window, sometime, come skippin' through the window, sometime.

Free, go lily, sometime,
Come skippin' through the window,
    sometime,
Gonna h'ist my window, sometime,
Come skippin' through the window,
    sometime. *(Repeat)*

Farewell, Sweet Jane

MAUDE THACKER, BALLAD SINGER OF TATE

THE STARK old classic British ballads, carrying their stories of love, jealousy, and murder on haunting modal melodies, are the oldest stratum of the folk-song tradition in the north Georgia mountains. They, and the romantic broadside ballads that went along with them, were widely known and sung a generation or two ago, but they have faded from the memories of most folk singers and musicians, who tend to favor instrumental music, railroad songs, love lyrics, and similar genres that were encouraged rather than superseded by the advent of radio and records in the twenties and thirties. It is true that several Child ballads were recorded commercially by early hillbilly artists, and a few of the older ballads and songs from this source as well as from family and local tradition crop up in the repertoires of many of the Georgians we met in our quest for folk song. But we had been looking without success for a "big" singer, one with a large store of the old ballads, when we met the late Tom Quinton of Talking Rock in Pickens County, an educator, storyteller, and collector of folklore and artifacts. He knew an interesting fragment of "The Farmer's Curst Wife" (Child, no. 278), and his mother, Kate Quinton, sang "Barbara Allen" (Child, no. 84), the best remembered of the British ballads in America; but when we asked about more such ballads, Tom lamented that most had died with an earlier generation. He did suggest that we talk to Maude Thacker, an older woman with a good memory for local history. Although she is a cousin of his, and he had known her all his life, Tom did not know whether she knew any songs or could sing. She proved to be the most prolific and interesting ballad singer we have met in Georgia.

We found Mrs. Thacker in front of her neat home on the edge of Tate, Pickens County's famous marble-quarrying town. She was the image of an old-time mountain woman, in a print dress, her hair in one long braid down her back; her wrinkled face looked like an animated apple-faced doll. "Yes, I know *lots* of old songs," was her immediate response when we told her what we were interested in. She was able to sing several ballads and songs from memory that day; but others she had to "unriddle," recall bit by bit and write down in a school copy book, or "ballet book." These we recorded on several subsequent visits. Her repertoire, acquired almost entirely from her father before 1920, is a cross-section of British-American folk song as it existed in the southern highlands during their period of relative isolation: Child ballads and British ballads from the broadside tradition; British and American lyric songs; native American ballads and humorous songs; and folk hymns and moralizing pieces of nineteenth-century origin. Unlike many traditional singers, she sings very few late-nineteenth-century sentimental parlor or popular songs, and only one or two modern country pieces learned from the radio.

While we were the first people to come to her door asking for ballads, Maude has earned a considerable reputation for wine making, an art she taught herself, although she had helped her father distill brandy when she was a girl. Her wine recipes appear in Joseph Earl Dabney's *Mountain Spirits II,* and her photo, in color, graces the book's cover. Now past eighty, she is still able to range over the mountains picking fox grapes and muscadines to make the wines that people come to taste from several states around.

Maude Mae Thacker grew up in a log house at the foot of Hendricks Mountain, one of the southernmost of the southern Appalachians, only forty-five miles north of Atlanta. Today a wealthy development, Bent Tree, covers the former family land, and the house has long since disappeared. Maude went up there with her brother recently to look around. "I used to know every pig trail," she commented. "Hit's changed, I reckon. Creek's still there. Golf course is there, the ninth hole is right up near the old house." They found the rocks their mother had set under the porch; Maude wanted to take one as a souvenir, but her brother dissuaded her—"Said I'd get snake-bit."

As a child Maude was very much a tomboy, and at the time when her younger brother was too young to do much work, she had to do much of the outdoor work on the farm. It was only after she married that she learned to cook and sew, unlike her younger sisters, who learned the traditional women's tasks. Maud wore overalls," 'cause you can't get about in a dress. And we'uz on that mountainside, a-plowin'. I generally wore what my daddy wore out, down on the knees, just cut 'em off, plenty long for me to plow in. . . . Yeah, and my daddy sawed the plow handles off and let 'em down, so I could reach 'em good. My brother, he could cover, but he couldn't lay [the rows] straight—I had to lay the rows off. We raised all of our stuff. We owned most of the Hendricks Mountain. . . . Our land went nearly to the top, and we used to go up there and saw board timber, and turn the blocks loose, and they'd roll plumb down to the foot of that mountain. Knock down trees! We got out boards, and split the boards in seven, and peel tanbark, haul that to Jasper [the county seat] and sell it." Maude also hewed cross-ties, and she drove steers, hauling wagonloads of timber to a sawmill where her father worked.

Maude was especially close to her father, despite the fact that he lived away from home during much of her childhood: he fired the boilers that powered the quarry machinery at Marble Hill, several miles away, and he lived in a little house over the boilers, coming home only on weekends. At these times she would often go off squirrel hunting with him. "Me and him'd take our dinner and go all day on them mountains. And he'd siiiiiing! He didn't have to sing a song to me but twice, till I knowed it. He just knowed all kinds of songs." Born in Pickens County in 1865, Eli Fields learned many of his songs when he was a convict laborer in the coal mines of Tennessee. He served two years there, before he was married, for refusing to inform on a friend who burned the house of a man who "reported

stills." Maude remembers that he had a clear voice that could be heard from the top of the mountain. He also sang to his babies, and when he "set up" all night with the dead.

Her father made brandy, which he sold for five dollars a gallon to people who came to the house, including, Maude recalls, one preacher! I asked her if he could pretty much get away with that, or if the "revenue" was a problem.

"Oh, the revenue'd get you if he could."

"Where'd they come out of? Atlanta?"

"No! Jasper! Ridin' horses. They rode up to our house one time, and said, 'Eli, where's your still?' And pa said, 'It's under the floor.' They never did look. They thought he's just a-jokin'. He wasn't. They turned and went back." Another time, "the revenuers cut my daddy's still down. . . . He happened to be on the hill, a-cuttin' wood, and the still was under a bank, and they was just a-watchin' the smoke, and they didn't look straight ahead. If they had, they'd-a seen my daddy. When he seed 'em comin', he just set down. They just went under that bluff, and he come up the ridge. He was give out. 'Hey, get that malt out of here! The revenuers done cut me down, be over here in a few minutes.' Us kids begin to sack that malt out and hide it under logs, out in the woods. . . . They didn't know whose still it was."

Maude's mother used some of their whiskey for "homemade medicine. She'd get a big quart bottle and fill it with herbs, pour whiskey over 'em." Among the herbs were ginseng, rattle root, and lady slipper. "Me and my brother, we had a little bitty round bottle, had a string tied around it, go in my daddy's keg, and let that bottle down there, guggle, guggle, guggle. We'd get the pure stuff! Without any herbs!" Maude remembers a time when she took her two younger sisters "up in the loft, made 'em both drunk! I couldn't get 'em back down the ladder. I had to call my mamma, and raise a plank. Had to let 'em down through there. And I let Fanny down, she couldn't stand up. And mamma said, 'You come down right now!' And she was standin' at the foot of the ladder, and she had a hickory stick about that long, and she wore that out on me! Me and my brother wouldn't get drunk, we'd just take a sup," Maude went on to explain. She got in trouble a lot, and "got more whuppins than any. Any time any of them got a whuppin', 'cause I'd butt in and then she'd pour it onto me. . . . Last time, I was bigger'n she was. She whupped me with a peach-tree sprout about that long! Yeah!" That time she had hit her brother with a rock because he wouldn't let her drive the mule. On another occasion she threw a snake at her sister. "I didn't work till dark much, but one night I had to. I'd throwed a snake on my sister and was afraid to go home, and I plowed till dark, took the trace chains off, hung 'em up, got the mule by the tail. . . . Mamma didn't whup me. Too dark to go out and get a hickory stick. I was a-plowin', plow got awful heavy, and raised up, there's a big old king snake at the foot of the plow, wrapped around the beam. I unwrapped it. And my sister, lived beside of us, she'd been gettin' our peaches, papa said don't pull 'em, the trees was young. I threwed that king snake on her, told her to leave our peaches alone, but she run before I had time to tell her anything. Went to the house just flyin'."

Obviously Maude had no fear of snakes, though "all the rest was afraid of 'em." One of her main amusements as a girl was to catch snakes to "put on a show" for the other children. She would "pick them up, throw them around." At one time she had twenty-two in a box in a tree.

Maude got to the fourth grade at the one-room Sharp Top School. "We had to cut wood for the heater. We didn't have it like the kids have it now. I liked to go to school, 'cause I got to play ball, fight with the boys." Maude explained that she fought to protect her kid brother. She was brought up in the Baptist church, and remembers that they wouldn't have "string music in their churches, these Baptists. Well, a piano's got strings, ain't it? Yeah, I was raised a Baptist, but I tell you what I b'lieve in—what's right!" She says they would have turned her out of church if she had gone to a "reg'lar dance. . . . And some woman asked a preacher about dancin', he said, if you want to dance, get off to yourself, dance all you want to!" As she spoke Maude was in her kitchen, offering samples of her wines to us, and she told us, "I dance around this table nearly every night." She did go to one square dance as a girl, up in Murphy, North Carolina. "I 'uz afraid my mother'd kill me," she recalled. I asked her where she learned the lively flatfoot buck-dance steps she does, and she replied, "At home. We 'uz goin' celebratin' one Christmas. Nobody didn't know I could dance. We got to dancin' at a neighbor's house, and I danced, too." They had a fiddle, a guitar, an accordion, and a banjo at the gathering. Maude was learning the organ at this time, and she played along. At seventy-nine Maude was learning the newest style of dancing at a carnival at Pickens County School. Maude thought about her late cousin Tom Quinton, who was then assistant principal of the school, as she recalled the occasion. "Pore Tommy. . . . They was a-discoin' down there, and I didn't know what discoin' was. And I said to my granddaughter, 'Lets go in and watch 'em—I want to see how they do that.' I like to see people dance, to tell you the truth of the business. We went in, and Tommy was there. Here he come, just a-flyin', grabbed me, made me dance with him. He was a sight."

Both her parents died in 1920, and Maude and her sister left home to work in the cotton mills down in Canton, Georgia. The sisters were courted by two brothers, whom they married. Maude's husband, Hubert "Red" Thacker, was a marble-mill worker, though he later became an ordained minister. They had a daughter and a son, and moved up to Knoxville, Tennessee, for a time before coming back to Pickens County. A widow for several years, Maude now lives with her bachelor son, Ed. She has kept the memory of her old songs alive by singing them first to her children, then to her three grandchildren, and finally to her five great-grandchildren. Today she still performs a number of pieces on her ornate parlor pump organ—"Little Brown Jug," and "Sherman Will March to the Sea," but when she sings, it is her unaccompanied voice that carries the story, the old-time way. Not particularly introspective or analytical, she declines to comment on why people in the old days favored ballads of jealousy, murder, treachery, and warfare, except to offer that she was never scared by them, and that her father liked war songs, and "songs about people a-killin' people." Of course a few songs were of happy love, and there were comical pieces like "Once I Had an Old Grey Mare" and "Calomel" in the family repertoire.

Maude's songs do mean a lot to her, and she recognizes their rarity and value; she wishes her voice were not cracked with age and that she could sing them as she used to. "Lots of times I go to bed at night, sing 'em to myself, just whisper. I wrote all them off, to give to my daughter. She's got 'em, but I don't guess she can sing ary one of 'em."

The Famous Wedding

Sung by Maude Thacker; Tate, Pickens County, April 25, 1981. Despite the similarity of its title to "The Fatal Wedding," this is a different and less frequently encountered piece; Cecil Sharp collected it as "Awful Wedding"

from Mrs. Moore at Rabun County, Georgia (Sharp, 2:83). A cryptic and ironic love song, Mrs. Thacker's version begins with the willow and ends with a dove, both symbols of unhappy love. The air is decidedly Scottish.

♩ = 73

The weep-ing willow is a very fine flower, it does blossom eve—ry year; young men and girls love and spend many hours and of-ten do their ru-in bring.

1. The weeping willow is a very fine flower
   It does blossom every year;
   Young men and girls love and spend
      many hours
   And often do their ruin bring.

2. Last night I was at a famous wedding
   Where the female proved unkind;
   The liquor was bought and the supper
      prepar-ed,
   And every one led a sing-a-song.

3. The very first song was my own true
      love,
   This is the song that he sings to his
      bride:
   "I'm troubled in my mind and changed
      in my notion,
   'Cause that I didn't get my own true
      love."

4. My true love she sits at the head of the
      table,
   And every word was remembered well.
   To bear it any longer she was not able,
   And down at her true love's feet she
      fell.

5. "Oh where shall I go, where shall I tarry
   To forget my own true love?"
   Right down by her graveside, oh there
      will retire,
   Mourning like some harmless dove."

Spoken: Lonesome (dove).

Betsy
(Laws M20)

Sung by Maude Thacker; Tate, Pickens County, August 2, 1980. Maude Thacker has a lovely tune in the dorian mode for this ballad of lovers' forced separation; the song comes from the British broadside tradition. It seemed, until the abrupt final line, that poor Betsy might have survived in America. Maude's version is the first reported from Georgia. See Laws I, p. 189; and Eddy, p. 218 (Ohio); Brown, 2:254 (North Carolina); Pound (Nebraska); Randolph, 1:235 (Missouri).

Oh Betsy is a lady fair, just lately came from weekly share; there bein' a mer - chant in the town, beautiful Betsy to him was bound.

1. Oh Betsy is a lady fair,
   Just lately come from weekly share;
   There bein' a merchant in the town,
   Beautiful Betsy to him was bound.

2. All on one Sunday evening as I've
       heard tell,
   He said to Betsy, "I love you well,
   I love you better than I love my life,
   I do intend to make you my wife."

3. His mother a-being in another room,
   Hearin' what her son said to Betsy,
   She was dissolved [resolved] all in
       her mind
   How to disappoint her own son's design.

4. So early next morning before she rose,
   She said to Betsy, "Put on your clothes,
   Put on your clothes and go with me
   To wait on me two days or three."

5. They rode and they rode till they came
       to the town,
   They rode to Mr. Gordon's and there
       put down.
   A ship being ready all in that town,
   Beautiful Betsy to Virginia was bound.

6. His mother a-making such quickly
       return,
   And who should she find but her
       only son.
   "You're welcome home, dear Mother,"
       he said,
   "But where is Betsy, your waiting
       maid?"

7. "Oh son, oh son, didn't I plainly see
   How great your love was to Betsy?
   Don't love her no more, for it's all
       in vain,
   Betsy is sailing the raging main."

8. Oh mother, oh mother, you've proved
       unkind;
   You have ruined this fair body of mine.
   You've caused me to weep, you've
       caused me to mourn,
   You've caused me to die and leave
       my home."

9. Then after seeing her own son lie dead,
   She rung her hands unto her head;
   Saying, "If it would please the Lord to
       send him breath again,
   I'd send for Betsy way o'er the main."

10. Betsy is sailing the salt sea;
    God send her safe to Vergisty [Vir-
        ginny?];
    She is more tender-hearted than a dove,
    She weeped and she mourned, and they
        both died for love.

Maude Thacker. (Tate, 1980.)

Lord Thomas

("Lord Thomas and Fair Annet," Child, no. 73)

Sung by Maude Thacker; Tate, Pickens County, August 23, 1980. Maude learned this ballad from her father. At one time one of the most *widely distributed of the classic British ballads in America, by the beginning of the 1980s it must be considered a rarity, especially a version*

with a complete text and excellent, if typical, tune. The expression "Don't run her down to me" in the eighth verse is an interesting

Americanism. See Child, 2:179–99; and Brown, 2:69 (North Carolina); Brewster, p. 58 (Indiana); NLCR, p. 73 (Virginia); Cox II, p.

45 (West Virginia); Davis I, p. 191 (Virginia); Davis II, p. 123 (Virginia); Fuson, p. 49 (Kentucky).

1. Lord Thomas he is a gaily man,
   He keeps the king's white hall.
   Fair Ellender is a beautiful bride,
   Lord Thomas he loved her well,
      well, well,
   Lord Thomas he loved her well.

2. "Oh mamma, oh mamma, come
      riddle me now,
   Come riddle me unto one;
   Whether I should go to fair
      Ellender's wedding
   Or bring the brown girl home,
      home, home,
   Or bring the brown girl home."

3. "The brown girl has both house
      and land,
   Fair Ellender she has none;
   My advice to you, Lord Thomas,
      my son,
   Is to bring the brown girl home,
      home, home,
   Is to bring the brown girl home."

4. He mounted on his milk-white
      steed,
   And rode to fair Ellender's door;
   And none so ready but fair
      Ellender herself
   To rise and let him in, in, in,
      To rise and let him im.

5. "What is the news, Lord Thomas,"
      she said,
   "What is the news?" said she.
   "I've come to invite you to my
      wedding,
   Which is bad news to me, me, me,
      Which is bad news to me."

6. She mounted on her milk-white
      steed
   And rode to Lord Thomas's gate;
   And none so ready but Lord
      Thomas himself
   To rise and let her in, in, in,
      To rise and let her in.

7. He took her by her lily-white
      hand,
   He led her into the hall,
   Seated her down among the
      ladies,
   Among the ladies of all, all, all,
      Among the ladies of all.

8. "Is this your bride, Lord Thomas?"
      she said,
   "Is this your bride?" said she.
   "She is a beautiful bride,
   Don't run her down to me, me, me,
      Don't run her down to me."

9. The brown girl having a little pen
      knife,
   Both keen and sharp;
   Between the long ribs and the short
   She riddled fair Ellender's heart,
      heart, heart,
   She riddled fair Ellender's heart.

10. He took the brown girl by her hand,
    And led her out in the hall;
    Drew out a sword, cut off her head,
    And he kicked it against the wall,
       wall, wall,
    And he kicked it against the wall.

11. He placed the brown girl on the
       floor,
    Fair Ellender to his breast,
    Saying, "Here's the death of three
       true lovers,
    God send their souls to rest,
       rest, rest,
    God send their souls to rest.

12. "Oh mother, oh mother, go dig my
       grave,
    Dig it long and deep;
    Place fair Ellender in my arms,
    And the brown girl at my feet,
       feet, feet,
    And the brown girl at my feet."

King William, Duke Shambo

("The Battle of the Boyne")

Sung by Maude Thacker; Tate, Pickens County, August 23, 1980. Maude Thacker's incomplete version of this eighteenth-century British broadside ballad is its first appearance in the southern tradition; she learned it from her father who, she says, knew the whole piece. First reported in Peter Buchan's Scarce Ancient Ballads *(Peterhead, Scotland, 1817), it describes the defeat of James II by William of Orange and his general, Duke Frederick Schomberg, at the Battle of the Boyne in 1690.*

July the first at the break of day in one thousand six hundred and twenty, King William, Duke Shambo, and his commanders prepared to fight King Jeems and his

The subsequent Protestantization of Northern Ireland and the migrations of the Scotch-Irish to Pennsylvania and the southern Appalachians were important consequences of this struggle. Samuel Bayard collected a burlesqued version in Pennsylvania with lines he said could be guaranteed to make Catholic Irish fighting mad (Korson, p. 47): "Ten thousand micks were killed with picks." Bayard comments that the beautiful "Boyne Water" air has been used for "Barbara Allen." O'Neill includes "Boyne Water" in Music of Ireland (no. 45), and Maude Thacker's melody is clearly part of this widespread melodic family. Brewster (p. 314), collected a fragmentary text without tune in Indiana, from a man who learned it from an Irishman in the 1880s.

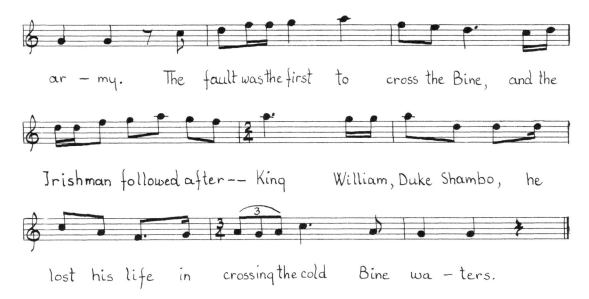

ar — my. The fault was the first to cross the Bine, and the Irishman followed after -- King William, Duke Shambo, he lost his life in crossing the cold Bine wa — ters.

1. July the first at the break of day
   In one thousand six hundred and
      twenty,
   King William, Duke Shambo, and his
      commanders prepared
   To fight King Jeems and his army.
   The fault was the first to cross the Bine,
   And the Irishman followed after—
   King William, Duke Shambo, he lost his
      life
   In crossing the cold Bine waters.

2. King Jeems a-being Shambo's spy
   Saw his horse with him was falling
   He reined his horse with a heavy rein,
   And to his men he call-ed
   Saying: "Brave, brave boys don't be
      dismissed [dismayed]
   At the loss of one commander,
   For the Lord shall be our King this day,
   And I'll be your commander.

3. King Jeems in his tents in his silence
      repose,
   Were thinking of very little danger;
   Bold Massas rode with his brave troops,
   And the elements roared like thunder.

Maude Thacker Recording Her Ballads. (Tate, 1980.)

Sweet Jane

Sung by Maude Thacker; Tate, Pickens County, April 25, 1981. This song of happy love is animated by lilting Irish melody. Hedy West collected an almost identical text, sung to a different melody, from Lula Prather Denson of Pickens County, who died in 1961; West performed it on Vanguard LP VRS-9124. The song is also known in the Ritchie family of Kentucky, and Brown (2:608) prints a North Carolina version; he states that the song originated in "California gold fever times." See also Combs, p. 206.

"Farewell, sweet Jane, for I must go a-cross the foam-ing sea; my trunk is now on John-son's board with all my com-pa-ny."

1. "Farewell, sweet Jane, for I must go
   Across the foaming sea;
   My trunk is now on Johnson's board
   With all my company."

2. She wet my cheeks with flowing tears,
   And then I kissed her hand,
   Saying, "Think of me, sweet Willie dear
   When you're in some distant land."

3. My bosom felt a feeling then,
   It'd never felt before;
   I went on board with Johnson's men
   And left my native shore.

4. For two long years we labored hard,
   A digging of our well;
   We lived on bread and salted lard
   But did not lose our health.

5. We loaded up our trunks with gold,
   And then I thought of Jane;
   An anxious thought did onward roll
   As I a-crossed the main.

6. For two long weeks we sailed along
   Across the mighty deep;
   I thought one night we all was gone,
   Our captain was asleep.

7. Until at length we shoved in sight
   Of our own native town;
   The our good captain did command
   To take the writing down.

8. I say a crowd of lovely girls
   Come marching to the ship;
   I saw sweet Jane with all her curls,
   And I begin to skip.

9. I ran and met her on the walk,
   My soul was filled with charm;
   Both was so full we could not talk,
   I caught her in my arms.

10. We marched along the marble walk
    Up to her father's door,
    Where everything was neat and clean
    Where we stood on the floor.

11. The parson read the marriage law
    Which bound us both for life.
    Now Jane is mine without a flaw,
    A sweet and loving wife.

I Am a Poor Wayfaring Pilgrim

Sung by Maude Thacker; Tate, Pickens County, August 1, 1980. Found more often as "Poor Wayfaring Stranger," this is one of the best known American camp-meeting spirituals. Mrs. Thacker's text is similar to that of R. E. Winsett (Radio and Revival Specials, *1939),* *but it contains substitutions, notably, "But I have a home in yonder city." This line is in Merle Travis's "I Am a Pilgrim," but it is not normally a line of "Wayfaring Stranger." The Travis song, however, may have been based on "Wayfaring Stranger."*

♩ = 72

I am a poor way-far-ing pilgrim, I'm a trav'lin' through this world be-

-low, but I've a home in yonder city, in that bright world to which I

go. I'm go-ing there to meet my father, I'm go-ing

there no __ more to roam; I'm __ just go - ing o-ver

Jordan, I am just go - ing o-ver home.

Mrs. Thacker's tune is unusual in that it opens on the fifth instead of the tonic. A close variant that also opens on the fifth appeared as "Fulfillment" in the Sacred Harp *(1844), set to a different text. Surely the tune is of Anglo-American folk origin. Related tunes are* commonly found as *"I Was Born in Old Virginia," "Come All You Fair and Tender Ladies,"* and others.

Early publications of the text (without tunes) occurred in 1858 (Bever, The Christian Songster), *and 1867* (Revival and Camp Meeting Minstrel). *The first publication of the text with the minor tune usually found today may have been that of W. T. Dale,* Times of Refreshing *(1893). John Garst has reported on early publications in* The Hymn *31 (1980): 98–101. See also Riddle, p. 94.*

---

1. I am a poor wayfaring pilgrim,
   I'm trav'lin' through this world below,
   But I've a home in yonder city,
   In that bright world to which I go.
   > I'm going there to meet my father,
   > I'm going there no more to roam;
   > I'm just going over Jordan,
   > I am just going over home.

2. I know dark clouds will hover o'er me
   I know my pathway's rough and steep;
   But golden fields lies out before me,
   Where wearied eyes no more
   > shall weep.
   > I'm going there to meet my mother,
   > She said she'd meet me when I come.
   > I'm just going over Jordan,
   > I am just going over home.

3. I want to sing redemption's story
   In concert with the blood-washed
   > throng;
   I want to wear a crown of glory
   When I get home to that bright land.
   > I'm going there to meet my school-
   > mates,
   > I'm going there no more to roam;
   > I'm just going over Jordan,
   > I am just going over home.

4. I'll soon be done with troubles and
   > trials,
   This form shall rest beneath to sod;
   I'll soon lay down this cross of denial
   And enter in my home with God.
   > I'm going there to meet my Savior,
   > Who shed for me His precious blood;
   > I'm just going over Jordan,
   > I am just going over home.

Granny Thacker Dancing. (Charcoal, 30″ × 22″, 1982.)

Once I Had an Old Grey Mare

Sung by Maude Thacker; Tate, Pickens County, August 23, 1980. This comical song seems to have been well known in north Georgia; we recorded a good version from the Chancey Brothers in Gilmer County. Maude's version has a particularly well developed story line.

This purely southern song was recorded commercially by Kentuckian Buell Kazee in the 1920s, and Norman Blake based his recent recording on this. For other variants, see Brown, 3:217; Henry, p. 410; Roberts, p. 190; Sharp, 2:326.

Once I had an old grey mare, once I had an old grey mare, once I

had an old grey mare, saddled her up and I rode her there.

1. Once I had an old grey mare,
   (three times)
   Saddled her up and I rode her there.

2. When I got there she was very tired,
   (three times)
   She lay down in the old church yard.

3. When the preacher begin to pray,
   (three times)
   The old mare shouted in a weepin' way.

4. She taken a notion to be baptized,
   (three times)
   You ought to 've seen that river rise.

5. When the preacher led her in,
   (three times)
   The preacher shouted and the old mare grinned.

6. When the preacher led her out,
   (three times)
   You ought to 've seen that old mare shout.

7. She lived a Christian ever since,
   (three times)
   She never has broke the old cross fence.

8. She said she'd live a Christian life,
   (three times)
   She'll make some old hoss a good old wife.

Barbara Allen

(Child, no. 84)

Sung by Maude Thacker; Tate, Pickens County, August 2, 1980. This is certainly the most widely known and sung of the old British ballads throughout the English-speaking world. We have recorded three good texts and tunes in north Georgia, from Kate Quinton in Pickens County and from Vaughn Eller in Towns County (see Flyright LP 546), and this fine if typical version from Mrs. Thacker. Hedy West recorded a version she learned in north-central Georgia on Folk Legacy LP FSA-32. Library of Congress LP AAFS L54, *Versions and Variants of Barbara Allen,* presents thirty recorded examples and Charles Seeger's exhaustive musicological analysis. See Child, 2:276–79; and Brewster, p. 99; Brown, 2:111; Byron, p. 8; Cox II, p. 96; Davis I, p. 302; Davis II, p. 182; Fuson, p. 62; Henry, p. 80; Morris, p. 283; Roberts, p. 95; Sharp, 1:183.

It was in the plea-sant month of May, when the greenbuds they were swellin', young

Wil-lie on his deathbed lay, for the love of Bar-b'ra Allen.

1. It was in the pleasant month of May,
   When the green buds they were
     swellin',
   Young Willie on his death bed lay
   For the love of Barbara Allen.

2. He sent his servant to the town,
   And sent him to a dwellin'
   Saying, "Here's a letter my master sent
     to you,
   If your name be Barbara Allen."

3. She took the letter out of his hand,
   And then she laughed and lingered;
   You'll never see another better day,
   For you'll never get Barbara Allen.

4. So slowly, slowly she got up,
   And slowly she went to him;
   She slowly passed the curtains by,
   "Young man, I think you're dying."

5. "Oh yes, I'm sick, and very sick,
   My heart is almost broken;
   But you'll never see another better day,
   For you'll never get Barbara Allen."

6. She started on her high way home,
   She heard the corpse a-coming;
   And ever' knock the death bell give
   Was: "Woe to Barbara Allen."

7. She went on home that very day,
   "Mother make my bed long and narrow,
   Sweet William died for me today,
   I'll die for him tomorrow."

8. Willie died on Saturday night,
   Barbara died on Sunday;
   The old woman died for the love of both,
   And was buried on Easter Monday.

9. Willie was buried in one church yard;
   And Barbara in the other.
   A rose bush sprung from Willie's grave,
   And a briar from Barbara Allen.

10. They grew and they grew to the old
      church wall
    Where they could not grow any higher.
    They tied themselves in a true love's
      knot
    To make young people wiser.

I Used to Do Some Frolickin'

JAKE STAGGERS, BLACK BANJO-PICKER OF TOCCOA

DURING THE NINETEENTH CENTURY the five-string banjo developed from a crude plantation instrument of African descent, through a period of popularization in traveling minstrel and tent shows, into a favorite of southern musicians, black and white, for playing song accompaniment and dance tunes. Jake Staggers was born in the last year of the century, at a time when black musicians, who had figured most importantly in the evolution of the banjo's picking styles and repertoire, were dropping the instrument in favor of the guitar, better suited for the blues and rags that were then coming into fashion. Jake was drawn to the banjo, however, and, starting at ten years, learned to play from his older brother Hansell, a friend named Jesse Godine, and Garnett Spencer, a white man. He learned on a homemade instrument made out of a tin pan with a cat-skin head, though ground-hog and even fish-skin heads were also used at the time.

Born in Oconee County, South Carolina, Jake Staggers has lived the last fifty years across the Tugaloo River, in Toccoa, Georgia. His working years were spent on railroad section gangs and in construction work; he drove an egg truck for a time. He was a sought-after musician in the community, playing for both black and white dances, in churches, at corn shuckings and hog killings. Christmas season would see him going through the streets of Toccoa playing a banjo hanging from his neck by a rope, parading to a dance with other musicians to the light of "flambeaux," torches of bottles and kerosene-soaked rags on long poles. In his old age he is a dignified and reflective man, comforted by a close and loving family and appreciative friends; but he is also anxious about the crime and social disorganization of the modern world, worse in his mind than the sporadic violence that marked his backwoods youth.

When we met him he had not played in years because of arthritis, but he told us he had been "dreaming about playing again." He has practiced his rhythmic drop-thumb frailing banjo style and his highly improvisatory singing of his interesting repertoire of preblues dance pieces, railroad songs, and spirituals. He is the only active black banjo picker we know of in Georgia, and the flavor of his life and music comes across best in his own words. When we talked with him at his home in a Toccoa housing project in April 1981, I started by asking him how he got started in music.

"That's all right. First, when I was ten years old . . . in Walhalla, South Carolina. My brother had two banjos, and I'd have him tune 'em up. And he'd leave, I picked one till it go down [out of tune], and I'd go get the other 'n. And somebody come by and tune it back up. Then I got to tune it myself."

I wondered whether there were several people in the community who played.

"Oh, yeah," he answered, "lot o' people played. The old songs, y'know. They had no songs like you got now, all these fancy songs. We had all these old breakdowns, y'know. . . . Blues, and things, lot of people played on guitar, not played on no banjer."

He said he was ten years old when he played his first square dance. I asked him what that was like.

"All night. I could go to the house today. Madison, South Carolina. Played 'Garfield.' That's the first thing I played. 'Garfield.' Ha! Old 'Garfield.' "

"Who did you learn 'Garfield' from?"

"My brother. I don't know where he got it at. He worked on the railroad a long time ago, y'know. Thought of a song, pick it up and sing 'em. I'd make banjos out of a board, tack me some nails, tack it

Jake Staggers and His Family. (Toccoa, 1981.)

in the end of it and tighten it, spool thread and tighten it, put a bridge on it. . . . Have that, and played a jew's-harp, played a French harp [harmonica], play a stick, bow it like that, tie a can, put it to your mouth, and play a tune."

He was referring to the primitive Afro-American mouth bow, which he called "bow'n arra' stick." "You can play a tune on it," he repeated.

"You think you could make one yet?"

"Yeah, what you do, get a stick of wood, bend it down, tie a string to it. Gotta be a good string, else it'll break, kick you in the mouth, see!"

"Did you ever hear anybody play the quills? Little pipes that you put in a row?"

"Nah." Then he remembered: "I used to see that, too, but I never did play it. I can play a single one. I can blow a single whistle. I used to make them out of cane. . . . I can blow a train song, mock a train, anything. . . . And I used to beat straws all night." This was the practice, going back to slavery times, of beating straws on the strings of a fiddle as the fiddler was playing.

"Now you used to play all the way up into Rabun County?"

"Yeah! And I used to play up on Panther Creek. I used to play for white folks all the time. I used to make my livin' when I was single playin' banjo for white folks and colored, y'know. You get a big tip, back then. Take yo' hat and go 'round, y'know. Some of 'em put a dollar in it, some of 'em put a penny!" We laughed at that. Jake remembered playing on Panther Creek "for the sheriff, when he fust married, all night up there. Twenty-five dancin' at one time. It's about fo' miles from here to Panther Creek. They had a big house up there to dance in. . . . I commenced playin' at sundown, I played for 'em till daylight."

"Did you play by yourself?"

"By myself! Sho! And I carried two sets of banjo strings—you could get a set . . . then for fifty cents—and if I break one, put one back on, while they rest and eat, and then I go right back. That big house is still there. . . . Oh, I used to make a lot of music in my day, down in the country, Lavonia, Carnesville. I used to go in there and play banjo, all around. After I got sick I laid it down." He looked at his old instrument leaning against the wall, without pegs or strings, its head torn and burnt. "That was a good banjo. One time I used to drink some, way back, I had two children on my lap, I was playin'

the banjo, and went to sleep, I was smokin', and the cigarette ashes fell on the head and caught fire! That's why it's got the hole in it. I used to drink, y'know, way back yonder, drink the little toddy along. I was workin', come in drink a drink, get my old banjer and set under that big tree and play. People come by the road—come by the road and stop. Mailman stop, listen at me play. Fust thing I know I have a yardful of people. Then they come back at night and they want to dance some, and I let 'em dance. Some of 'em bring a guitar, they play that. I been through with women—with banjo pickin', I used to didn't care about nobody, 'cause I couldn't be beat, on back then! My fingers good and limber, and I don't care who was playin', I walk in, and they stop. 'Give it to him! Let him play,' all like that. I say, 'We'll all play together.' We'd go playin' together, some'd break a string, I'd go right on. Lot of times I'd get there, and I'd go beat that head like I'm beatin' the banjo, they never did tell the difference, y'know! Boy! Be a crowd on the floor. I used to have a good time, all the days out."

"What do you think's different about the old-time music from modern music?" I asked.

"I don't like that fancy stuff. I like that old-time banjo pickin' and guitar pickin'. . . . These young folks they like this jazz music—they don't know nothin' about no frolic like we used to frolic."

When I asked if any young people know about it, Jake said that they don't know how to go through a set. "I used to pick banjo and call a set at the same time," he recalled.

"What are some of the figures you'd call?"

"Swing corner; promenade; wind the ball; head and foot. Dance around, put a woman in the middle, and you dance around her like a turkey gobbler. We used to have fun! White and black, get on the flo' at one time and dance."

I wondered if they ever just sang at frolics, with no instruments.

"Naw, less'n you pat. I used to do a lot of pattin' and they'd dance, buck dance. . . . I got a girl up No'th, she can dance as good as anybody. She never have been beat, turned down! I used to buck dance. Ball the jack. I used to dance on my hands. Get up and swing the girl right on! Yeah, man, I used to do some frolickin'. That's right!"

"Sounds like good times," said Fred Hay, who was along that day.

"It was good times. Somebody come by with a big jug of corn liquor—whaaaaa! Po' out a glass half full, and people did cut right!

After a while, you'd hear a pistol shoot in the house, and people run out the do'! Yeah! One time me and her," indicating his wife, "were out behind a big ol' tree, big as that heater, over in South Carolina, this side of Westminster. And I had that banjer in my han', and somebody shot the lamp off the table with a shotgun. I run out the do' behin' that big tree, and they shot that tree about five or six times. Me and her got behind that tree."

"Were they trying to shoot you, or just anybody?"

"No! Jus' shoot, they didn't care. Outlaw crowd come break up the dance, this side of Westminster. Boy, we was frolickin' that night. This fella—he come out of the chain gang—had hands this wide. And he weighed three hundred pounds. Now he was some stout guy. He was wearin' the ball and chain, had the chain around his neck, then a chain around his leg, and a big ball . . . tied to his leg."

It sounded to me as if Jake was saying the man dragged the ball and chain to the dance, and I asked if he had the ball and chain right there.

"No. He got out, worked his time out, they turned him loose. He done got out of the chain gang, then, he come to that party. Boy, he stabbed that girl right there, right down the side of the neck, cut her throat, busted her heart wide open."

"When was that?"

"I was about thirty-six years old. Long time ago."

"What year were you born?"

"I'm eighty-two now. Count for yourself. Twentieth of June I'll be eighty-three. Yessiree."

I asked if he knew any long old tales that people used to tell.

"I know my grand-daddy told me, he had a yoke of steers, and he goin' to North Carolina, camped along the road. Had a little old fice [dog], little old fice kep' a-growlin', he never did see nothin'. He's cookin', and he's up and around, got his stuff cooked, little fice's gone. And a gre't big bear is standin' beside the wagon. He went taken go climb a tree! He reach and got his fiddle and he climbed a tree, and he put the fiddle right up in that tree, and the bear shakin' that tree. And after a while a lot of wildcats come, and panthers, and they went to scratchin' 'round that tree, and the tree begin to weave like that, and he thought about that fiddle. And he take that bow and draw it 'cross that fiddle, and they went to jerkin' their feet out, and one pulled his shoulder out and left it there! He got his feet hung in a root, and up on there, couldn't get it loose, tear it loose. That's all what saved him. That fiddle! Say, he's playin' the las' tune he played on that fiddle, all the way he's goin then. Had them old steers, weavin' on the road. Little old dog come out o' the woods, caught up with him, he put him in the wagon. He played that fiddle all along plumb to North Carolina. Yeah boy!"

Jake said his grandfather never told him what tune he had been playing.

Jake Staggers. (Toccoa, 1981.)

Seventy-four

Sung by J. C. "Jake" Staggers with five-string banjo; Toccoa, Stephens County, April 18, 1981. One of the first songs that Jake Staggers learned, this is the Tugaloo River–area variant of the widespread family of railroad songs that includes "Reuben's Train," "Train Forty-five," "Nine Hundred Miles," and "Five Hundred Miles"; compare with George Childers's version of the last named, p. 173. The verse beginning "Set you in the shade" also relates it to the banjo song "Red Rocking Chair," part of the white banjo picker's repertoire but, like the present piece, once the common property of white and black singers.

Five hundred miles from my home ———————, five hundred miles from my home, dar - ling, five hundred miles from my home.

1. Five hundred miles from my home,
   Five hundred miles from my home,
      darling,
      Five hundred miles from my home.

2. There's seventy-four, blow,
      station, blow,
   Blow like she didn't want to blow
      no mo',
      Blow like she didn't want to blow
      no mo'!

3. Darling, darling, what mo' could I do?
      What mo' could I do?

4. Set you in the shade, give you all
      I made,
      Honey babe, what mo' could I do?
      Honey babe, what mo' could I do?

5. Honey, honey, I ain't gonna leave town,
   Gonna lay 'round town till the pay train
      come back,
      Honey babe, you're on my min'.

6. Baby, baby, honey babe, what mo' could
      I do?
   I set you in the shade and give you all
      I made,
      Honey babe, what mo' could I do?

7. Baby, baby, what mo' could I do?
   Ain't gonna leave till the mail train
      come back,
      Honey babe, what mo' could I do?

Garfield

Sung and narrated by J. C. "Jake" Staggers with five-string banjo; Toccoa, Stephens County, April 18, 1981. Jake Staggers learned this unusual cante-fable, or spoken narrative interspersed with sung elements, from his older brother Hansell, who picked it up as a railroad worker; presumably human life was cheap enough on the rough section gangs to be taken in a dispute over cigars. The white North Carolina collector-performer Bascom

Sung:

Oh, Gar-field, kill'd a man, kill'd a man, kill'd a man, Little Gar-field,

Spoken:
Smoked a two-hundred-dollar ci-gar, Big Garfield, Little Garfield smoked a fifty-dollar cigar. One mornin' soon he got up went down the road, y'know, met Big Garfield, y'know,

Sung:

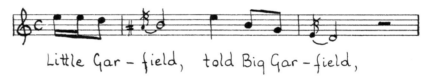

Little Gar-field, told Big Gar-field,

Spoken:
My cigar smokes the best, y'know, Little Garfield told him, mine smokes the best, his wife gettin' breakfast, y'know, went after Big Garfield,

Sung:

Where are you goin', Big Garfield? I'm goin' down the road. Feelin' bad, Lord

Spoken:
Little Garfield turned 'round, y'know, told Big Garfield, my cigar smokes the best, Big Garfield shot him in the side, y'know,

Sung:

Shot him in the side.

Spoken:
He fell on the groun', turned 'roun', and said,

Lamar Lunsford sang and recited this piece, also to banjo accompaniment (Library of Congress recording AFS L29, Songs and Ballads of American History and the Assassination of Presidents); Lunsford's version associates the story with President Garfield's assassination by Charles Guiteau, although the incident is described as a small-town street attack. The similar melodies in Lunsford's and Staggers's versions are characteristically black, and it is probable that this composition originated as an Afro-American response to the assassination. There is a related fragment, "My Frien' Garfiel'" in Henry, p. 439.

Sung:

Don't let my loving wife know it, don't let my loving wife know, Lord, don't let my loving wife know.

Shot him in the side.

Spoken:
He turned over, looked over, y'know, and said:

Sung:

Shot him in the side, shot him in the side, killed Big Garfield, shot him in the side. Oh, Lordy me,

oh———, Lordy me. Oh, Lordy me, oh———, Lordy me———.

Sally Ann

Sung by J. C. "Jake" Staggers with five string banjo; Toccoa, Stephens County, July 25, 1981. Though this song is clearly of black origin, it has in large part moved into the white repertoire, where it is performed as a banjo piece in both the old-time and bluegrass modes, and as a fiddle or string-band piece, sometimes sung, sometimes not. The only recent black performance is that of Lacey Phillips of Caldwell County, North Carolina, who plays it in the drop-thumb style on banjo, without singing (Physical Records 12-001).

White performances are numerous, a few being Wade Ward (Virginia, Folkways FA 2363); Tommy Jarrell (Virginia, County LP 748); Junie Scruggs (North Carolina, Folkways FA 2314, a prototype of the well-known Earl Scruggs instrumental version). We have recorded versions in Georgia from W. Guy Bruce, and from Lawrence Eller, who sings:

*Up the road and down the creek, me and Sally
    fell asleep,
All night long with Sally Ann, all night long
    with Sally Ann.*

Ray Knight sings a version that L. D. Snipes favored:

*Sal got a sugar lip, so they say,
Shake that big foot, Polly Ann,
Shake that little foot, Sally Ann.*

*Now Susie in the bed with a hog-eyed man,
I'm going home with Sally Ann.*

The sexual references in this song are frank enough. Cliff Carlisle, who recorded "Sal Got a Meatskin" for Penacord (25639), said that the "meatskin," also in Staggers's text, is a maidenhead, though the alternate meaning can be a slab of fat pork (NLCR, p. 79).

I got a su-gar foot down the road, I got a sugar foot down the road,

I got a su-gar foot down the road, I got a su-gar foot down the road.

1. I got a sugar foot down the road,
   I got a sugar foot down the road,
   I got a sugar foot down the road,
   I got a sugar foot down the road.

2. Down the road, darlin', down the road,
   Down the road, darlin', down the road,
   Down the road, darlin', down the road,
   Down the road, darlin', down the road.

3. Sift the meal and save the bran,
   Sift the meal and save the bran,
   Sift the meal and save the bran,
   Goin' to the weddin' with Sally Ann.

4. I'm gonna marry Sally Ann,
   I'm gonna marry Sally Ann,
   I'm gonna marry Sally Ann,
   I'm gonna marry Sally Ann.

5. *Repeat 4.*

6. *Repeat 3.*

7. Sal got a meatskin laid away,
   Sal got a meatskin laid away,
   Sal got a meatskin laid away,
   Grease John's wooden leg every day.

Frolic. (Charcoal, 22" × 30", 1983.)

How Long the Train Been Gone?

Sung by J. C. "Jake" Staggers with five-string banjo; Toccoa, Stephens County, April 27, 1980. This is a previously uncollected song, *although the railroad image has been used in black spirituals such as "This Train Is Bound for Glory," and "I'm Goin' Home on the*

Come and go with me _____, come and go with me _____, come and go with me.

How long the train been gone _____? How long the train been gone?

How long the train been gone _____? Come and go with me.

Mornin' Train." Although many black preachers considered the banjo a worldly instrument inappropriate for church music,

Jake has been using his banjo to accompany this song, as well as "Old Time Religion," for as long as he can remember. Occasionally he

will use the "How long the train been gone?" refrain as a sort of coda to his performance of "Garfield."

Refrain:

Come and go with me, come and go
    with me,
Come and go with me.

1. How long the train been gone?
   How long the train been gone?
   How long the train been gone?
   Come and go with me.

2. Got my mother and gone
      (three times)
   Come and go with me.

3. How long the train been gone?
      (three times)
   Come and go with me.

4. It been very long gone,
      (three times)
   Come and go with me.

5. Got my father and gone,
      (three times)
   Come and go with me.

6. Dark cloud risin' in the Eas',
      (three times)
   Come and go with me.

7. Mother, when you gonna rise?
      (four times)

8. I'm gonna rise in that Judgment Day,
   Rise in that Judgment Day,
   Rise in that Judgment Day,
   Come and go with me.

9. How long the train been gone?
      (four times)

Up the Oak, Down the Pine

Sung by J. C. "Jake" Staggers with five-string banjo; Toccoa, Stephens County, July 25, 1981. This previously uncollected "reel," or frolic tune, is typical of its type: one or two simple couplets sung repeatedly over a rhythm laid down by an instrument. It provides a link between the old plantation dance songs and the later country blues.

Up the oak, down the pine,
Up the oak an' down the pine,
Up the oak an' down the pine,
Tell my mama I'm down the line.
    Oh, Lord, tell my mama I'm down the line.

Oh, mama, I'm goin' home,
Oh, mama, I'm goin' home.

Down Yonder

THE TANNERS OF DACULA, SMOKY JOE MILLER,
UNCLE JOHN PATTERSON: SKILLET LICKER
MUSIC OF THE PIEDMONT

GORDON TANNER welcomed his old friend Smoky Joe Miller and Uncle John Patterson, the "Banjo King" from Carrollton, into the "oblong concern of a chicken coop" back behind his home on the outskirts of Dacula, Georgia. He had converted it into a music room, and he explained, "We run the chickens off, brought some half-stumps in." "I'm a country boy and feel right at home," said Uncle John. Actually the now-famous building is well fitted out, with a carpeted area at one end for the musicians, old photos and more recent trophies lining the walls, and an assortment of upholstered chairs and two oil-drum wood stoves provided for the comfort of the folks who gathered on Friday evenings to hear Gordon fiddle the tunes he had recorded with his father's renowned string band, Gid Tanner and the Skillet Lickers. In these sessions Gordon was joined by his son Phil on guitar and friends of Phil's on bass, banjo, and electric guitar—this group, which they called Skillet Lickers II, was "hard to classify" in Phil's words, as their music had become an amalgam of the old-time style and bluegrass, with some contemporary country ideas thrown in.

Yet Gordon kept returning to the ebullient Georgia fiddle-band music that his father and others played on some of the first commercial country, or "hillbilly," recordings back in the 1920s; and this warm Saturday afternoon in 1979 he had set up before our microphones the typical old-time string band, with "one on the fiddle, one on the banjo, and one on guitar," as Uncle John declared. "This is the first time I played with Gordon Tanner, but I played a thousand times with his dad." John was explaining why he had no trouble falling in with the old numbers. He was in typical form, his bare feet patting out a beat, his bare fingers picking and strumming his old

S. S. Stewart, the banjo muted but not dulled by a towel behind the head. Gordon's fiddle began to wail out, then whispered, then chopped out a breakdown rhythm, and he smiled and cocked his head back in a pose reminiscent of his father's old photographs. Joe Miller's guitar line was well salted with runs learned first hand from Riley Puckett, the guitar picker of the original Skillet Lickers—runs that, as Gordon put it, "give you a blood transfusion!" These three veterans of Georgia's great age of old-time string music were putting their lifetimes' experience into some of the finest recordings of that style to come out of the red-clay hills and pine woods of the Piedmont in years.

We eventually produced the tapes recorded at this session into an LP for Folkways records (*Down Yonder*, FTS 31089), and this recording, a half-hour television documentary ("Down Yonder," produced for Georgia Public Television by Clate Sanders), and folk festival performances, were bringing Gordon Tanner much-deserved recognition in his last years. In 1980 Gordon and Phil performed at the Smithsonian Festival of American Folklife on the Mall in Washington, D.C. In July 1982 Gordon and Phil, along with Joe Miller, appeared at the National Folk Festival at Wolf Trap Farm, and then Gordon and Phil went up to the Brandywine Festival in Delaware, where Gordon was to have been reunited with Lowe Stokes and Bert Layne, two veterans of the original Skillet Lickers, whom he had not seen in over fifty years. The day before the festival Gordon suffered a heart attack, and two days later he died. The sorrow felt by Gordon's family and musical friends on his passing was to a degree tempered by the knowledge that he had died doing what he loved the most, keeping the old-time music going.

Uncle John Patterson, Gordon Tanner, and Smoky Joe Miller Taking a Break During Recording Session. (Dacula, 1979.)

Born in 1916, Gordon Tanner lived most of his life in Gwinnett County, where his father was a farmer, Saturday-night fiddler, and frequent participant in the fiddlers' conventions in nearby Atlanta. Gordon remembered the time in 1924 when he heard his parents discussing a proposition by Frank Walker of Columbia records that Gid go up to New York and cut some recordings; Gid said he would go if he could get a certain "blind boy" to go with him. A few weeks later Gordon was listening to the Gid Tanner–Riley Puckett duo on the "little grindin' Victrola" his father brought back from New York.

Gid expanded his recording group into the famous Skillet Lickers, which included Clayton McMichen, Lowe Stokes, Fate Norris, and others. Gid played a rough and flavorful old-time fiddle, but the more skillful fiddling of McMichen and Stokes was featured on the Skillet Lickers' recordings. Gid, however, was a warm and extroverted entertainer, and his exuberance and showmanship sparked the group's music. He was much sought after for live shows, and, as Gordon told it, "he'd be full time [in music] till things got shallow, then he'd bounce back on the farm. He always kept two mules at home, and a milk cow, and raisin' two hogs a year, but he never hesitated to unhitch the mules and get his fiddle and go, whenever there was a request for him."

It was difficult at times to assemble the Skillet Lickers for live performances, so Gid Tanner often recruited other musician friends and members of his family for shows close to home. Of Gid's children Gordon was "strongest with the musical talent," and Gid fitted out his shy red-headed son with thimbles to play rhythm on a washboard; Gordon would also be asked to sing songs like "It Ain't Gonna Rain No More" and "Letter Edged in Black," dance a buck and wing, and play straight man to his dad's jokes. Gordon remembered going to Atlanta with his father on a wagon, and seeing Gid attract a huge crowd in front of some merchant friend's store with his fiddle, only to be moved on by the police. As Gordon told it, "The law has to come in, the streetcar is blocked—and made him put his fiddle up. Of course me, small as I was, it scared me. Of course, it didn't scare my daddy. . . . He'd scramble around and put his fiddle up, we'd walk around the corner, do the same thing, and I was scared to death the law was coming again. . . . But that's the way it was. They was hungry for that kind of music."

Gordon recalled other occasions when he had to provide an impromptu "second" on his dad's banjo when Gid was playing at a courthouse square or similar setting. "He'd give me the banjo, and had a clamp on it . . . by the thumb string, and right below there were two fingers, and that was G chord, and he said, 'Hold that right there!' He knowed I could beat time on anything. I would play that, you know. . . . He didn't have time to be teachin' me. Had to get goin'! 'Course, a lot of his songs, you had to be quick to get in another chord anyway! So . . . I learned that I wasn't wigglin' my fingers up and down there too much, and somebody might find out I wasn't playin'. So I begin to feel bad about that, and then the fiddle created a lot of interest, and I wound up bein' a fiddler."

Gordon's first modest goal on the fiddle was to play a recognizable tune. At fourteen he was playing "Georgia Wagoner" with his father and Riley over the radio in Covington, Kentucky. During his high-school years Gordon played in occasional contests and joined his dad playing for Gene Talmadge's 1932 gubernatorial campaign. His fiddle playing progressed quickly; though his father was still his chief influence, he learned much from McMichen and Stokes, both through occasional personal contact and through the Skillet Lickers' records, which were at the Tanner house.

By 1934 Stokes and McMichen had left the band, and Gid was asked by RCA to reassemble the Skillet Lickers to cut some sides in San Antonio, Texas. Riley Puckett went along, and Ted Hawkins was added on mandolin. Gordon, a seventeen-year-old student at Dacula High, was told by his dad, "You gonna be out of school for a week—talk to your teacher." Gordon assumed that he was being asked along just to help drive: Riley was blind, and Hawkins, as old as Gid, didn't drive.

Gordon recalled the trip vividly. "We didn't drive at night, so it took us three days. We'd get up early and drive as long as daylight'd last, then [we'd lodge] in a boardin' house or tavern. We'd have to take whatever we could. . . . One place we stopped, the sidewalks were made of boards, like a Western town. . . . We was drivin' an old '30 Chevrolet. It was already four years old, and my daddy had done a lot of travelin', and it was wore out, the front end was out of line, and I'd be give out in four hours, and he'd take over. . . . Every long hill, he'd say, 'Son, cut the motor off, save all the gas you can.' We went into this San Antonio hotel [the Texas Hotel], the oldest hotel in San Antonio, and this here recording set-up was in, looked to me it was big enough for a basketball court. And no furnishing in it. . . . And we was out almost in the middle of it, settin' around one mike.

We didn't rehearse, and so this man got us spaced around it. 'Course I was at the mike, my daddy in back, and Riley on the left, Ted on the right. So he begin to name out things he wanted us to play."

In his characteristically self-effacing manner, Gordon had told how he, as a high-school student and basketball player, and spare-time musician, had come to be lead fiddler for the most celebrated string band of the era. When I asked if he really didn't know he would be playing until he was at the mike, he replied, "Well, I sensed that I might be privileged to play one or two numbers . . . but I did play lead on everything that was played." Among the twenty-four sides cut at that historic session, the Skillet Lickers' last, were some of their most popular numbers, "Back Up and Push," "Soldier's Joy," "Tanner's Hornpipe," "Flop-Eared Mule," and a full-length and still definitive version of "Down Yonder." Gordon's name was not on the labels, though his picture appeared with the group in an RCA publicity brochure. For years he respectfully deferred to the assumption of many that his dad was playing lead fiddle. Though Gid never did claim to have played "Down Yonder," Gordon remembered having "coached my daddy in learnin' to play it after I saw that it was selling. I said, 'People's gonna ask you to play it wherever you go.' But I never could get him to get the double stops. He would 'single-out' strings." Yet "people would say, '*Nobody* plays "Down Yonder" like your daddy!' I said, 'That's right.' I never did have no reason to try to steal the credit, because I was lucky to be on."

Gordon graduated from high school in 1936. Though he was offered a basketball scholarship to North Georgia College, he would have had to go into debt to buy the required uniforms, so he decided to stay at home. He married later that year, and he and his bride, Electra, worked at chopping cotton for seventy-five cents a day to pay the rent on the house they later bought and where Mrs. Tanner still lives. Gordon also sharecropped with his father, drove a school bus, and later went to work for General Shoe Company in the county seat of Lawrenceville. Even at $9.45 a week such jobs were hard to find in the midst of the depression, and Gordon was not inclined to leave it for the uncertain life of a professional musician, especially after the couple's first child was born. He worked his way up to being a foreman at General Shoe, and later worked at Georgia Boot in Flowery Branch until his retirement in 1981.

Gordon continued to play with his father in the area, and at church on Sundays. In 1956 he tried his hand at making violins, and he mastered this difficult art. During his retirement he spent much of his time in his small shop, hand-crafting his exceptionally fine instruments. After spending hundreds of hours on each one, he would give it to a close friend or member of his family.

Gid Tanner died in 1960, and in 1968 Phil and several of his friends organized the Junior Skillet Lickers, later called Skillet Lickers II, and persuaded Gordon to play lead fiddle for them. This group has kept the name and the music going. They were no purists, however, and used a bluegrass banjo and electric guitar; Gordon provided the smooth modern fiddle licks appropriate to the bluegrass and country tunes they performed along with the older Skillet Lickers repertoire. The group performed frequently at Georgia festivals and fiddlers' conventions; at the Georgia Mountain Fair at Hiawassee, Gordon won the "King of the Mountain Fiddlers" crown.

The old-time music scholar Norm Cohen has pointed out that Gid Tanner, forty at the time he started to record, was older than Puckett or McMichen, and unlike these men, who absorbed popular and jazz influences into their music, "his orientation was toward traditional music" ("The Skillet Lickers: A Study of a Hillbilly String Band and Its Repertoire," *JAFL* 78 [1965]). Gordon inherited this love for the older material from his father and knew a good portion of the traditional songs and tunes played by Gid and others in the Skillet Lickers' circle. Like his father, Gordon could sing along with the fiddle, though on slow songs his voice seemed closer to Riley Puckett's rich tone, full of sentiment. Though he did not have Gid's penchant for extroverted comedy, he was a warm and communicative performer and had surpassed his father's technical ability on the fiddle even by the 1934 session. The good response to his music up to the time of his death had convinced Gordon that the old-time music could still speak to present-day audiences. "It's genuine," Gordon told me, "not a fad, something that blooms up and goes away, and you talk about it years ago, that come up like a storm, and went on."

JOE MILLER is a longtime friend of the Tanner family, and though he was "never a member of the regular Skillet Licker band," he did many shows with "Mr. Gid and Riley" in the forties. He was born in Walton County in 1918, and his family wanted to instill an interest in music in him at an early age. His mother made him a gourd fiddle fitted with strings of wires unwound from a sieve, and a cornstalk bow. When he was four or five his uncle bought him a twenty-five-cent Marine Band harmonica. Joe says, "The next time he came to visit, I was playing that thing, and it just thrilled him to death! So that fall he gathered in his crop and bought me several more, in different keys. I thought I was really uptown! I'd tote three of them in my pocket. People would give me nickels and dimes to play. . . . I was so little, you know, the curiosity."

It was the guitar that most attracted him, and a few years later his parents "ordered a 'leven-dollar ninety-five-cent Bradley Kincaid Hound-Dog guitar, and that was my start. Mother's brothers would come by and play some once in a while. And . . . the late Arthur Tanner [Gid's youngest brother] would come by and tune up for me and sing a few songs, show us a few chords. . . . And on those long winter nights around the fire we'd parch peanuts and pop corn, and I'd thump on that old guitar."

When he was six or seven Joe heard Riley Puckett for the first time, and thereafter he took every opportunity to go to Skillet Lickers shows. "I was always hanging around the side of the stage . . . to catch what I could. Riley just took my fancy as a guitar player, and it never changed." Joe remembers that Riley had the most unusual style of playing "of anybody I ever saw. He never moved his arm back and forth; his arm stayed steady on the instrument, and all the work was in his wrist and those two fingers, and I don't know how in the world he did it. He was blind, you know, and it was a unique process he developed while learning, that I never did see anybody duplicate. He was the fastest on those runs—that's why he got those multiple runs . . . go back and forth so fast." Eventually Joe learned how to play these distinctive runs with the flat-pick.

Joe recalls Puckett as a "moody-type feller, like all blind men I've ever had any experience with, and I have been associated with a good many. He was very sensitive, very emotional, you just had to understand him and kinda lean toward him a little bit. Some people couldn't get along with Riley because he was easy to get his feelings hurt, but if you can stop and realize what a unique separated world a blind man lives in, you can understand why, you know." Joe can speak from some personal experience—although not blind, his vision has always been considerably impaired. "But I always loved Riley," he continued. "He was always a nice quiet-type feller, and sociable, but he did have moods. . . . He'd get places where he wouldn't have

much to say, be down and out. *Then,* really, was when Riley did his best performing, yeah, when he was in one of those moods, felt like he was kinda left out . . . he'd get the blues, but when it come his time to sing on the stage, buddy, he always took the cake. When Riley would thump that guitar and say his first few words, every little child that was cryin' out through the audience would be quiet, you could hear a pin drop, and before he finished, especially the ladies, you could see 'em reach in their purse, get their handkerchief to dry their face. He could sing your heart out, he could reach you."

Gid Tanner, on the other hand, "was a live wire and a natural-born comedian. Everything he did was funny, and it 'most always was ad lib, too. . . . He was just as great a personality off stage as he was on. When you'd come to know him one time, you knew Gid Tanner. . . . He was always ready to make music and have a good time. Yeah, he was a great performer." Joe, who later worked as a side man with Puckett and Tanner, remembers that "Mr. Gid could take the show as a fiddler and comedian, and Riley could take it as a singer, and it seemed like there was always an unseen contest going between him and Riley for the honors. And it always was amazing to me, because I enjoyed both of them. That's one thing that made them great. They had the deep-seated desire in their soul to entertain the audience, and to make them love the show. I guess that's in the heart of all musicians."

Joe's first professional experience was with the Tennessee fiddler Charlie Bowman. "Charlie had moved south into Atlanta and had started a barn dance on WGST at the old Erlanger Theater on Peachtree Street, and I had come up with a young friend of mine that I'd taught to play guitar by the name of Everett Spain. He and I did harmony yodels back in those days. . . . Charlie gave us a break and put us on the air, and we were on the WGST Barn Dance every Saturday night."

By this time Joe had decided that music was one vocation open to a person with extremely poor eyesight. In 1939 he went up to Chattanooga, Tennessee, to play on station WDOD with Chester Anderson and Kentucky Evelyn. He was guaranteed five dollars a week, which "didn't leave much to play on" after he had spent two dollars for groceries and three dollars for a one-room apartment with a bed, a two-burner stove, and a little table and chair. Sometimes there would be a small bonus above the guarantee, sometimes not. After a few months of this penurious life, "my shoes would get to ramblin', I'd get to thinking about things back home. . . . I'd get homesick and was ready to give it up."

In the early forties he went on the road again, this time with Fisher Hendley and the Rhythm Aristocrats out of Columbia, South Carolina. At his audition Joe had amazed Hendley with his ability to seemingly set the strings ablaze with note-for-note fiddle tunes and lightning-fast runs, and earned the nickname "Smoky Joe."

Back in Georgia Joe worked with Gid Tanner, whom he considers "the most honest, the most congenial man I ever worked with in show business. . . . I played with him up to the time I got married, and some for good old brotherly love after that." His marriage was in 1943, and shortly thereafter he went to work at the Carwood overall plant, a job he held until his retirement in 1981. He got the calling to preach in 1951 and was ordained by the North Georgia Conference of the Congregational Holiness church. For the last twenty-six years he has had a radio ministry, first out of WIMO, Winder, then WMRE and now WKUN, both in Monroe.

His wife, Nellie, died in 1981, and Joe lives with his elderly parents in a big house in the Walton County village of Campton; he gives music lessons in the tiny music store he keeps in the side room. Music was the cement for his friendship with Gordon Tanner, whom he considered dear as a brother. "There's a bond like that between most musicians. . . . It's the best recreation I have. [Some] go to their football games . . . hoot and holler their head off—just give me my old guitar and two or three of my good friends, brother, I'm in heaven!" Another of Joe's good musical friends is mandolinist Newman Young of Monroe, with whom he does Blue Sky Boys–style vocal and instrumental duets.

Though he is a religious man and often sings and plays gospel music, Joe Miller continues to love the secular folk songs and parlor songs of an earlier day. For him, they express "the early pioneer life of people in America, their heartaches and sorrows. . . . Back in those days when a tune came out, it usually had an authentic background. . . . They sang about things that were tragic, and some love songs. But I remember as a young child sitting around the fireside, and hear musicians sing these songs on phonograph and radio, it just seeded in my soul. And at a tender age I could just weep when they'd sing those beautiful songs with that pretty harmony, telling those sad stories. I guess I'm living in a changing age, and it breaks my heart to see those old songs put back on the shelf, and the younger generation doesn't know about it. And I'm persuaded to believe that if it's introduced to them . . . it would touch their heart. It made a better person out of me. I'm sure of that."

JOHN PATTERSON died in the spring of 1980. He was a warm and outgoing southern gentleman of the old school. Not one to adopt a "shucks, I can't pick" attitude, he was well aware that he was a master stylist and technician on the five-string banjo. He will be missed by his many friends, and the growing number of people who are coming to appreciate his importance in the story of southern old-time music.

He learned to pick "Shout Lulu" on his mother's lap when he was three years old. If his first tune was typical for southern banjo pickers, his very early start and subsequent spectacular career were not. Bessie Patterson was a champion banjo player, and when she died in 1924 she had already schooled her fourteen-year-old son in the basics of his extraordinary style, a combination of up-picking with chordal brushes and three-finger melody playing; on her death bed she had him promise never to let anyone beat him playing a banjo. John got his first chance to defend his mother's title a month later at the Fiddlers' Convention in Atlanta's city auditorium. He found himself up against Rosa Lee, the daughter of Fiddlin' John Carson, later to be known as "Moonshine Kate." The full story of this epic contest has been told by Uncle John in his own words in the notes for his banjo LP (*Plains Georgia Rock,* Arhoolie 5018) and by Gene Wiggins in both prose and poetry ("Uncle John Patterson, Banjo King," *The Devil's Box*, Tennessee Valley Fiddlers' Association, vol. 13, no. 3). Rosa Lee had already played John's best piece, "Spanish Fandango," so the sixty-seven-pound boy, wearing a shirt made out of a flour sack and a pair of his "granddaddy's pistol pants" picked "Hen Cackle" so spiritedly that "old Gid Tanner, and even John Carson . . . got to cackling and got to crowing," as John recalled. In the finals John was allowed to play "Spanish Fandango," and he won. "And from that time till now I've managed to take care of myself," he said in recent years. He had been national champion and had never lost a contest.

Uncle John—he wore the "Uncle" since boyhood—had been playing with the famous fiddler Ahaz Gray, like the Pattersons a resident of Carroll County on Georgia's western edge. He later teamed up with John Carson, as well as many other noted Georgia string musicians, in the 1932 Talmadge campaign; he met Gordon on some occasions when Gid Tanner was along, but he remembered that Gordon was doing more driving than playing.

After Gene Talmadge's election, John, who had been a sharecropper, became the governor's bodyguard. John Carson was made elevator operator in the statehouse, and the two musicians often played together in the statehouse and at Talmadge parties. Following Talmadge's defeat in the early forties, John went to work at Lockheed Aircraft as a hydraulics engineer. Music was not neglected during the following years: John toured with Smiley Burnett in 1952, and in 1962 he played his banjo composition "John Glenn Special" in a five-hour marathon, exceeding his goal to play it as long as the astronaut was in orbit! John had politics as well as music in his blood, and he served in the Georgia General Assembly from 1968 to 1974 as representative from Carrollton.

John was an all-around musician, adept on the fiddle, piano, and musical saw, as well as the banjo. After losing his picking index finger in an accident in the fifties he simply shifted the lead to his second finger. Before his Arhoolie record, on which he was backed by his son James on guitar, he recorded little—one disc in 1931 and one in 1947 with his Carroll County Ramblers. His recordings with Gordon and Joe will stand as a tribute to a great old-time musician.

Before he died, John had been teaching his banjo style to his grandson Gregg, and it remains to be seen whether this style, certainly as complex as Earl Scruggs's immensely popular style—and more interesting in its syncopated treatment of melody—will be continued in practice.

THERE IS NO QUESTION about whether the remarkable Tanner family of Dacula will keep their brand of music alive. Before Gordon's death, Phil and his son, Russ, were joining their guitar and "doghouse" bass to Gordon's fiddle in a family string band. Nowadays Phil and Russ continue to play the old-time music as third- and fourth-generation Tanner family fiddlers, and the chicken-coop music room is still the setting for lively Friday-night picking sessions. Russ, who shows an amazing resemblance to youthful photographs of his great-grandfather, is making rapid progress on the fiddle, and may carry the sound of Gid Tanner's Skillet Lickers well into the twenty-first century.

Hand Me Down My Walking Cane

Sung by Gordon Tanner (lead) with fiddle, and Joe Miller (tenor) with guitar, banjo by John Patterson; Dacula, Gwinnett County, October 13, 1979. Issued on Folkways FTS 31089. This popular nineteenth-century comic song is a parody of camp-meeting pieces. It owes much of its continuing popularity to the April 17, 1926, recording of Gid Tanner and the Skillet Lickers (Co. 15091-D); Gid used his falsetto, "double-barreled voice" for the "all my sins" line. See Brown, 3:430.

Oh, hand me down my walkin' cane, hand me down my walkin' cane, hand me down my walkin' cane, I'm gonna leave on the midnight train, all my sins been taken away, taken a-way.

1. Oh, hand me down my walkin' cane,
   Hand me down my walkin' cane,
   Hand me down my walkin' cane,
   I'm gonna leave on the midnight train,
      All my sins been taken away, taken
      away.

2. Yonder comes a man across the field,
   Yonder comes a man across the field,
   Yonder comes a man across the field
   Kickin' up dust like an automobile,
      All my sins been taken away,
         taken away.

3. Mary wept, and Martha moaned,
   Mary wept, and Martha moaned,
   Mary wept and Martha moaned,
   Susie got choked on a chicken bone,
      All my sins been taken away,
         taken away.

4. Now if I die in Tennessee,
   If I die in Tennessee,
   If I die in Tennessee
   Send me back by C.O.D.,
      All my sins been taken away,
         taken away.

Goodbye, Little Bonnie, Blue Eyes

Sung by Gordon Tanner with fiddle, guitar by Joe Miller, and banjo by John Patterson; Dacula, Gwinnett County, October 13, 1979. Issued on Folkways FTS 31089. This is a traditional southern folk song, known in the Carolinas and Georgia. It shares its tune with "There's More Pretty Girls than One," and a verse from that song crops up in Gordon's version, which he remembered singing "when my daddy begin to put me in front of the public, I guess when I was around five years old, or six." He learned it from Nora Day, an aunt on his mother's side. "They were around the organ a good bit, and they sang. . . . She had two brothers, and they played the banjo some, that's just home, around the fireplace, and I believe she wrote down and had me to learn that song." Arthur Tanner recorded "My Bonnie's Blue Eyes" in 1927, but the side was not issued. See Brown, 3:334.

Goodbye, little Bonnie, blue eyes, goodbye, little Bonnie, blue eyes, I'm go-ing out West where I can do best, goodbye, little Bonnie, blue eyes.

1. Goodbye, little Bonnie, blue eyes,
   Goodbye, little Bonnie, blue eyes,
   I'm going out West where I can do best,
   Goodbye, little Bonnie, blue eyes.

2. The train is rollin' around,
   The train is rollin' uptown;
   The train is rollin' to carry me away,
   Goodbye, little Bonnie, blue eyes.

3. My trunk is done packed and gone,
   My trunk is done packed and gone,
   My trunk is packed to never come back,
   Goodbye, little Bonnie, blue eyes.

4. You promised to marry me,
   You promised to marry me,
   You promised that you would marry me,
   Down under that coconut tree.

5. I asked your father for you,
   I asked your mother too;
   I asked them once, I asked them twice,
   I asked them good and nice.

6. Now there's more pretty girls than one,
   There's more pretty girls than one,
   There's more than one, there's more
      than two,
   But none in this world like you.

7. The train's done come and gone,
   The train's done come and gone,
   It's gone, gone, to never come back,
   Goodbye, little Bonnie, goodbye.

8. Goodbye, little Bonnie, blue eyes,
   Goodbye, little Bonnie, blue eyes,
   Goodbye, little Bonnie, don't cry,
      if you do,
   You'll spoil your beautiful eyes.

Smoky Joe Miller, Art Rosenbaum, and Gordon Tanner. (Charcoal, 22" × 30", 1977.)

Three Nights' Experience

("Our Goodman," Child, no. 247)

Sung by Gordon Tanner with fiddle, guitar by Joe Miller; Dacula, Gwinnett County, December 19, 1981. Issued on Folkways FTS 31089. This comic British ballad has been *widespread in America, in urban as well as rural tradition (my father learned a version as a boy on the streets of Paterson, New Jersey). It was recorded by several early hillbilly perform-*

The first night when I got home, drunk as I could be, I found a hoss in the stable where my hoss ought to be.

ers, including the Skillet Lickers, at their last session in San Antonio, in 1934 (Bb B-5748), under the title "Three Nights' Drunk." Gordon had heard it performed by his father, who used his "double-barreled voice," or falsetto, for the woman's part, and by his uncle, Arthur Hugh Tanner; he did not know "how it rebounded into my family." See Child, 5:88–95; also Belden, no. 13 (Missouri); Brewster, p. 155 (Indiana); Cox I, no. 30; Davis I, p. 505 (Virginia); Finger, p. 161; Henry, p. 119; Morris, p. 317; Randolph, 1:228; Sharp, 1:257.

---

1. The first night when I got home, drunk
     as I could be,
   I found a hoss in the stable where my
     hoss ought to be.

   "Now come, my wife, my dear little
     wife, explain this thing to me
   How come a hoss in the stable where
     my hoss ought to be?"

   "Oh you blind fool, you blind fool, can't
     you never see?
   It's nothing but a milk-cow your granny
     sent to me."

   "I rambled this wide world over, ten
     thousand miles and more;
   Saddle on a milk-cow's back I never
     have seen before."

2. Second night when I got home, drunk
     as I could be,
   I found a coat on the rack where my
     coat ought to be.

   "Oh come, my wife, my dear little wife,
     explain this thing to me.
   How come a coat on the rack where my
     coat ought to be?"

   "You blind fool, you blind fool, can't you
     never see?
   It's nothin' but a bed-quilt your granny
     sent to me."

   "I rambled this wide world over, ten
     thousand miles and more;
   Pockets in a bed-quilt I never have seen
     before."

3. Third night when I got home, drunk as
     I could be,
   I found a head on the pillow where my
     head ought to be.

   "Now come my wife, my dear little wife,
     explain this thing to me;
   How come a head on the pillow where
     my head ought to be?"

   "Oh you blind fool, you blind fool, can't
     you never see?
   It's nothing but a cabbage-head your
     granny sent to me."

   "I traveled this wide world over, ten
     thousand miles and more;
   Moustache on a cabbage-head I never
     have seen before."

The Lonesome Hungry Hash House

Sung by Gordon Tanner with fiddle, guitar by Joe Miller; Dacula, Gwinnett County, December 19, 1981. Issued on Folkways FTS 31089.

Gordon learned this comical take-off on the state of boarding-house dining in the South before the day of Ramada Inns from his father;

There's a place down the street where the tramps an' the hoboes meet, a place they call that se—cond-class ho—tel; oh, the bill of fare was read, two new boarders they fell dead, in that lonesome hungry hash house where I stay. Oh, the

it was recorded for Columbia as "Hungry Hash House" by Fate Norris and the Tanner Boys in Atlanta on March 14, 1926, but was *not released. It was recorded as "All Go Hungry Hash House" by Charlie Poole and His North Carolina Ramblers, Co. 15160, reissued on* *Old Timey LP 100; see NCLR, p. 236, for this version. The tune is the serviceable "Little Old Log Cabin in the Lane."*

bis-cuits they were wooden, they had sawdust in the puddin', the ba-by had both hands in the soup; oh ___, the eggs they were matched, if you touched them, they would hatch, in that lonesome hungry hash house where I stay.

1. There's a place down the street where
       the tramps and hoboes meet,
   A place they call that second-class hotel;
   Oh, the bill of fare was read, two new
       boarders they fell dead,
   In that lonesome hungry hash house
       where I stay.

Chorus:
Oh, the biscuits they were wooden, they
    had sawdust in the puddin',
The baby had both hands in the soup;
Oh, the eggs they were matched, if you
    touched them, they would hatch,
In that lonesome hungry hash house
    where I stay.

Second chorus:
Oh, the butter it was bald, if you touch
    it it would squall,
The hound dogs would lick out your
    plate;
And the sausage rolled on wheels, if you
    touch 'em, it would squeal,
In that lonesome hungry hash house
    where I stay.

Wall in Gordon Tanner's Chicken-House Music Room. Skillet, 1920s Photograph of Fiddlin'
John Carson and Gid Tanner in Tree-Stump Frame by Gordon, and Mirror Made from Gid
Tanner's Mule Harness. (Dacula, 1977.)

The Tanners. Three Generations: Gordon, Russ, and Phil. (Dacula, 1977.)

Stagolee Was a Bully

(Laws, I15)

Sung by Uncle John Patterson with five-string banjo; Carrollton, Carroll County, March 25, 1978. Uncle John had not thought of this song in thirty-five years when he sang it for us; he had tuned his banjo in D (f#DF#AD), a tuning corresponding to the open "Sevastopol" guitar tuning used by many black musicians, and he thought of this fragment he had heard his mother sing and play on the banjo "when I was very small." Fuller versions of this song

1. Stagolee was a bully, and old Bull Lyons
      was, too;
   Stagolee shot Bull Lyons, and shot him
      through and through.

2. People 'round the White House wrung
      their hands and cried
   When they got the message that old
      Bull Lyons had died.

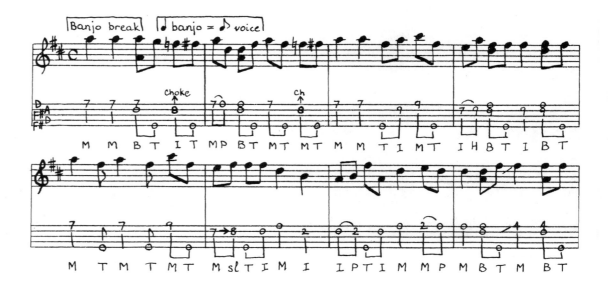

of black origin tell the story of Stagolee killing Billy Lyons over a John B. Stetson hat. The white West Virginia recording artist Frank Hutchison recorded it in 1927 (reissue, Folkways FA 2951), and black guitarists Mississippi John Hurt and Furry Lewis also recorded it in the late 1920s. See Laws II, p. 240; Dunson, p. 54 (Hutchison version); Lomax I, p. 93; Odum and Johnson, p. 197, for a Georgia version; Scarborough, p. 92. Abrahams, pp. 123–36, gives an extensive discussion of the black "bully," the Stagolee character, and several variants of the ribald toast, or rhymed narrative, that celebrates his exploits.

Arkansas Traveler

Gordon Tanner, fiddle and dialogue, Phil Tanner, guitar and dialogue; Dacula, Gwinnett County, 1977. Issued on Folkways FTS 31089. This bit of American folk theater was first published by Oliver Ditson and Company of Boston in 1863 and attributed to Mose Case, an itinerant musician, though the fiddle tune was in print by 1847 and both the tune and the skit were presumably in oral circulation. The sheet music was accompanied by the explanation: "This piece is intended to represent an Eastern man's experience among the inhabitants of Arkansas, showing their hospitality and the mode of obtaining it."

Country entertainers have relished the story of the farmer getting the best of a city slicker, and the Skillet Lickers were no exception. According to Gordon, " 'Arkansas Traveler' is a deal that always opened my eyes. I'd hear my daddy and uncle [Arthur Hugh Tanner] play that from the stage, and setting around the house. . . . It would tear the audience up. . . . So when Phil was growin' up and settin' under our feet and all, he'd hear me and Papa Tanner do it. We'd do it from the stage. Well, first thing I know, well, Phil—I was playin' it, and I said, 'Son, I'm gonna ask you a few questions.' He answered every one! Done knowed it." Today it is a mainstay of Skillet Licker II shows. Gid Tanner and Riley Puckett recorded it in 1924 (Co. 15019-D), and it was recorded by Clayton McMichen and Dan Hornsby in 1928 and by Earl Johnson in 1927 (reissue, County 514). See also Ford, p. 46; NLCR, p. 232; and Roberts, p. 183.

(Fiddle plays whole tune)

Traveler (Gordon): Hey, stranger, where this road go?

Farmer (Phil): Well, I been livin' here all my life, and it went anywhere yet, I don't know it.

(Plays coarse part)

Traveler: I mean, where does it fork at?

Farmer: Oh, it don't fork, it just goes on top of the hill and splits all to pieces.

(Plays coarse part)

Traveler: Well I'm lost, and I'd like to spend the night.

Farmer: Well you can't stay here.

(Plays coarse part)

Traveler: Listen, I'm a long ways from home, I'd like to spend the night anyhow.

Farmer: Well, knock a dog there off a bench and have a seat!

(Plays coarse part)

Traveler: Hey, that corn out there looks mighty yellow.

Farmer: Oh, yeah, we planted the yellow kind.

(Plays coarse part)

Traveler: What I mean, it don't look like you gonna make but a half a crop.

Farmer: Oh yeah, that's right, we just workin' on halves.

(Plays coarse part)

Traveler: Well, how'd your 'taters turn out?

Farmer: Oh, they didn't turn out, me and Betty had to dig 'em out!

(Plays coarse part)

Traveler: Whoa, look out! Head that cow!

Farmer: Oh she's already headed, thank you.

Traveler: Well turn her, then!

Farmer: She's already turned, hairy side out.

Traveler: Well, speak to her, you fool!

Farmer: Good mornin', cow.

(Plays coarse part)

Traveler: Squirrels very thick in this country?

Farmer: Oh, yeah, they're just about as thick as my wrist.

(Plays coarse part)

Traveler: Hey, you have mighty dry eatin' around here.

Farmer: There's a bucket of water over there. Wet it!

(Plays coarse part)

Traveler: Well, do you have knives and forks, silverware, and stuff, you know, to eat with?

Farmer: No, we don't.

Traveler: Well how do you do, then?

Farmer: Very well, thank you, and how are you?

(Plays coarse part)

Traveler: How long you been livin' here anyhow?

Farmer: You see that mountain over yonder?

Traveler: Yeh.

Farmer: That was just a hole in the ground when I first moved here.

(Plays coarse part)

Traveler: That creek down there very deep?

Farmer: There's water slim to the bottom.

Traveler: I mean, can anything cross it?

Farmer: Yeah, my old geese, they cross it every day.

(Plays coarse part)

Traveler: Hey, as I said, I've traveled about a good bit, and I'm lost, but I don't seem to find much between you and a fool!

Farmer: 'Bout the only thing I see is that fiddle there!

(Plays whole tune)

I Wish I'd Bought a Half a Pint and Stayed in the Wagon Yard

Sung by Gordon Tanner with fiddle, guitar by Joe Miller, and banjo by John Patterson; Dacula, Gwinnett County, October 13, 1979. Issued on Folkways FTS 31089. If "Arkansas Traveler" tells of a city slicker's adventures in the country, this song recounts a country boy's adventures in town. The town was evidently Atlanta. Joe Miller explained that the hero "had made his little crop, went to get it ginned,

Now I'm a jolly farmer, last night I came to town; I brought a bale of cotton, I'd worked the whole year round. I put my mule in the wa-gon yard, I bought a bottle of gin. I went out to see the 'lectric lights and watch the cars come in.

get it cashed in, but he . . . wanted to celebrate a little, but he got in trouble." Today Atlanta is a metropolis of skyscrapers and expressways whose suburban sprawl is transforming nearby Gwinnett County, though Gordon's home on the eastern edge of the county is still quiet and rural. A half-century ago, the electric lights and cars of the city were enough to tempt a young sharecropper. This song was recorded by Lowe Stokes and His North Georgians in 1929 (Co. 15557-D), though Gordon felt his uncle Arthur Hugh Tanner was in the group and probably composed the song. In any event, Gordon learned it from Arthur's singing.

1. Now I'm a jolly farmer, last night I
        come to town;
    I brought a bale of cotton, I'd worked
        the whole year round.
    I put my mule in the wagon yard, I
        bought a bottle of gin.
    I went out to see the 'lectric lights and
        watch the cars come in.

2. I met a dude out on the street, the clock
        was striking nine;
    He said, "Come on, you hayseed, take a
        drink, it's mine."
    I must have bought a dozen drinks, it
        hit my pocketbook hard.
    I wish I'd bought a half a pint and
        stayed in the wagon yard.

3. Now I'm a deacon in a hard-shell
        church, down near Possum Trot.
    If the sisters hears about this spree, it's
        bound to make them hot!
    I went out on a party, I led the pace that
        kills;
    When I woke up the gang was gone and
        left me all the bills.

4. I found them over on the corner, near
        Salvation Hall;
    That drunken bunch was over there
        singing, "Jesus Paid It All."
    They put me out in a dry-goods box,
        and Lord, my pillow was hard.
    I wish I'd have bought me a half a pint
        and stayed in the wagon yard.

5. Now listen to me, farmers, I'm here to
        talk with sense:
    If you want to see the 'lectric lights,
        peep through the fence.
    Don't monkey with those city guys,
        you'll find them slick as lard.
    Just go and buy you half a pint and stay
        in the wagon yard!

Gordon Tanner and Smoky Joe Miller. (Dacula, 1978.)

Prettiest Little Girl in the County

Played on fiddle and sung by Gordon Tanner, guitar by Joe Miller; Dacula, Gwinnett County, December 19, 1981. A widespread fiddle tune, this piece is very similar to "What're We Gonna Do with the Baby-o." The original Skillet Licker side was cut on April 10, 1928, by Gid Tanner, Riley Puckett, and Clayton McMichen. Gordon sang the following couplets to the fourth line in the musical transcription:

Prettiest little girl in the county-o,
Papa and mama both said so.

All dressed up in calico,
I'm gonna take her to the party-o.

I can get her if I want her,
I can get her if I want her.

Down Yonder

Played on fiddle by Gordon Tanner, guitar by Joe Miller, and five-string banjo by John Patterson; Dacula, Gwinnett County, 1978. Issued on Folkways FTS 31089. The enormous popularity that this tune enjoys springs from the March 29, 1934, recording by the Skillet Lickers, in the Texas Hotel in San Antonio, with Gordon playing lead fiddle (Bluebird B-5562). Reissued several times, it eventually sold over a million, and RCA kept it in print into the 1960s. A discography compiled by John Edwards and provided by the John Edwards Memorial Foundation at UCLA lists "Down Yonder" as recorded by McMichen's Melody Men in Atlanta on November 6, 1926 (Co. 15130-D). Gene Wiggins has pointed out (John Edwards Memorial Foundation Quarterly 55 [Fall 1979]: 146) *that the song was actually written by L. Wolfe Gilbert, the man who had written the words to "Waiting for the Robert E. Lee" in 1912. Gilbert published "Down Yonder" in 1921, and that same year it was recorded by the Peerless Quartette. This record was possibly McMichen's source.*

Gordon did not remember a full-length recording before his own, however: "I was enthused over learning to play fiddle, and my surroundings was, of course, my daddy, and other musicians, and what records might be brought in. Now as I learned to play, I would spin a record occasionally, but this record, if I recall, it was a dialogue record—it was the Skillet Lickers' 'Corn Liquor Still in Georgia,' or it could have been on the 'Bee Hunt', or the dialogue 'Possum Hunt on Stump House Mountain.' Well, they would talk a while, then they would play. Anyway, McMichen played 'Down Yonder,' or Lowe Stokes, one. It wasn't labeled . . . I learned it, and any time I was around other musicians, I would play it."

Uncle John Patterson was also unaware that "Down Yonder" was a popular song before it became a fiddle tune, and in a story Gordon had not heard, he told his version of how the tune came to be titled. It seems that John was with Gid Tanner, Lowe Stokes, Fate Norris, and some others at the Fiddlers' Convention in Atlanta in the twenties. "I was there with the banjo, and I was very small. I just wanted to be around, play with 'em. They'd say, 'Come on in, Uncle John.' I'd be sort of timid, and set down, and you talk about banjo, fiddle, and guitar, we'd tear it apart! So I broke a string. They'd been workin' on this tune for a long time, and nobody knew what they was playin'. And I broke a string, and I says, 'I got to go down yonder and get a string.' And they said, 'That's it, "Down Yonder"!' And I went down on Decatur Street and got a string to go on the banjo."

"That's history," Gordon commented.

"Heavenly Light Is Shining on Me." The Eller Brothers and Leatha Eller on the Mountaintop.
(Oil and alkyd resin on canvas, 66" × 72", 1978.)

"My Number Will Be Changed." Doc and Lucy Barnes, Naomi Bradford, and the Gospel Chorus of Athens. *(Oil and alkyd resin on canvas, 66" × 78", 1978.)*

Jake Staggers Beside the Railroad. (Oil and alkyd resin on canvas, 52" × 54", 1980.)

"I Am a Stranger on My Way." Howard Finster of Pennville. *(Oil and alkyd resin on canvas, 76" × 72", 1983.)*

Let's March Around the Wall

MR. HGT AND DOC BARNES:
THE LAST OF THE OLD WORK SONGS

THE HARD PHYSICAL LABOR of the Old South proceeded to the cadence of black voices singing surging and powerful work songs: the timber-stowing and cotton-screwing shanties of the seaports, the cotton-chopping songs of the plantations, and the hammer songs and track-lining songs of the railroads, all of which followed the West African pattern of leader and chorus, call and response; there were also the freer field hollers and mule-driving cries. Some of the work songs were religious, some profane; at times they were ironic, at times laced with veiled or overt protest against slavery and the oppressive labor systems that followed slavery; sometimes they reflected pride in work and admiration for work heroes like John Henry and Po' Lazarus. The twentieth century, with its mechanization of work, has seen the demise of the work-song tradition—in the early thirties John and Alan Lomax found strong survivals in the penitentiaries of the South where gang-labor persisted, and in recent years examples of the work song in active practice have been recorded in prisons in Mississippi and Louisiana. In Georgia the old work songs have virtually died out except as they are remembered and resung by older men who heard and used them in earlier years.

Two such singers are Mr. HGT and Doc Barnes of Athens. One warm summer evening I met them in Doc's backyard to learn about and to record the track-lining and railroad work songs Doc had heard years ago, and the pick-and-hammer songs that Mr. HGT had sung and led on jobs in his youth. Like Doc, Mr. HGT is a church deacon—these days he uses his rich, deep voice in service of the Lord and is leader of three church choirs—and he preferred not to attach his name to his recordings of these tough-sinewed secular songs, with their occasionally "rough" verses. Yet as he talked about the work songs a double pride came into him: the old John Henry pride in the triumph of a man's physical strength and spirit against great odds; and the pride of the singer, able to inspire his fellows and move the spirits of listeners with his art.

He remembered the days when he learned the work songs: "I'd like to sing . . . spiritual singin', but the *other* kind of singin', that's 'way back when you were—beatin' a dog with a 'simmon tree! The world was on fire, then. They put that fire out, on them jobs!"

I asked him about the jobs.

"Right. I was highwayin' back then, and I learned those songs from different ones on the highway. You know, cuttin' roads, you know, and things. I was in my twenties. That was in the thirties, I know. We cut that Monroe highway, and that Greensboro highway . . . from Watkinsville to Greensboro. I wasn't nothin' but a boy on that there."

He learned some of the songs when he worked with pick and shovel on WPA crews, from older men. "Some of them had been in prison, and been out—and I was workin' with 'em. Convict songs, all that kind of stuff, we used to call it. . . . We used to do mo' pickin' with a pick and shovel than some folks do with a back-hoe now. . . . I worked on the post office here in Athens. That was in 1939, and '40. . . . Me and a fella named Leroy. . . . He used to sing that old song, 'Hamma tamma damma ramma'. . . . And we picked that whole basement out. Folks used to come around and look at us pick! And he's dead and gone, now. I was a young fella, then. I know I was in my teen-age, 'cause I married when I was seventeen, and I was workin' there when I was eighteen or nineteen. He would lead that.

. . . He would sing his song, and I'd sing mine. Befo' that I worked on highways. Curtis . . . was a fella I learned the songs under, and he dead and gone. . . . They just make the day go a little faster, when you get to singin', make you feel like workin', just old work songs."

Mr. HGT is still working, and even today snatches of the old songs come to his lips on the job. At our evening recording session he had to take a pick, spin it like the rotors of a helicopter above his head, and send it thudding down into a pile of red dirt in his friend Doc's yard before he could start the song about how old John Henry died on the mountain.

And Doc, who knows several hundred spiritual songs, and learned the art of carving walking sticks with African snake and lizard motifs from his father, is still mildly amazed that he can remember the old work spiritual, "Let's March Around the Wall." After singing it, he said, "Like that. See what I mean. But, you know, what a person should keep, they forgets. What I mean, somethin' will mean somethin' to 'em, they forgets it."

Let's March Around the Wall

Sung by Brady "Doc" Barnes; Athens, Clarke County, July 3, 1981. Doc heard this old spiritual performed as a work song years ago, in the part-singing style referred to in the chorus. See Arnold, p. 117; and White, p. 98.

1. Oh, come along boys, let's march
      around the wall,
   I don't want to stumble, great God, I
      don't want to fall.

   Chorus:
   My leader, my tenor, my bar'tone,
   God, forever stand.

2. Sister Mary, she wo' three links of
      chain,
   And ever' link was in my Jesus name.
   One was the Father, one was the Son,
   One was the Holy Ghost, and they all
      made one. *(Chorus)*

Doc Barnes Blowing the Quills. (Athens, 1980.)

My Captain Paid Me Forty-one Dollars and a Quarter

Sung by Mr. HGT; Athens, Clarke County, July 3, 1981. This hammer or pick song was performed with a pickax, in a simulated work situation. The singing is rhythmically very *free, set against the regular sound of the pick striking the ground (↓) and the plosive exhaling (whah!).*

oh, part-ner her hips so broad.

My li'l wo-man whah! she got a ring tied all around her shoulder whah!

shine-a like gold whah! and it shine-a like gold. whah!

1. My cap'n paid me   whah!
   Forty-one dollars and a
        quarter   whah!
   To get a pair of shoes   whah!
   Oh, partner   whah!
   To get a pair of shoes   whah!

2. I got a woman   whah!
   She got legs jus' as   whah!
   Big as anybody   whah!
   Her hips so broad   whah!
   Hips so broad   whah!
   Oh, partner   whah!
   Her hips so broad   whah!

3. My li'l woman   whah!
   She got a ring tied all around her
        shoulder   whah!
   Shine-a like gold   whah!
   And it shine-a like gold   whah!

Hamma-Tamma
Damma-Ramma

Sung by Mr. HGT; Athens, Clarke County, July 3, 1981. Mr. HGT helped dig out the foundation of the Athens Post Office with pick and shovel in 1939, before he began earning a quarter an hour more for running the concrete mixer. Songs would "make the day go faster," make the picking "go easier and get more willingness." This song was led by Mr. HGT's partner, Leroy. According to Mr. HGT, Leroy

"didn't have nothin', just the two words, just said it over and over, and the pick be soundin', you'd hear the pick hittin' the dirt. . . . Leroy used to sing that there, and when the picks'd go up and come down, we'd be right together, workin' automatic, like workin' by machine. . . . That's the reason they used that 'hah' in there, hit the same time."

Hamma-tamma (hah) damma-ramma, (hah)
Hamma-tamma (hah) damma-ramma. (hah)
Oh, hamma-tamma (hah) damma-ramma. (hah)

Work Gang with Picks. (Charcoal, 22" × 30", 1983.)

Old John Henry Died on the Mountain

Sung by Mr. HGT; Athens, Clarke County, July 3, 1981. In addition to the great ballad (see Neal Pattman's version, p. 188), the steel-drivin' man has been celebrated in an extensive family of work or hammer songs. Several of these are given in Johnson, pp. 71–83, and Chappell, pp. 97–103; Perdue lists a Georgia work song from the WPA Collection, p. 54.

Mr. HGT's fine song begins with a reference to John Henry, then shifts to a first-person account of a man escaping from the chain gang. The line "Anybody ask you was I runnin' " occurs in the hammer song "Take This Hammer," and this song is distantly related to the work song–banjo songs "Swannanoa Tunnel" and "Yew Pine Mountain."

This performance is characterized by a highly ornamented vocal line, with the final long notes of each phrase sung with much more vibrato than the other notes.

Ol' John Henry   whah!   died on the
   mountain   whah!
Ol' John Henry   whah!   died on the
   mountain   whah!
He was a-whuppin' steel   whah!   oh,
   pardner   whah!
He was a-whuppin' steel   whah!

Ain' gonna tell nobody   whah!   my
   right name   whah!
Gonna tell nobody   whah!   my right
   name   whah!
My name is Sam   whah!   and I don't
   give a umh   whah!
Oh, pardner   whah!   and I don't give
   a—   whah!

Anybody ask you   whah!   was I
   runnin'   whah!
Anybody ask you   whah!   was I
   runnin'   whah!
Now tell 'em no   whah!   tell 'em I's
   flyin'   whah!
Oh, pardner   whah!   tell 'em I's
   flyin'   whah!

I run 'cross the   whah!   Blue Ridge
   Mountain   whah!
I run 'cross the   whah!   Blue Ridge
   Mountain   whah!
'N when the sun went down
   whah!   oh, captain,   whah!
'N when the sun went down   whah!

Track Lining

Told and sung by Brady "Doc" Barnes, Athens, Clarke County, July 3, 1981. Doc remembers the chant of the track-lining crew and the musical ring of steel on steel as if it were yesterday. See Library of Congress LP AAFS L8 and L52; Botkin, p. 746; Hurston, pp. 322–23.

Spoken:
You know how people used to work on the railroad track with the steel bars, linin' the track, you know. Old Jed Ealy . . . he was the line-man, otherwise, he was the head of the track. They had a bossman, Cap'n Ball was they bossman. And them niggers—I tell the truth, I say "niggers"—I just say that, you know! They had those long steel bars, they had about six or eight of them, you know, and just like this here is the track, and you have cross-ties ever so far apart . . . those nig' get those bars, I tell you the truth, could play a tune with those iron bars just as good as you could sing a song with 'em. Cap'n Ball had a thing, you know, peepin' through, he'd say, "This track is out of line—it gotta be lined!"

Chanted:
"All right, boys, get your bars."

Spoken:
That's Jed, he's the lead man . . . they'd get them bars, you know, he just start a song, and all of them would get the bars set.

Sung:
Ain't but the one train ridin' this
    track   whah!
Run down to Macon an' right straight
    back   whah!

Ain't but the one train ridin' this track   whah!   run down to Macon an' right straight back   whah!

Spoken:
Now I'm tellin' you what I stood and watched! My daddy's baby brother, he was with 'em too. And man, they could take them iron bars:

Sung:
Ain't but one train run this track,
Run to Athen' and Macon right
    back   whah!

Spoken:
And they had some of the prettiest tune. Wasn't no music [instruments] 'round there nowhere, but they could make them iron bars, right on the edge of that track. . . . I'm tellin' you what I know. They could make music with them iron bars, and when they get through, it was lined. And they had a big ol' man, Cap'n Ball, he was about 250, and he'd spy down there, and he'd say, "Jed." And he'd hold up one finger, that'd mean about another inch, you know,

Sung:
Jus' move it boy,

Spoken:
And he'd do thataway, that'd mean half!

Sung:
Pick it up, line-man   whah!
Jack the rabbit, Jack the bear,
Boys can't you move it jus' another
    hair?   whah!

Spoken:
I used to follow them up! In that time . . . they was hand cars, you had to pump! Had a handle on this side, handle on this side. . . . Take fo' men, when the front would go down, the back would come up, and I'm tellin' you, they could hustle on that thing! Now they got motors on 'em, but then, whoosh! sailin', too! You get them fo' men stout, and got power, good Godamighty, they could make thirty miles an hour. The section gang, with the hand car. I never will forget that.

Shout, Lulu

W. GUY BRUCE OF SCREAMERSVILLE

W. GUY BRUCE NEVER DREAMED that at the age of eighty-five he would be leaving his little house and watch-repair shop out in the country near Trion, Georgia, to fly up to Washington, D.C., to pick banjo, "pat some foot," and sing "Shout, Lulu" for the crowds at the Smithsonian Festival of American Folklife. It was not that he had never traveled—Guy had ridden his motorcycle to Miami in the fifties, and, an avid baseball fan, he had once gone up to New York to see his favorite team, the Yankees, play. He simply did not believe that people up north would be interested in the old-time down-home music he had learned as a boy. "If you want a good banjo-picker, get Roy Clark," he suggested to the festival staff person who called him long distance to invite him to perform. She and I finally convinced him that it was his style rather than that of the TV star that was wanted, and after a week at the festival he realized that there is indeed an appreciative audience for his exuberant picking and singing.

A few months later he was reflecting on the ups and downs of his kind of music. "This stuff I used to know lots of, y'know, Art, whenever I learned to pick—when I got up in my twenties and early thirties, banjer pickin' died out; all I picked was square dances, and just picked a piece or two, never picked for nobody to listen at, for thirty years."

I asked him why he thought old-time banjo picking died out. "Well . . . it's just like everything else, y'know. I tell you . . . along about when I'd been pickin' banjer about six or seven years, along come what we called talkin' machines, the graphanolas, I think they called them then, they had a gre't big ol' horn, and the record's about the size of a bakin' powder can. . . . That hurt banjer pickin'—and fiddlin', too. . . . And then in the early twenties the radio came in; well, people just went wild about those things. And then, I believe it was along in the late forties, when television come in . . . that still got it worse. . . . Well, after they all come in, got kindly sorta wore down, why, then, banjer-pickin' commenced comin' back in style. . . . [Earl] Scruggs, he got it started a whole lot, his style . . . and people now, they just like to hear it. And a lot of these things I've knowed for seventy years, y'know, why it's new to some people! It just comes and goes."

Most of what Guy Bruce knows—and as well as banjo picking, that includes unaccompanied ballad singing, telling of tall tales and ha'nt tales, reciting of bawdy toasts—he learned from local tradition before the advent of the electronic media. Age has not dimmed his memory of his store of lore and music, and it is hard to imagine that his skill at banjo picking and his verve and style in singing and tale telling were ever much sharper. He is a man of small stature and strongly expressed opinions, and his independent-minded frontier spirit is that of a man who has lived his life among the long ridges of Georgia's northwestern corner, on the approaches of Lookout Mountain, the Tennessee River, and the West.

I inquired about his ancestry, remarking that Bruce is a Scottish name.

"My granddaddy Bruce *was* a Scotsman, you see. And my granddaddy Worthy, that's my mother's daddy, he was an Irishman. He was born in the United States, but he was of Irish descent. He was a great big fella. I never did see him. . . . He died before my daddy and mother was married. . . . He—I heard grandma tell about it—

Gordon Tanner, Phil Tanner, and W. Guy Bruce at the Smithsonian Folklife Festival.
(Washington, D.C., 1980.)

helped build that railroad through Acworth, Georgia."

"You talk about him being a fighter."

"Oh, yes, at three o'clock Saturday afternoon, they'd knock off and go to town, get their groceries on the handcar. They'd get a few drinks, he'd get in a fight with somebody, y'know, called it 'fist and skull,' they used their fistes, they'd tie up thataway in a fight, they'd just make a ring around them, and when the one got enough, he'd holler, 'Enough!' And they pulled the other man off of him. They'd shake hands and get 'em another drink. I wouldn't have liked such pastimes as that, but, now, he liked it."

Guy describes his father, Will Bruce, as being "as hard as a pine knot." He was five feet five inches tall, "about two inches taller than me. He got up at four o'clock in the morning. When there's 365 days in the year, that's how many times he got up at four o'clock—when it was leap year, he got up one more time. Worked from daylight till dark. . . . He planted cotton and corn, like everybody else." When Guy was a "little bitty thing," he made a cotton sack out of a flour bag and helped pick cotton. And "whenever I was little, I'd have to carry in wood, store wood for my mother, and whenever I got to any size at all, dad put me on the other end of a cross-cut saw. Everybody burnt wood. And down there at Trion, this little old cotton-mill town, everybody cooked with wood. My daddy, that's how he got his spendin' money—his farm was covered up in pine, and he'd cut it up in cordwood, let it dry, and goshamighty, that'd heat up a stove." Guy's mother, Annie Worthy Bruce, was "just a housewife. She worked in the fields, too, when she could get any time." His parents were inclined toward music only to the extent that his father played French harp (harmonica) occasionally, and his mother sang shape-note hymns in church.

Guy's memories of his boyhood around the turn of the century are most often expressed in the form of tales, either true anecdotes, tall tales told as true, or stories told to him of supernatural occurrences. They usually begin, "Whenever I was a boy." One tall tale told as autobiography suggests that Guy thinks of himself as a clever fellow who can put mind over matter, like the heroes of many old folk tales. He told it with relish at the Smithsonian Festival.

How He Got the Cow Out of the Well

"BACK WHENEVER I was a young feller, everybody had a well out in the country, and had to dig it. Had to dig it with a pick and shovel. Didn't have no such thing as well-drilling outfits. So dad, he started him a well, and got it down twelve, fifteen feet deep. Cattle was a-runnin' outside, and he was a-diggin' it outside the yard. And so the milk cow come around there that night, and somehow she fell in. Next mornin', he went out, she was layin' in the bottom of the well. Didn't seem to be hurt, but of course, couldn't get her out. She was an awful good cow, give lots of good rich milk. Dad went to huntin' around, send for neighbors to come and he'p him, go get ropes to try to pull her out. I said to him, 'If you just let me down in there, I'll get her out.' He said, 'Son, you can't get her out.' I said, 'You just take a plow line, let me down in there, I'll show you.' Well he did. . . . I was just a little old feller, I was always small, and he let me down in there, and I went to milkin' her, and I just kept milkin' her, and that good rich milk—I kept milkin' till I just floated her out the top.''

How His Daddy Milked the Old Cow to Death

"WHENEVER I was a young feller, y'know, people, when they wanted to make whiskey, the law . . . wouldn't get out and hunt nobody down, and nobody wouldn't turn you up to the law, or anything, so if you wanted to make whiskey, you'd go out in the woods and find you a branch, and put up your still! Well, there's a feller, he's gonna make some whiskey, and he put up a still about a quarter-mile from our house, back in the woods, and back then the hogs and cattle just run outside, and you had to have a fence around your fields. . . . And these fellers, whenever they put up their still, and filled their barrels up with beer, y'know, to work it off where they could make their whiskey, they'd just cut poles and build a little old fence around it. Sometimes the cows would pull it down and get in there. So late one afternoon about sundown dad looked out and seen the old cow comin', she's just a-reelin'. He said, 'That old cow pushed down John's fence, yonder, and drink his beer up. She's drunk. I'll get the bucket and milk her before she gets down. He went out and went to milkin' that old cow, and doggone if he didn't milk her till he just killed her! He happened to taste of the milk, found out she's givin' nothin' but egg nog, and he just milked her to death!"

A Witch Tale and a Ha'nt Tale

As GUY REMEMBERS IT, his family "used to sit around the house when I was a little boy, and grandmother lived with us, and father and mother, them and her'd tell, they'd call 'em ha'nt [haunt], witch tales. Yeah!"

"Tell one of them," I suggested.

"Well, they'd sit around and tell them dad-blamed tales, and I had to sleep in the back room, and there wasn't no light in there, and I'd be afraid to go to bed. I was a little old boy about eight or nine years old. I heard my grandmother tell about a little boy, I forget his name, and he was a-settin' by the fireplace—everybody had a fire-place, you know. . . . And somebody'd bored auger holes through the rocks in the chimney, y'know, and he commenced to screamin' that some old lady in the community—everybody said she was a witch—that she was a-pullin' him through that auger hole! So he got in a bad shape. So what they'd do for that, they had muzzle-loadin' rifles, y'know, and they'd run a silver bullet, they'd mount some silver money, hard money then was silver, and wasn't like it is now—junk. . . . They'd melt that down, run a silver bullet, draw the witch's picture, and if they shot her through the hand, she'd have a sore hand. I wondered why in the dickens they didn't shoot her through the head! They wouldn't shoot the woman, they'd draw her picture and put it up out there, and shoot maybe through her hand. Well, that'd break the spell. Yeah, that beat anything I ever heard tell of."

I asked Guy if it made any difference how well the picture was drawn.

"No. Back then, nobody couldn't draw, they'd just draw a picture and say it was the old woman, put her hand up, and shoot it through there! I just thought to myself, why in the dickens they didn't just shoot her through the head. If that would make a hole in her. Now, such stuff as that.

"They'd say such and such house is ha'nted. They'd tell such tales as this: There was a feller one time a-traveling, and he stopped at a house, wanted to stay all night. Feller told him he didn't have room— 'I've got a house out there, it's empty. You can stay out there, but it's ha'nted.' Feller said, 'Well, I'll stay out there.' He went on out there, hadn't been there but a little while, commenced gettin' dark. Had an upstairs to the house, said he heard somethin' a-slidin' around. Directly he looked around, there's a coffin comin' . . . come sliiiiiiidin' down the stair step, and slid out on the floor, and popped and cracked a little, and he said, 'Well, there's a pretty good place to eat my supper on.' He set the stuff he had to eat down on it and went to eatin', and he heard a bull upstairs, bellerin' and a-takin' on, and directly a big old spotted bull come down them stairs, just a-bellerin', you know, and he just got down there and he pawed and he pawed, and he finally went out the door. Feller said, 'Well, maybe that's all of it. I'll eat my supper now.' He started his supper, and the coffin begin to pop and crack, and he said 'Wait a minute, wait a minute! Don't bust open with my supper on you. You'll ruin my supper. Wait till I get my supper off of you.' Well he took his supper off of it, opened up, and there lay a man. And the man said to him, 'I've got a whole lot of money hid down yonder in the apple orchard under such-and-such a tree.' Said, 'If you go down there and get that—' told him his wife's name, 'and carry it to my wife and children, there won't be nothing else seen here.' The man went the next morning and got that, so there wasn't nothin' else seen there.

"Now such dad-blamed tales as that!" Guy added.

At this point Guy's son, Guy Jr., asked him to tell the "true story about the Indian, the root doctor . . . who came to your house when you were little, and picked up the pot on the trail across the hill."

"Oh, yeah, well that was an old—he claimed to be an herb doctor, diggin' up herbs, he was an Indian. That was just above Screamers-ville, right there in the Jug Holler. I imagine I was about thirteen, might not be that old. Anyway, after he left, there was a trail that went over the ridge from one house to another, down through a place called the Houston Holler, and right beside the trail he dug a little trench."

Guy told that they found the trench, and there was a puddle, and a mark of a jug, and he assumed that the Indians had buried gold or silver there, years before, and left a sign known only to themselves.

Catamount Story

I ASKED Guy where Screamersville was.

"Whenever I's a boy they called this community Screamersville. Right up above where I lived, there was a place called Jug Holler. They said they's an old man used to live up at the top of the holler, used to make jugs, and they called it Jug Holler. He made 'em out of clay, and he had a kiln somewhere where he'd burn 'em, and made 'em, these reg'lar old stone jugs, I call 'em. They wasn't stone, of course—made 'em out of clay, as hard as stone.

"Back whenever I's a boy, I was pretty well up, about fifteen or sixteen years old. And I'd been down to a place called Martindale Holler—the houses wasn't close together . . . and goin' down there afoot, that was about the only way we had of traveling. So . . . I was possum huntin' . . . back several years before that with my daddy, heard a catamount squallin'. They make a funny kind of racket, hear it again, you know it!"

"What's a catamount?"

"Well, it's a member of the cat family, sort of like a panther. Only they don't scream—a panther screams just like a woman. And I was a-comin' down there, through Martindale Holler, on my bicycle, and I'd fiddled around till it got dusky dark. And I'm a-comin' down through there, and I got nearly to the end of it, and one of my tires was a-gettin' low, and I had a pump, a bicycle pump, and I stop and leaned it up agin an ol' stump, I's a-pumpin' up that old bicycle, and there's somethin' squall right up aside of the hill . . . went like that thing I heard when I was possum huntin'. I had plenty of air in that tire! I didn't see it, and I didn't want to see it." Its cry made his hair stand up on his head and lift his hat up.

During his courting years Guy had other occasions to go through the holler on his way to "playin' parties," where "they'd play 'Skip to My Lou' and such as that." He always carried two stones in his pocket to protect himself against the catamount.

How to Lay Out a Man

STILL ON THE SUBJECT of scary memories of his boyhood, Guy told about the custom of "laying out" the dead.

"You know, when anybody died, there wasn't no undertaker. Did you ever help lay out a man? I have. The neighbors went in and washed him and dressed him, you see, and set up with him, you see, of a night. I never could see much sense in that myself. When a man gets dead, he ain't goin' nowhere without somebody takin' him. But they'd set up with him, and they'd tell tales . . . and they'd hear chains a-draggin' around the house, such tales as that. I was a little old kid, had to sleep by myself, I's afraid to go to the back room and go to bed. Beat all I ever heard tell of!"

A Foxfire Tale and a Snake Tale

AT THIS POINT Guy Jr. prompted his father to "tell about Uncle Tom . . . and the foxfire."

"Foxfire? It wasn't him, it was the grandpa where he was stayin', and his name was Bell. And around Dahlonega, back then, you'd see them mineral lights of a night. My daddy back then, his name was William—they called him Will, and his cousin was about his size, named Will Bell. My grandmother died when my daddy was little, and his brother went to Arkansas, come and got him, carried him back to Dahlonega, he was stayin' with his aunt and uncle, and that boy, he said of a night when it was cloudy, and kind of drizzlin' rain, said you could see lights—that's gold country, and kind of mineral lights." These lights were known as foxfire.

"His cousin, Will, was just as scared of them things as he could be, and if he had to get up of a night, you know, then, you didn't have a bathroom, you just went to the door. They was just livin' in an old hut; I've lived in old houses by jingo, that you could look up and see the stars! Look down and see chickens under the floor. Paw said they come a rain, and it was leakin' in on his uncle and aunt, and they just got up and took the bed off the bedstead, and put in on the floor by the bed. And his cousin had to get up during the night, he didn't know his daddy and mother was there, went to the door, he got there, he said he got up, and he just kept his eyes shut right tight, and just feel around, and the boy's daddy just reach up, grabbed the boy by the ankles, and said, Whaaaaaaaaaaaaa! The boy's uncle had to get up and wash. He was wet all over!

"And my daddy said that boy, if he got scared, he'd just go to cussin' just as hard as he could cuss, and he's afraid of snakes. His uncle had taken in an old field, and it was growed up in sassafras sprouts, and they'd cut them sprouts, and big old long sprouts was layin' there, and they'd planted it in corn. Well, back then you didn't have nothin' to get that sod broke up with, that broom-sage sod, and it wasn't broke up good, and they was a-hoein' corn. And he turned over a big old sod, and a big old long black snake run out of it—aha!—and run right between that boy's [the cousin's] legs, and he just stood up on his hoe handle, seemed like a minute. Just stood up on that hoe handle, and when he come down, he come down a-cussin' and a-cuttin'! And he said his aunt [the boy's mother] just grabbed up one of them great old long sprouts, old sassafras sprouts, and lit in on him, and whithered him for cussin'! He never paid no attention. He just cussed and he cut till he cut that snake up into little bitty pieces! About that long! Ever' time he'd hit him he'd cuss. His mother was a-pourin' away to him."

Guy says these incidents would have occurred around 1875, when his father was eight or ten years old.

WHEN HE WAS ABOUT TWELVE, Guy started picking the banjo. When I asked what kind of banjo he learned on, he answered, "Banjers then was just banjers. Banjers then didn't have a name . . . and wasn't as good as they are now. . . . I could play a tune on any one I picked up. I never did chord, so it didn't make no difference to me. . . . Lot of 'em 'd make them out of old cigar boxes and first one thing and another. Cigar boxes then was wood."

"What kind of hide would they put on them?"

"Kill a cat!" Guy answered without hesitation. "Kill a cat and tan its hide. My brother-in-law . . . if he happened to burst his banjo head, if he could find a big old tom cat and get him to kill him, he'd cut his head off, skin him just quick as he could, then he'd just split his head open and get his brains and go to rubbin' that on the furry side of the skin, and that hair'd just be a-slippin' off o' there, and why he could kill the cat this morning and late this afternoon it'd be on the banjo so he could pick a tune on it!" He laughed. I had heard about this practice from several other old-time banjo pickers in the Appalachians. I asked if the banjos in those days were fretless.

"They had frets on the neck, but lots of people pulled 'em out, or filed 'em down smooth. They couldn't pick with 'em on there, you see. They done a lot of slurrin' with their fingers. The first banjo I ever owned cost me two dollars and a half. There's an old banjo picker, he's still livin', be ninety-four next December, and he tried to get me to take the frets out. I wouldn't do it."

Guy learned from this man, Oscar Brown, and another man in the community. "I started out to frail. I can't frail to do no good now. I'm plumb out of business on that." He was referring to the downward stroke, variously called rapping, clawhammer, framming, and in Georgia, frailing. I asked him what he calls the thumb-and-finger style he now uses.

"I don't call it nothin'. Just old-timey banjer pickin'."

I knew he played for square dances, and asked about other occasions when he would pick the banjo. "Well, back then," he answered, "there wasn't any music, and if a feller could make music, people just naturally liked to hear it. And there was an old fiddler moved in our settlement, right up in the country—that was before I was married, I was in my teens, a boy! And we'd go to the neighbor's house, and we'd walk two miles, and that was in the fall of the year, and play music till midnight—not midnight, bedtime. And everybody'd sit just as quiet and listen. They thought that was just wonderful . . . you can't comprehend how it was. . . . Most anybody that went anywhere then walked, you see. And I rode a bicycle a whole lot in my lifetime."

"Did you take the banjo with you on the bicycle?"

"Yeah, I'd tie it on the handlebars and light out! I finally got a motorcycle, rode that till I was fifty-nine years old, children got at me to sell it, and my wife [did too]. Last one I owned, I bought in 'fifty, a Harley Davidson, that was the biggest one Harley made, I rode that rascal to Miami and back. Yeah! I didn't take my banjo with me."

Music was just a pastime for Guy, and he worked on the farm until he got married at twenty-one. He made extra money by taking fresh meat from the farm down to the mill town of Trion and selling it from his wagon for six to eight cents a pound. I asked him if he ever worked in the mill.

"Yes, but the day that I went to work in a cotton mill, that's the day I hunted an excuse to quit." He had an exceptional understanding of mechanical things, and his usual job in the mill was fixing machinery; but he could not tolerate the oppressive supervision of the foremen. One time he was on an upper floor, and the boss complained that he hadn't been able to find him. Guy exploded: " 'It don't make a damn to me how long it took you nor nothin' 't all about it!' I said, 'To hell with you! I don't care nothin' about your time nor nothin' else.' I said, 'I'll go fix your machine, but don't go bellyachin' to me about how long it took you to find me and this that and t'other, don't go goin' on me about it!' He never said no more. I said you just tell me if such and such a machine is out of shape. I stayed there about four or five months. I guess it got on my nerves. I don't like to work for the other man no how."

Guy's temperament was much better suited for self-employment, and for most of his life he has "fooled around with watches and clocks."

"I just started up myself. . . . I don't know whether you believe it, I believe a man has a talent. And to fix anything, I had a talent for it. I could look at a machine that I had never seen, if there was somethin' that wasn't a-workin'. . . . I could look at it and find the trouble. Watches, I just liked to fool with 'em, you see. I didn't have any money to buy me no tools. I got me up some little tweezers, little old pliers, and screwdrivers. . . . So I had to do all that cleanin' out by hand, and I got a dollar. A man, if he got a dollar a day for his work, workin' out, he was a-doin' fine. I don't mean eight hours, I mean a day! Well, I charged him a dollar to clean out his watch, wasn't any kickin' about it. But if I was to charge a man now what he made in a day to clean out a watch, he'd go through the top of his house! That shows how things have changed."

I asked Guy when he began fixing watches.

"I started out when I was about seventeen. And I'm five years older than the century. That'd be five from seven, be 1912, wouldn't it? I still fool with 'em. I got watches out there, and clocks, in the shop, now. I don't solicit no work, but friends that know me, they don't let me quit. Feller asked the other day, 'Want you to tell me what I'm goin' to do when you quit fixin' clocks.' I said, 'You got to do the best you can.' "

Guy's children are married, with families of their own. Only his son, Guy Jr., followed music, and plays fiddle and guitar with his father. Guy's first wife is dead, and when he was eighty-seven he and his second wife were divorced. He found he did not like living alone, and married for the third time a few months later. He is not unhappy about some of the changes that have come about during his lifetime: "Used to be if you was talkin' about a bull, you'd have to say 'male cow.' Nowadays, if you're talkin' to a woman about a bull, you just say bull. That's what he is! People was finicky about their speech whenever I was young. I like it the way it is now. You can talk plain. If a woman was pregnant, she wouldn't any more talk to a man, nor get out where anybody could see her when she was showin'. . . . Just like she'd done somethin' awful. Awful wrong. And she wouldn't of no more told a man that she was pregnant than she'd-a tuck wings and flew off! Now I look back on it, it beats ever'thing I ever seen."

One thing that has not changed is W. Guy Bruce's music, which has remained much the same as when he learned it early in the century. He courted his new wife, Minerva, by playing the banjo for her. I asked if she had a favorite tune. "No," he answered, "she likes all the old pieces."

Greenback

Sung by W. Guy Bruce with five-string banjo; Welcome Hill Community, Trion, Chattooga

County, April 25, 1981. "Greenback" seems to be the north Georgia form of this animal song, presumably of black or minstrel-show origin. Chesley Chancey sang a similar version he had learned from Land Norris. The tune closely resembles "Once I Had a Fortune" as

played and sung by the Bogtrotters and others in the Galax, Virginia, area, as well as "Whoa, Mule, Whoa." Perdue, p. 40, gives a version of "Gwine On Down to Town" with the "Raccoon's got a bushy tail" verse.

1. Raccoon up a gummy stump
   Possum in a holler
   And a pretty girl at my house
   Fat as she can waller.

   Chorus:
   Higher off o' the greenback
   And higher off o' the change;
   Higher off o' the greenback, boys,
   Can't get away with me.

2. Raccoon's got a bushy tail,
   And the possum tail is bare,
   And the rabbit's got no tail at all,
   But a little bitty bunch of hair.   (*Chorus*)

3. Possum up a 'simmon tree,
   Raccoon on the ground,
   And the raccoon says to the possum
      "Won't you shake them 'simmons
         down."   (*Chorus*)

4. Possum got a round tail,
   Beaver's tail is flat;
   And the rabbit's got no tail at all
   But he can't he'p that!   (*Chorus*)

5. Junebug comes in the month of June,
   And the lightning bug's in May;
   The bedbug comes at any old time,
   But he comes here to stay!   (*Chorus*)

W. Guy Bruce. (Welcome Hill, Trion, 1980.)

The Lily of the West
(Laws P29)

Sung by W. Guy Bruce; Welcome Hill
Community, Trion, Chattooga County, April

25, 1981. *This first-person narrative from the British broadside tradition gained some currency in the nineteenth century in America through such songsters as* Uncle Sam's Army Songster *(Indianapolis: n.p., 1862). Guy sings it in the typical* parlando rubato *ballad-delivery style; he learned it years ago from Harve Adams, a "great big man" with a "deep voice." See Laws I, p. 263; Belden, p. 132 (Missouri); Eddy, p. 147 (Ohio); Sharp, 2:199 (Kentucky); and Randolph, 2:76 (Arkansas).*

Oh it's I'm just down from Illi — nois some pleasure for to find, a handsome girl from Ar-kansaw, most suitable to my mind; her cheeks was red as ro — ses, her eyes did pierce my breast, they called her handsome Mary, the Li-ly of the West.

1. Oh it's I'm just down from Illinois some
   pleasure for to find,
   A handsome girl from Arkansaw, most
   suitable to my mind
   Her cheeks was red as roses, her eyes
   did pierce my breast,
   They called her handsome Mary, the
   Lily of the West.

2. I courted this fair damsel, her love I
   thought I'd gain
   Too soon, too soon, she slighted me,
   which caused me grief and pain;
   She deprived me of my liberty and stole
   away my rest,
   I was betrayed by Mary, the Lily of the
   West.

3. I walked out one mornin', about a mile
   in yonders grove;
   I spied a man of low degree conversing
   with my love;
   He sang to her so handsomely as she
   lay on his breast,
   He sang to handsome Mary, the Lily of
   the West.

4. I shouldered up my rifle, my dagger in
   my hand,
   I quickly rushed upon him and bravely
   made him stand
   I cast like a desperado, my dagger
   pierced his breast—
   All this was caused by Mary, the Lily of
   the West.

5. Oh it's now that I'm convicted and sen-
   tenced I will be,
   If ever again in this wide world I gain
   my liberty,
   I'll travel this wide world over, I'll travel
   to the West,
   And there I'll murder Mary, the Lily of
   the West.

As I Walked Out
One Morning in Spring

Sung by W. Guy Bruce with five-string banjo; Welcome Hill Community, Trion, Chattooga County, April 25, 1981. Guy learned this British lyric folk song with its fine Scottish melody from Harve Adams, who also taught *him this unusual 6/8 time banjo setting, a rhythm rarely attempted on the instrument in this century. See Brown, 2:436, for a North Carolina text without tune; and Sharp, 2:189, for a Tennessee version.*

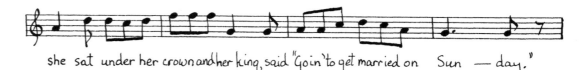

1. As I walked out one morning in Spring,
   I spied a fair maiden so sweetly did sing
   As she sat under her crown and her
        king,
   Said, "Going to get married on Sunday."

2. Last Saturday night she went to town
   To buy green ribbon and a new-fangled
        gown,
   Inviting all the ladies around
   To come to her wedding on Sunday.

Shady Grove

Sung by W. Guy Bruce with five-string banjo;
Welcome Hill Community, Trion, Chattooga
County, April 25, 1981. One defining
characteristic of the older styles of Appalachian
fiddling and banjo picking is the use of various
traditional tunings suited to the old modes
and keys. Chesley Chancey told us he would
need four banjos to do a show properly, meaning
that he would have each in a different tuning
in order not to have to retune on stage. Guy
is the only banjo picker we have met in Georgia
to use the old "mountain minor" tuning, suited
to tunes in the dorian mode—he calls it "Shady
Grove key" and uses the fFGCD (tuned a whole

Sha-dy Grove, sugar Betty Ann, Shady Grove I say,

Shady Grove, sugar Betty Ann, bound to leave this place.

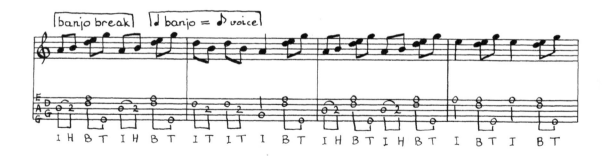

tone higher) of the more common gDGCD, in order to have more open strings of the sung melody. (Sidna Myers of Hillsville, Virginia, plays the haunting "Twins Sisters" in this present tuning on Rounder 0028.) After playing this piece, Guy said: "I just picked that up whenever I was a sprout, you might say, in my banjer pickin', way back yonder. Heard somebody pick it, asked 'em how they tuned the banjer, said they tuned it in 'Shady Grove' key. We didn't know nothin' about F and G and C, and D. . . . We'd just tune the banjer in 'Shady Grove' key, or 'Shout Luler' key, or 'Cabbage' key, or 'Greenback' key." Guy explained that when you knew those keys, you were a banjo picker. He learned "Shady Grove" from an old fiddler named Perkins in his early years as a musician. For a Kentucky version, see Rufus Crisp, Folkways LP FA 2342. See Sharp, 2:37 for "Betty Ann"; also Brown, 3:552; and Ritchie, p. 46.

1. Shady Grove, sugar Betty Ann,
   Shady Grove I say,
   Shady Grove, sugar Betty Ann,
   Bound to leave this place.

2. Shady Grove's a pretty little girl,
   Mighty hard to please:
   She went to sleep by herself one cold
       night,
   And I hope, by jinks, she'll freeze.

3. *Repeat 1.*

Shout, Lulu

Sung by W. Guy Bruce with five-string banjo; Welcome Hill Community, Trion, Chattooga County, September 20, 1980. Guy's exuberant performance of this banjo song is reminiscent of Uncle Dave Macon at his best. It certainly is the most exciting rendition I have recorded, and I have recorded several, as this song is much more current in the tradition than its absence from printed collections would suggest. In Georgia I have recorded it from John Patterson, Lawrence Eller, the Chancey Brothers, Mabel Cawthorn, and Jake Staggers; and I have collected it as well from Pete Steele in Ohio and Smoky Mountain Cass Moore, a migrant farm worker in Michigan, originally from North Carolina. The Ellers' performance can be heard on Flyright 546; see also Rufus Crisp's version, Folkways FA 2341. Guy has in his excellent text some verses from the lullabye "Hush Little Baby"; these occur in another banjo song, "Say, Darling, Say," sung and played by Ernest "Pop" Stoneman on Folkways FA 2315. Guy explained that "bumzeray" in the last stanza of his version means "the old billy goat's mean!"

When I get sick and I have to go to bed, send for little Lulu to hold my head.

Shout, Lulu, shout, Lulu, shout, shout.

1. When I get sick and I have to go to bed,
   Send for little Lulu to hold my head.
       Shout, Lulu, shout, Lulu, shout, shout.

2. Shout, little Lulu, sing and pray,
   You gonna die some rainy day,
       Shout, Lulu, shout, shout,
       Shout, Luly, shout, shout.

3. Shout, little Luly, shout your best,
   Your old grandma's gone west!
       Shout, Lulu, shout, Lulu, shout, shout.

4. How many nickels will it take
   To see little Lulu's body shake?
   Two little nickels and a dime,
   We'll see little Lulu shake and shine.
       Shout, Lulu, shout, shout,
       Shout, Lulu, shout, shout.

5. Shout little Lulu, shout your best,
   Granny's got her head in a hornet's nest,
       Shout, Lulu, shout, shout,
       Shout, Lulu, shout, shout.

6. Hush, little baby, and don't say a word,
   Papa will buy you a mockin'-bird.
   If that mockin'-bird don't sing,
   Papa will buy you a diamond ring.
   If that diamond ring turns to brass,
   Papa will buy you a looking glass.
   If that looking glass gets broke,
   Papa will buy you a billy goat.
   If that billy goat runs away,
   Whoopee, bumzeray!
       Shout, little Lulu, shout, shout,
       Shout, little Lulu, shout, shout.

"Shout, Lulu, Shout." W. Guy Bruce at the Georgia Folklife Festival.
(Charcoal, 22" × 30", 1983.)

The Rovin' Gambler
(Laws H4)

Sung by W. Guy Bruce with five-string banjo; Welcome Hill Community, Trion, Chattooga County, April 25, 1981. This song derives from the British "Roving Journeyman"; in America it became associated with the reckless and randy Civil War soldiers and veterans, as in "The Blue-Coat Man," Brewster, pp. 342–43. In its present form it is widespread throughout the middle South. Samantha Bumgarner of North Carolina recorded an instrumental version, "Gambling Man," in the early 1920s. Guy Bruce has known it as long as he has picked the banjo. He sometimes sings a refrain after a verse, made from the last line of the verse and the basic melody, as: "Lie my money down, lie my money down / Whenever I meet with a deck of cards I lie my money down." See Belden, p. 375; Brown, 3:79; Henry, pp. 98–99; Laws, 2:221; Randolph, 4:835; Roberts, pp. 108–9.

♩ = 113

I'm a rov-ing gamb-ler, I gambled down in Town; when-ev-er I meet with a deck of cards I lie my money down.

1. I'm a rovin' gambler, I gambled down
    in town;
   Whenever I meet with a deck of cards I
    lie my money down.

2. Hadn't been in Washington for many
    more weeks than three,
   When I fell in love with a pretty little
    girl, she fell in love with me.

3. She took me in her parlor, she cooled
    me with her fan,
   She whispered low in her mother's ear,
    "I love this gamblin' man."

4. "Daughter, oh dear daughter, how do
    you treat me so,
   To leave your dear old mother and with
    a gambler go?"

5. "Mother, oh dear mother, I know I love
    you well,
   But the love I have for this gamblin'
    man no human tongue can tell."

6. I gambled down in Washington, I
    gambled up in Spain;
   I'm a-goin' down to Georgia to gamble
    my last game.

I Don't Know How We Made It Over

THE BROWN'S CHAPEL CHOIR OF BISHOP

BROWN'S CHAPEL is a country church outside Bishop, Georgia; its members are in large part the descendants of slaves who worked on the cotton plantations around. When it meets on the fourth Sunday of every month, the old "Dr. Watts" hymns are lined out and sung in the surge-singing style that black singers adapted from the whites long before blacks were allowed to organize their own churches. And the traditional spirituals are sung as well, by the congregation and by the choir of four women and one man, one of the most impressive vocal groups we have heard. Most choirs from rural and small-town black churches in Georgia still dip back into the well of traditional spirituals for their repertoires, but very few sing these in the old *a capella* way, and with as much soul-stirring artistry, and almost overwhelming dignity and poignancy, as the Brown's Chapel Choir. All but one of the choir's members have moved up the road from Oconee County to Athens, a few miles to the north, and it was in his home in Athens on the Plaza, a street of well-kept houses, that we talked to Otha Cooper and to Imogene Riggens. Cooper, a widower, is the bass singer of the group. Riggens sings lead and is the youngest member, the only one who was not in the choir when it was organized over thirty years ago.

When I asked Imogen Riggens what one has to do to be a good sacred singer, she said, "You have to pray a lot, too, to be a good singer."

Cooper took it from there: "You got to have that talent, got to have the voice to produce, and then, you know, meditate with the Lord, and as you grow in grace, you get stronger. But, I mean, it's gotta be a God-given talent."

I remarked that I felt the choir put more feeling into their singing than did most modern gospel singers.

"Well," Cooper said, "after we got to going without music (instrumental accompaniment), we rearranged the songs, put a little salt and black pepper on it, you know. Sing it with a feelin' on it, you know. And you have to get a little of God's grace in there, you see, to be able to put the program over, and I mean, when you put your heart and mind—trust in God, and put your heart and mind on it, and ask Him to help you, He ain't gonna let you down."

I asked about the time they sang with instruments.

"Oh, yeah. One of the leaders of the group when we had musicians—our first leader, she passed, Moselle Bell. She had a God-given talent." Her favorite songs were "Sweet Home," "I Don't Know Why I Have to Cry Sometime," and "I Don't Know How We Made It Over." I asked if Cooper had learned these songs from her.

"I knowed 'em way before then. See, I *been* knowin'—I came out of a singin' family. Well I was raised around a Christian altar—family altar. 'Cause my father was a minister, and my mother, she was a faithful member up until her death."

A man who had played guitar and piano with Cooper in jubilee quartets, played with the Brown's Chapel Choir when it was formed. I asked when he left the group.

"Seven or eight years, or probably longer'n that. Me and him was ordained as a deacon the same time. He lives right across the street over there, but, you know how some people just turn back."

"Does he still play?"

"No, he don't study about nothin' like that. . . . He got stuck on the bottle, and every dollar he gets, that's where he put it. He's not there by himself—there's plenty mo' with him! Plenty mo' in the boat with him."

I observed that singing without accompaniment had brought them back to the way people used to sing in the old days.

"That's right," Cooper agreed. And my older brother, 'sides me, he sung until he had a heart attack. He could 'double-bass' where me and the rest of them leave off, he could pick it up. I wish you could've heard it when he's in there. That would carry you to the way we used to sing, when we first started out."

When I asked who the singers had been in his family, Cooper replied, "All my people could sing. On both sides. All of 'em could sing. But all of 'em dead. I don't have but one aunt livin' now. All of 'em got offspring—they still singin', but none of 'em is around here, you know." I asked if he had known his grandparents. "Sure, I knew them. I remember my great-grandma. Sho' did. I used to sit down and listen, talk, you know, when I was small. I used to sit down and listen at her talk about how she came along, and all. Such as, she was fifteen years old when they said she was free. I mean, she could tell you somethin'. You could set down and listen all night. I could, 'cause I was interested in what she said. I mean she could tell some things that're unbelievable. . . . The people back then, when they would ship them over, they would sell 'em, and they would have to wear the same name as whatsonever, you know. She used to tell me about how they used to do them. And sucha things as that."

He preferred not to go into the specific brutalities of slavery he had heard from his great-grandmother. I offered that it was a pretty hard system.

"It ain't no pretty hard. It was *rough*. Of course, quite a while ago."

I changed the subject back to songs and asked if he remembered any particular spirituals his grandmother sang.

"No, just the songs we been singin' all our lives."

"Same ones."

"Same ones. Went on back, generations, yeah. People were more sincere back then, than they is now. 'Course you find a few now that's sincere, but most of them, they done drifted away from the plan of Salvation. . . . They figure they're gonna have time to get back, but you never know. Just one step between life and death, you see. You don't know when you gonna make that last step. . . . You gonna live to see a lot of things that the Bible predict, come to pass. I have. I lived to see it. When I was goin' to grade school, the teacher was sayin' they was workin' on a gadget, you could sit in your livin' room, and a person could be a thousand miles away, and his picture would come up on a screen, and if you know that person you recog-

nize who he is. So we went back home, told our parents, they said, 'That teacher don't know what she talkin' about.'" He laughed. "Well, you know, it's a long time comin' but it finally come. She said, scientists was workin' on inventin' the television at that time. . . . I never thought I would see cars replace mules and wagons. They used to drive mules and wagons from Bishop to here. That's the most transportation they had. . . . You didn't hardly ever see a car. On Sundays, them that had buggies would ride in the buggies. Hitch up the wagon, fill it full of straw, and that's the way they'd ride to church. You'd see mules tied around in the church yard."

"What year were you born?"

"1918. But I came up in the Cross. Don't forget I didn't. My niece and nephew here, I tell 'em how we used to work, plow all day, plowed on my daddy's farm up until Friday, plow on a Saturday for somebody else, and at night, when sundown come, he'd give me fifty cents. They said, 'Well, I jus' wouldn't work for it!' I said, 'Yes, you would, too. Come along when I did, you didn't know no better.' Nobody didn't have nothin'. Back then, times was rough!" He told about how people back then grew their food, and each family raised a hog each year. They kept milk cool in a well or spring. "People have come from a long ways," he said, alluding to the old spiritual.

I said that people might have to use some of the old knowledge again.

"Well, my wife, she didn't want to go back to the old days, but if it had been lef' to me, I'd have me a little farm now. I could go back now, get four or five acres, just somethin' to raise a vegetable garden, somethin' like that, I get a kick out of it."

Cooper recalled the country dances of his youth: "At that time, well, the adults, they would have a all-night fish fry. What they did back there then, they would clear all the furniture out of the room, and then they would have a dance, what they would call 'set.' They would dance all the way around—they didn't have no piano, some would have an organ, or a guitar. All they had was guitars and organs. And the ones makes the music, they'd be over here in this corner, and the one be over there, be like the preacher, sort of like they call 'teachers,' they'd be pattin' their hands. . . . Go 'round in a ring, and each partner'd get out and dance. Till they get all the way 'round."

I asked if church members attended these gatherings.

"Oh, no! They wouldn't be church members, church members

Brown's Chapel Choir. Viola Watkins, Beatrice Robinson, Otha Cooper, Imogene Riggens, and Lily Mae Davis. (Athens, 1980.)

didn't go to nothin' like that. The worldly crowd. The church members, they was more strict back then than they is now. Nawsir, that's the worldly crowd. Church members, they didn't do nothin' but go to church, and they'd have meetin' at night. Back then they had them oil lamps, you know, set on the wall. . . . But they would have meetin', and that church'd be full up.

"Back befo' World War II," he continued, "you couldn't stir people around here with a—man, people 'round here like ants. Anywhere you go, you couldn't go to a rural area, everywhere you see'd be a house, and a houseful of people, and they have a bunch of children—jus' peoples everywhere. But after World War II they went to emigratin' out of here, go in the service, and they went north, to work in the factory. They hadn't been used to makin' no money. 'Course I went to buildin' the first apartments here . . . workin' for thirty cents an hour. . . . I was just a common laborer. I didn't go into the buildin' business for myself till after World War II." His kin "scattered all over the country, that's right. They jus' goin' wheresonever the work was. That's the way they emigrated."

"Do you keep in touch with them?"

"Well, some of 'em, but mos' of them is dead, now. Some went to every state in the Union. All my peoples, most of them is dead. Cousins, things like that. They still a few of them scattered around. We stay in touch about once a year. Christmas cards."

Emigration, social upheaval, and death have taken their toll on community as well as family; yet the Brown's Chapel Choir has kept a nucleus of singers with a strong shared tradition and common roots in the church and the land. I spoke further with Otha Cooper about his life as a singer and the aesthetic of unaccompanied singing.

As we had encountered very little singing out of shape-note books among black religious singers in north Georgia, I asked Cooper about this practice.

"The old heads did. I never did. . . . I used to sing with a male chorus, they sung notes. But the leader died out, and they went down. I wish you had been there when they sang the notes! I didn't know what they talkin' about! On every song they sing the notes first, and I just wait, till they get to the words. . . . When I was young I would hear a song about twice, or three times [and know it]. But, you know, I'm funny, I hear a song, and tomorrow, it just come to me, the words just come to me in my mind, the Lord just will it to me. People say I'm just musically inclined. . . . 'Course, some of the songs we used to sing, I done forgot the words, some of the jubilee songs, some of the old spirituals, too, 'cause we don't sing 'em, some of 'em, in so long." Although the choir can perform many songs, Cooper explained that jubilee quartets had to keep a larger active repertoire: "When we used to sing in a quartet, we used to have to sing 'bout eight or ten songs in a program. In the choir, we don't have to round up but two." Churches in the area periodically present musical programs at which choirs and groups from fifteen or more other churches are invited to perform two numbers each.

Like all first-rate Afro-American traditional singers, Cooper and the Brown's Chapel Choir are not musical archaeologists, preserving in a pristine way the songs and styles of the past; they constantly re-work and re-create the old material. He is aware, too, that they can reach back and perform the old antebellum spirituals that would not have lent themselves to performance in the accompanied quartet style. "Most of the songs we sing is real old," he explained, "but we make our own re-arrangements. There's plenty of those songs you can't sing if you sing with music [instruments]. It's got a different beat. I mean, we have to rhyme it so it'll coincide with just your foots—just foot-stompin'. And when you got the music, see, music cover up a whole lot. You can even stop, and the music carries it on for you. You can't do that, the way we sing, you got to—I mean, everyone *got to be in there.* When you stop, you can tell it. You got nothin' to cover up there, I mean, you just have to pour it out! But if you've got, on a fast beat, a piano playin', all she's got to do is jus' keep goin', and people wouldn't know the difference, they just think, well, they just got a break there. . . . I've seen them fall plumb flat, the music jus' keeps goin'. . . . But we jus' don't have the talent now we had when I was comin' along. I jus' don't know what it is, I mean, everything done made a change. You can't hardly find nobody can sing the different parts. Now when we first started singing quartet, we wasn't but four—if you get four persons now, and each one can sing their part, soprano, tenor, baritone, bass, if them four . . . can really sing, each one could master their part, that's all you need to sing. If four people . . . really know how to blend their voices together, it would be like a piano. Each one would be on a different voice, but the voice would harmonize as one. Now that's the way we started out."

I Don't Know How We Made It Over

Sung by Brown's Chapel Choir (Imogene Riggens, lead); Athens, Clarke County, January 19, 1980. This is one of the moving old-time spirituals that use the image of getting over, or making it over, to heaven, as a metaphor for deliverance from slavery. Mavis Moon, a singer in Doc Barnes's Gospel Chorus, sings the lines:

How we got over, how we got over, oh my Lord, Oh my soul looked back and wonder', how we got over.

This song, in its travels, has picked up some lines from "Amazing Grace."

Lord, you know then, I don't know, you know, church, I don't know just how we

made it o — ver, Lord, thank you, Jesus, God, I don't know, you know it

must have been the Grace of God. I said, Lord, thank you, Jesus, God

I don't know, you know, church, I don't know just how we made it o — ver,

Lord, thank you, Jesus, (God) I don't know, you know it must have been the Grace of

God. I said, Lord, Oh, Lord, well, I don't know, you know, church

I don't know just how we made it o — ver, Lord, thank you, Jesus, (God)

Solo

I don't know, you know it must have been the Grace of God. Some-

times I feel dis — couraged. Oh, yes! You know it seem like my work is in

vain.   oh, but the Ho — ly Spir-it ____ speak to me, re-
In vain,   Hm   Hm Hm   Hm   Hm Hm   Hm

- vive my soul a - gain.   I said
  Hm   Hm   Hm   Hm   Hm

Chorus:
Lord, you know then, I don't know, you
    know, church,
I don't know just how we made it over,
Lord, thank you, Jesus, I don't know, you
    know it
Must have been the Grace of God.
I said, Lord, God, I don't know, you know,
    church,
I don't know just how we made it over,
Lord, thank you Jesus, well, I don't know,
You know it must have been the Grace
    of God

1. *Solo:*
   Sometimes I feel discouraged

   Group:
   Oh, yes!

   Solo:
   You know it seem like my work is
      in vain

   Group:
   In vain,

   Solo:
   But the Holy Spirit speak to me, revive
      my soul again,
   I said *(Chorus)*

2. *Solo:*
   Through many dangers, toils and
      snares, I already come,
   Now it was Grace that brought me safe
      this far,
   Grace will lead me home. *(Chorus)*

Women in Church. (Athens, 1977.)

No Room at the Hotel

Sung by Otha Cooper; Athens, Clarke County, March 21, 1981. This touching retelling of Luke 2:7 is possibly a fragment of a longer religious ballad. Otha Cooper learned it from his mother, Blanna Cooper, and says it is "an old family song." The

There was-a no room, no room, they had no

room, there was-a no room, no room at the

hotel; you know the time had fully come

for o-ur Sa-vior to be born, there was-a no room,

no room, they had no room.

highly ornamented vocal line carries the story of the Holy Family's being turned away from the inn from the sympathetic point of view of "the help," as if it had

happened yesterday. Although it does not appear in any of the collections of spirituals, this song has had some currency; George

Mitchell recorded a version from James Lloyd in LaGrange, Georgia, and it was sung by Vera Hall of Livingston, Alabama.

1. There was-a no room, no room, they
      had no room,
   There was no room, no room at the
      hotel;
   You know the time had fully come for
      our Savior to be born,
   There was no room, no room, they had
      no room.

2. Now according to God's Word, there
      was a Virgin girl,
   The mother of King Jesus, she was a-
      wanderin' around one night;
   She was tryin' to find her a home for
      our Savior to be born,
   There was-a no room, no room, they
      had no room.

3. Church, I know those peoples they was
      wicked, and yet they did not know,
   That Jesus Christ He had shed His
      blood to save their sinful soul;
   You know for years they thought it was
      right to say, when they turned po'
      Mary away,
   There is no room, no room, had no
      room.

4. Well I know that mother she got worried,
      because she had no place to go,
   With the pain to be delivered of a man-
      chil',
   Oh she had been from do' to do', po'
      Mary didn't have no place to go,
   There was-a no room, no room, they
      had no room.

5. You know the bellboy and the porter,
      the waiter and-a the cook,
   They will be there release' at the Judg-
      ment, because they saw how they
      looked,
   Well they heard the manager say when
      they turned po' Mary away,
   There was no room, no room, they had
      no room.

Brown's Chapel Choir. (Athens, 1980.)

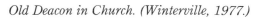
Old Deacon in Church. (Winterville, 1977.)

Welcome Home

Sung by Brown's Chapel Choir (Imogene Riggens, lead; Bea Robinson, first alto; Viola Watkins, second alto; Lily Mae Davis, soprano; Otha Cooper, bass); Athens, Clarke County, January 19, 1980. Like the better-known spiritual, "Sit Down, Servant," this song presents a moving conversation between Jesus, and the singer, one of His children, "coming home." Songs like this are monumental artistic achievements and powerful statements of faith and of humanity that came out of the black people's time of bondage in the South.

1. *Leader:* Welcome home,　*Group:* welcome home,
   Leader: Welcome home,　*Group:* welcome home,
   I wanna hear Jesus saying, welcome home;
   You been workin', yes you been toilin',
   Toilin' for a long, a long time,
   Come on home, oh, child, sit down and rest a little while.　*(Repeat verse)*

2. *Leader:* I been travelin' over hills, and over mountains,
   Lord, sometimes it seems like I can't go on.
   Then I hear a sweet voice, keeps on whisperin' to me,
   Sayin', one mo', one mo' mountain, and you'll be home.

3. *Leader:* Don't cry no mo',　*Group:* don't cry no mo',
   Leader: Don't cry no mo',　*Group:* don't cry no mo',
   I wanna hear Jesus say, don't cry no mo'.
   You been cryin', yes, you been cryin',
   cryin' for a long, long time,
   Come on home, child, sit down and rest a little while.

4. *Repeat 1.*

♩ = 84

Wel-come home, welcome home, welcome home, wel-come home, I wanna hear Jesus say – ing, wel-come home; you been workin', yes you been toilin', toilin' for a long, a long time, come on home, oh, child, sit down and rest a little while.

I Wish I Was a Mole in the Ground

CHESLEY CHANCEY, GEORGE CHILDERS,
AND MABEL CAWTHORN: BANJO PICKING AND
FAMILY STRING BANDS

I N HIS LAST YEARS Chesley Chancey had to get around on a wooden leg and one good leg; yet he managed to do some traveling with his younger brothers, Joe and Ralph, playing the mountain music they had learned as boys in Gilmer County. Chesley and Eva Chancey lived up a holler in the Boardtown section, several miles from the county seat of Ellijay; one room in their house was filled with yard goods that Eva used in the garment-making cooperative she formed with several other women when they became fed up with the low wages and bad conditions in the local textile mill. I visited "Bear," as he was called by his brothers, for the last time in June 1980, only a few days before his death. His banjo picking, and his memories of life and music making in the mountains, came through as strong and pure as the good moonshine whiskey he had made in his younger days.

He started by telling me that he played the jew's-harp at three then went on to the French harp (harmonica) and organ, before starting the banjo at five. I asked who the musicians were in his family. "Well," he answered, "it was handed down to me from my great-granddaddy, Charlie Simms . . . on my mother's side of the house, and fiddlin' Ira Simms, that was his brother." From Gilmer County, "they was raised partly in what we call Hell's Holler. And right across the hill over here there's a big creek we call Fightin' Town, and you go on just a little futher, turn up, and you go into the Devil's Den. Well this is so. So you can just lay it out from that. That's so."

"I don't doubt it," I found myself saying. "It makes sense."

"That's the truth, that's the names of that settlement back there: Fightin' Town Creek, the Devil's Den, and then Hell's Holler. And the next creek's Tongue Creek."

I asked if folks mostly farmed back then.

"Yeah, they farmed, and their livin' was give to them in these mountains. There's plenty of fish and plenty of game. . . . The mountains were full of wild hogs, full of big chestnut timber as big through as that television there—bigger. Chestnuts fell on the ground in the fall of the year, and a lot of places you couldn't walk for 'em, collect a pile of chestnuts, and their hogs, their cattle, their sheep and everything got fattened down on them, so they didn't have to feed nothin'. Just a little bit to get their stock through real bad winters. . . . 'Bout all they done is fish and hunt, and played music, drunk good whiskey."

I said I didn't know whether to ask about the whiskey or the music first, and he laughed. I decided to inquire about where he got his style of banjo picking.

"Well, I'd have to say that I picked my style up from a man we called—now we had *two* George Holloways—but I picked up my style from the one they called *little* George Holloway. And I switched from there to a feller by the name of Bob Watkins. And I switched from there to a feller by the name of Felton Looper. And then the rest of the tunes I play, some of them I made up myself, some I learnt from others."

I asked about Land Norris, who was from Boardtown, and made records in the early days of country recording, in the twenties. "Yes, I knowed Land Norris, knowed him well, but I never did try to foller his style none. He won the championship of Georgia, playin' the banjer, and they just shipped him up to New York. He went to makin' records." I sensed that Chesley felt that there were better banjo pickers around.

The Chanceys of Boardtown. Chesley, Ralph, Don, and Joe.
(Gilmer County, 1979.)

I wondered if they had small string bands back then.

"Most of the time," he explained, "when a man played then, it would be the fiddle and a five-string banjer, or just the banjer by itself. A five-string banjer is the only instrument you can entertain a crowd with by yourself. . . . Now people will get bored with a fiddle, but you can take a banjer, you can dance with it, play it, you can sing with it, and you can switch right over into sacred music, and still you're in line."

"Now some of the religious denominations didn't hold with the banjo," I commented, alluding to the prohibition by some churches of string music.

"Lot of them that don't hold with no music at all."

"But you weren't brought up to that? You were brought up that music was all right."

"Brought up that music was all right?" He thought about that. "Oh, I was brought up every way. Mostly brought up by the hair of the head. We wasn't a mean people," Chesley went on to explain. "Oh, if you'd come in and jump on us, we'd try to get you off, but we wasn't a mean people. If we wanted to get drunk, wanted to play music, we played music, half drunk. . . . 'Course I was only drunk one time in my life—got drunk when I was sixteen and stayed drunk till I was thirty."

He played a line of "Mulberry Gap" on his old Gibson banjo, and went on to talk about the cycles of the seasons in the mountains in early times: "My granddaddy . . . said the way people used to live here, in the spring of the year they'd plant all the corn, cane, ever'-thing it took to do 'em through the winter, and had plenty of apples. Every summer, before harvest time, why everybody'd go to church. Everybody. Them that didn't belong joined. And they'd have big baptizings, shout, what have you. And they'd go back at harvest time and gather all this stuff in, and every man'd make him his barrel of whiskey or brandy, and they'd drink that brandy or whiskey until spring, and play music and dance. Now that was the life they lived here in these mountains. So beat it if you can!"

Chesley talked about his own days of making whiskey: "When we first started out as boys, we didn't make much, but we got to where we's makin' *good* whiskey. Now most people made whiskey that wasn't too pleasant, but we didn't. We made it to drink. And sell.

But we knowed we was goin' to drink some of it, and for that reason, we made it good. And we'd make 100–125 gallons. . . . I think of one moonshine still that turned off 600 gallons a day."

I asked the inevitable question about the "revenue."

"Oh, they'd come in every once in a while and catch somebody, but they never did catch me. I was too wild." A lookout was generally posted on a ridge, and he would fire one warning shot in the air at the approach of the federal officers. Chesley used to haul whiskey to Dalton and to Atlanta. He knew a building in Atlanta where he could go if he was being pursued by the law. "Well, you know, if you got any holes shot in your car, why you'd just run [the car] in on an elevator that lifted up in the building. See, they knowed that car in the lobby, and when it come back down, all them bullet holes was stopped, new paint job, new tags, everything, and you was on your way."

He stopped making whiskey in the thirties, and worked as a builder, and farmed his land. He continued to play music, though it was not until 1957 that the Chancey Brothers as such was organized. "We played all those years, and it wasn't necessary to have a name. We just played. They got to calling us the Chancey Brothers and the Holloway Brothers. We had a fiddler, a little feller, and he was good, but he died, and that busted that band up. That was George Mings. I believe that the first band—I guess it would have to be in nineteen and twenty-eight, it was me and Claud Chapman and Oscar Land, and they called us the Boardtown String Band." Land played the fiddle, and Chapman the guitar and harmonica. Eventually the Chancey Brothers played on WLSB radio in Copper Hill, Tennessee, and did road shows up to a hundred miles from home, but gradually they tapered off. It was difficult to play and hold down jobs.

Chesley Chancey played in the typical index-finger-and-thumb up-picking style of the Georgia mountains; but his banjo playing had an unusually keen sense of melody, and he attempted difficult horn-pipes and fiddle tunes. It is unlikely that the rare old tunes he played will be picked up by the next generations.

ONE MOUNTAIN MUSICIAN who *is* teaching the old-time style to his offspring is George Childers of the Jerusalem section of Pickens

Bobby Childers and His Father, George Childers. (Jerusalem section, Pickens County, 1980.)

County, south of Gilmer County, in the foothills of the Blue Ridge. Recovered from a recent stroke, George plays shows locally, performing both bluegrass and old-time music with his sons Bobby, who usually plays guitar, and James, who sings. Bobby, a family man in his early twenties, is also learning banjo. George told us on a recent visit, "Bobby can pick banjer good."

I commented that, unlike most younger musicians who were learning the three-finger postwar bluegrass style, Bobby plays the early two-finger style.

"He don't play nothin' but two-finger. He can play every tune I play, and 'Using My Bible for a Roadmap' he can beat me so bad I won't even pick it without him, hardly. . . . He can pick out 'Lonesome Road Blues' good. Bobby's comin' right on. He plays just like I do."

Bobby is at least the third generation of Childerses to be a banjo picker. George remembers that his dad, Dave Childers, was "A-number-one. I couldn't play banjer like he could. But he wouldn't show me one thing."

"Why do you think that was?"

"I don't know. . . . He never showed me one thing in the world. He said, 'I learned it the hard way, so can you.' He said, 'If you want to play that banjo, you tune it. Get out here behind the house.' I just worked at it, and the first tune I ever picked was 'Cripple Creek.' I made that thing talk. Once in a while, I could get him to pick it up, play them old tunes like 'Ninety-seven,' 'Nellie Gray,' them old tunes away back yonder, 'Ground Hog' and 'Old Grey Mare.' "

George had started on "an old banjer with a lard-tub head on it, didn't have no good sound," and he recalls how he got his first good banjo, in 1928. "Right here, the other side of this big white church used to be a Baptist preacher lived there. . . . His wife wanted some blackberries in the spring of the year. . . . I was over there, seed this old banjer hangin' up on the wall, didn't have a string on it nor nothin', and old black pegs stuck up through the neck, and an old whittled-out peg for a thumb key. And I looked up there and seed that a-hangin' up there. She asked me how much I'd pick two gallons of blackberries for, and I said, 'How many gallons you take for that banjer up there?' She said, 'I'll tell you what I'll do: you pick me three gallons, and that banjer's yours. And I'll give you fifty cents to buy you a set of strings.' I said, 'You just sold your banjer.' Oh, I run

home as fast as I could, about a mile and a half, and I said, 'Mamma, I want you to help me pick three gallons of blackberries, I've got me a banjer.' She said, 'I'll do it.' We lit out down an old road, and the blackberries was just a-hangin' like this, like that, and it wasn't no time we had three gallons. . . . I told mamma, 'Let's finish fillin' this pan up. That's a real banjer.' I thought it was, because it had brackets on it." George walked twelve miles and back to get his Black Diamond strings in the town of Fairmount.

Soon after he "worked that banjer out," George was asked by his cousin Uncle John Childers to play for a square dance with him. "It was about eight or nine miles across that mountain, over to what they called Blalock Settlement. We lit out that evening about four o'clock, and by the time we got over there, it was time for the dance. Went in, they had Leonard Childers was pickin' guitar, John pickin' mandolin, I was pickin' five-string banjo, and Uncle Harm Childers was playin' the fiddle. This is at a big old mill house, they had just gathered in there, seventy-five or a hundred people. They'd drink a little, but they didn't get out of the way like they do now. Just danced all night, you never hear'd a bad word out of nobody. . . . We started, and them husky boys, got to dancin' around by me, and I's settin' and where a girl had been singin', she got up and went on the dance floor. And they got fifty cents, and they said, 'Water Boy, this belongs to you.' " George has never figured out why he was nicknamed Water Boy.

A half-century ago George began a musical friendship with another banjo picker which continues to this day, and he told me of their meeting: "First time I ever seen that old man, I wish you could have seen him, he had one of his britches about that high, and he had a little old Model A roadster, and he had that banjer. I seed a little old man comin' down the road, and had that banjo tied around his neck with a thread, and he'd walk a little piece, and start beatin' on that banjer. Galen Blue run a little place, that old buildin' wasn't but eight feet long. And he come over there, I asked, 'Who is that old man?' " They told him the man's name. "Well I lived over here and he lived over yonder. I said, 'No, I ain't never seen him before.' He'd been drunk, he wants more liquor, you know how it is, he drove up there, and he wanted to know, 'Any of you fellers got a drink?' I had a half-gallon in the little ol' car—and I wouldn't drink half a gallon in a year, I don't think. I told him, 'Let's see that old banjo you got there,' that old Sears Roebuck way back yander model. . . . I told him, 'Play me a tune on that!' He set down and played 'Yeller Bumblebee.'

I'm tickled in the mornin', tickled in the night,
Been tickled by a yeller bumblebee.

He done good on it. I went out there to the little old car and got my banjer, we got under that shed there, and I picked four or five with him, and he said, 'Tell you what I want you to do.' And I said, 'What's that?' He said, 'Just want you to go home with me. We'll go somewhere and find us a drink, if they's any around.' The revenuers had raided everything. And he said, 'We'll play all night. . . . I've got a cotton pile, and pick all night long.' I said, 'Suits me. Ain't got another thing to do.' I told my mother when I left home I'd probably not be back 'fore the next day. We went over there, and he had a little old cotton house about as long as this house is across, about eight foot wide, and we went over there, and he just kep' on, 'Boy, I've got to have a drink. Got to have a drink.' I said, 'I don't guess there's any liquor in this town. . . . The revenuers have raided every-thin'.' And there wasn't. They'd raided them, scared them all out. I said, 'Now if it's all right b'you, I'll give you a drink of this I've got.' 'Oh,' he said, 'that'd be just wonderful.' I said, 'Just wait a minute,' and I got out of that little old car, raised the trunk, reached down and got this can of liquor, I had it down there, didn't know if it's no 'count, been haulin' it three months. I said, 'If you like it, you just drink all of it you want.' You can believe he was drunk, time he got home, he was down that fur in that half-gallon can. But he never missed a string. And that was something that astounded me. We got down in that cotton pile that night, and played *all night long*. We'd just play a little bit, and lay down and rest awhile, and play again. And drink. We picked things like 'Blue Eyes,' just them old things like 'Turkey in the Straw'."

In 1930 George was in Tennessee competing against Tom Cat Payne in a banjo contest. The noted Georgia fiddler Clayton McMichen heard him play and told the officials, "I want to enter this boy in this contest." George at first "didn't no more figure to win that contest than you'd figure to jump over that tree. I guess I didn't have no confidence in myself, but I could just naturally pick a banjer, I was limber . . . and knowed how, too." Payne shook hands with

him. "He was a-gettin' pretty old, then. He told me, 'I wish you hadn't entered this contest, in a way. However, your music *is* interesting. . . . I never lost a contest in my life.' I told him, 'For seventy-five dollars I'll eat that banjo up.' "

"What tune did you play?"

"I played 'Coal Creek March,' 'Lonesome Road Blues,' and 'Shake That Little Foot, Sally Ann.' Tom Cat, he come out and played the banjo in every position, behind his neck—I can do that too—he got it down there and turned it, played it wrong-handed, every way a man can pick it. He was from Tennessee. I winned the contest on 'Coal Creek March,' I learned it from John Childers. Uncle Tom Cat had a different version, everybody has a different version of 'Coal Creek March.' My version must of tuck it. And when I got through playin' that, there's just silver dollars, fifty-cent pieces, ever'thing else layin' at my feet. They walked up and laid them up there, said, 'That's for the Water Boy.' Uncle Tom Cat told the judges, 'He beat me, absolutely. That's the first time that's ever happened.' Then me and Clayton McMichen had thirty minutes, and Lowe Stokes picked guitar. . . . That's where I met Gid Tanner."

George had occasion to play with Tanner later on, and says he even backed Riley Puckett on guitar on a record once. He left home for a time to play music on the road, but got homesick and came back. Most of his working life he was a sawmill worker, but he never let his music slip away. In the fifties he learned the bluegrass style of banjo, and even played with Earl Scruggs on a show in Ellijay; he says that Earl admired his old-time style and said he couldn't teach him a thing. Around home these days he is likely to be in overalls, bare-footed, an imposing man with heavy dark eyebrows and intense eyes, picking his old Vega banjo, an American eagle decal visible on the inside of the resonator through the transparent plastic head.

THE HEADLINE READ "If She Goes to Jail, What About Her Pets?" and the story told of an eighty-one-year-old Franklin County woman who had been accused of selling a small amount of marijuana. But what attracted our interest was the accompanying photo, which showed Mabel Cawthorn frailing a banjo and skillfully fretting it high up on the neck. We decided to look her up and found her old tin-roofed house on a hill above a river, off a county road near

Mabel Cawthorn. (Carnesville, 1983.)

Carnesville. A rough voice answered our knock: "Who's there?" We told her through the closed door, and although she could not have known our names, she invited us in. Dressed in a housecoat, Mabel began to build a fire in her wood stove against the December morning cold, indignantly declaring that she had never committed a crime; she had no use for marijuana and less for the man who accused her. (Later that day she told us, "I ain't in favor of sich as that! All this younger generation that's comin' up foolin' with that kind of stuff, if we have a war, we won't have a man can stand up and fight! We'd just be whupped, that's all there is to it.") We told her we hadn't come to worry her about any of that but wanted to hear her play the banjo. Her face lit up. "I *love* music!" she said. She produced two banjos from cases under her bed and had us get our fiddle from the car. Soon we were getting together on "John Henry" and "Living on the Hallelujah Side."

Mabel had scores of old photographs on her piano and covering the walls of the room, many of them showing her as a younger woman, with her banjo. I asked her how long she had been playing.

"Ever since I was eight years old. My oldest brother picked the banjer, and he 'uz off at work and he'd leave the banjer layin' on his bed, and I was a little smarty toddler, I'd go in there and get his banjer, and I kep' on and I kep' on. I went and got it one day and says, 'I'm gonna play the banjer.' He says, 'You can't play no banjer.' I says, 'I can, too. Listen at me, Tom, I'll show you what I can do!'" She played "'Corrina, Corrina, Where You Been So Long?'—that's his favorite song, that's a purdy song, too . . . and he jumped up and down and slapped his hands, and had all kinds of fits about it. He wasn't gonna hide his banjer no more."

Mabel grew up in a family of four boys and four girls, in Hart County. Her father, William Jeff Adams, was a good singer, and her mother, Mary Drucella Julie Ann Shaw, made music on the jew's-harp and was a fine dancer: "She'd do all kinds of dancin', different from what they do now, she'd put her heels and her toes together, and go all over the house." Her mother's brother, Albert Shaw, was "the greatest fiddler you ever heard, played all over the United States. Me 'n' him'd play together, we'd win a prize wherever we'd go, these fiddlers' conventions. Last one we had was here in Carnesville, at the courthouse. I 'uz makin' homemade soap, and they couldn't come to no conclusion up there [at the contest]. Uncle Al

got 'em to come after me, and I grabbed the old banjer and away we went!"

When Mabel played for square dances she always played "Shout, Lulu," which she still picks, along with another banjo song she learned from her brother, "Old Reuben" (see "Seventy-four," p. 79, and "Five Hundred Miles," p. 173):

Heard old Reuben say he was comin' home today,
He was five hundred miles away from home.

Love, if you say so I won't railroad no more,
I'll sidetrack my train and go home.

I'm goin' up north, gonna pull my britches off,
Gonna dance in this long shirt tail.

She remembers the tragic ballad "Little Mary Phagan" (see p. 231) and sentimental parlor songs and gospel numbers which she plays equally well on piano or banjo. She can beat a straw on the strings of a banjo when a friend like Oscar Peace comes around to play, and she can blow on the harp (harmonica) old-time pieces like "Lost John" and a version of "Hop Light, Ladies" which she calls "Run Here, Johnny, There's a Bug Done Got on Me."

When she was young, Mabel said, "ever'body used to play. They just quit, for some reason 'r 'nother."

"Why'd you keep on?"

She laughed. "I just liked it! Keeps me company! I stay here most of the time right by myself night and day, and my piano and my banjer keeps me company. I talk to my cats and talk to my dogs, and you think they was educated, tell 'em anything. . . . You take that ol' big red dog there, he'll git up on the floor on his hind feet and dance, when I'm playin'!"

A tough banjo-pickin' girl, widow of a moonshiner, Mabel is a latter-day Darlin' Corey, ready to fight for what she believes to be right. "I'm the first one ever took the needle treatments for being mad-dog bit, in Atlanta," she told us. "I don't never feel the 'fects of that, I'll tell you the truth, now, till somebody does something to me that they oughtn't to do, and git me *mad!* But when I do git mad, I'm mad. I'll fight a man quick as I will a woman." She recalled an incident that had occurred several years ago: "Man pulled up there in the yard [with] three girls, just what you might say nekkid, and he pushed them three girls out of that car, out there, and he drove off, left them girls. And them girls come on in the house, cryin'. . . . I didn't set down to sewin' machine that day, but I took some of my clothes the next day, and I made all three of them girls some clothes. . . . And I ain't never found out who that man was that brought them in the yard and pushed 'em out."

A few days later the father of one of the girls came to get them, early in the morning. "He come on after them girls, and he was gonna put them girls in the car . . . after he threatened to beat his girl up, and I just told him, 'John [not his name], now you ain't gonna do that on my premises, that girl ain't done nothin'. I wish you would leave 'em alone, so they can get some clothes on and get fixed up, like they ought to.' 'Oh, I'm gonna get them!' They's all settin' inside on the bed, scared to death, cuddled up like little kittens. I said, 'John, bein' as how you got a girl in there, you can take them, but,' I said, 'don't you put your hand on nary one of them girls.' He said, 'Mabel, you don't mean you'll fight me, do ye?' I said, 'Yeah, if you lay your gun down, I'll hide mine where I can't find it, John, and I'll fight you!' He was a gre't big man. He said, 'I'll just have to wait till some other time, I guess.' I said, 'I'd appreciate it if you was to.' " Then Mabel let him take the girls away. Mabel says the girls are now married and doing well. "You couldn't of stood there and these girls like you might say nekkid," she added. "You'd of took them girls in if you'd been like me."

I Wish I Was a Mole
in the Ground

Sung by Chesley Chancey with five-string banjo and Joe Chancey with guitar, and with Ralph Chancey on mandolin; Boardtown Community, Cherry Log, Gilmer County, October 22, 1978. This song was recorded in the twenties by North Carolina singer Bascom Lamar Lunsford (reissue on Folkways LP FA 2040), and later on a ten-inch Folkways LP, FP 40. Lunsford wrote that his version, learned from a schoolmate of his in Haywood County, North Carolina, is "a fine type of indigenous American banjo song extant in the Great Smoky and Blue Ridge Mountain region . . . and has numerous unrelated stanzas born out of the hilarity of mountain banjo picking." The Chancey Brothers' fine version, with two-part harmony, is more regular in rhythm than Lunsford's halting melody. See Brown, 2:215 (North Carolina); and Dunson, p. 84 (Lunsford's version); Lunsford, pp. 10–11.

1. Lord I wish I was a mole in the ground,
   Lord I wish I was a mole in the ground;
   A mole in the ground, turn this wide
       world around,
   Lord I wish I was a mole in the ground.

2. Lord I wish I was a lizard in the spring,
   Lord I wish I was a lizard in the spring;
   'f I's a lizard in the spring, I could hear
       my darlin' sing,
   Lord I wish I was a lizard in the spring.

3. I'll take you to your mamma next
       payday,
   I'll take you to your mamma next
       payday.
   I'll take you to the door and I'll kiss you
       no more,
   I'll take you to your mamma next
       payday.

4. Lord I wish I was a mole in the ground,
   Lord I wish I was a mole in the ground.
   'f I's a mole in the ground, turn this
       wide world around,
   Lord I wish I was a mole in the ground.

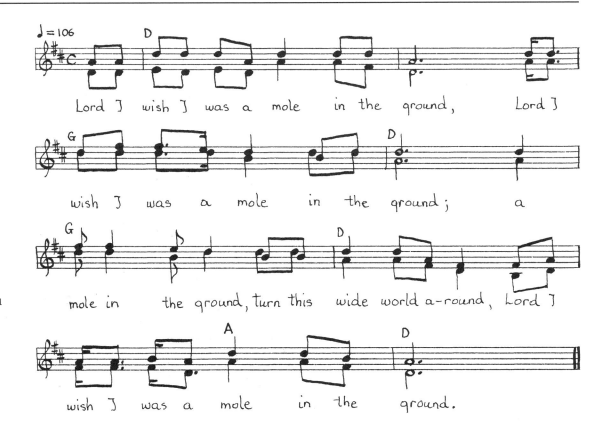

Shoot the Turkey Buzzard

Sung by Joe Chancey with guitar, Chesley Chancey with five-string banjo; Boardtown Community, Cherry Log, Gilmer County, November 11, 1979. The Chancey Brothers sing and play the best version we have heard of this mountain fiddle and banjo song, which seems to have been widespread in the Georgia Blue Ridge.

Shoot that turkey buzzard, shoot that turkey buzzard,

shoot that turkey buzzard, flyin' round the mountain.

Old hen cackle and the chickens flew, rooster swore that he'd go, too.

Shoot old Da-vy Dugger, shoot old Da-vy Dugger,

shoot old Da-vy Dugger, catch his wife an' hug 'er.

Shoot that tur-key buzzard, flyin' round the mountain.

Shoot that turkey buzzard, shoot that turkey buzzard,
Shoot that turkey buzzard, flyin' round the mountain.

Old hen cackle and the chickens flew,
Rooster swore that he'd go, too.

Shoot old Davy Dugger, shoot old Davy Dugger,
Shoot old Davy Dugger, catch his wife an' hug 'er.

Shoot that turkey buzzard, flyin' round the mountain.

Chesley Chancey. (Gilmer County, 1980.)

Mulberry Gap

Played by Chesley Chancey on five-string banjo; Boardtown Community, Cherry Log, Gilmer County, October 22, 1978. This is Chesley's banjo setting of a rare tune that was handed down as a fiddle piece in his family.

He tuned his banjo in one of the older mountain tunings, fCFCD (or, transposed, gDGDE), used by Gaither Carlton of Deep Gap, North Carolina, for "Ramblin' Hobo," and Hobart Smith of Saltville, Virginia, for "Last Chance."

Poor Ex-Soldier

Sung by Joe Chancey with guitar, Chesley Chancey with five-string banjo, Ralph Chancey with mandolin, and Don Chancey with bass fiddle, and fiddles by Gene Wiggins and Art Rosenbaum; Cherry Log, Gilmer County, *October 22, 1978. This plaint of the unappreciated veteran of World War I is set to the tune of "Knoxville Girl." It may derive from a Monroe Brothers recording of the thirties.*

1. I'm just a poor ex-soldier, a-broken
   down in doom;
   I fought all in the great World War for
   the old red, white, and blue.
   I left my parents and my girl, to France
   I did go,
   I fought out in the battlefield, in the
   howling sleet and snow.

2. I saw my buddy dying, and I saw him
   stop and groan,
   Although I haven't saw him in the battle
   all alone;
   Though we were friends when we left
   home, the hero of our land,
   But I came back and found no one that
   would lend a helping hand.

3. They called us wounded warriors, asking for shelter or bread,
   Although we fought in no man's land,
   and many poor boy is dead.
   So listen to my story and lend a helping
   hand—
   I'm a poor forgotten soldier boy who
   fought to save our land.

Five Hundred Miles

Sung by George Childers with five-string banjo; Jasper, Pickens County, June 23, 1980. This railroad song, in several of its myriad forms, has enjoyed wide currency in Georgia. In addition to the present song, we have recorded it as "Seventy-four" (see Jake Staggers's version in this collection, p. 79); as "Count the Days I'm Gone," from the Eller Brothers and Ross Brown (Flyright LP 546); as "The Train Song," from W. Guy Bruce; and as "Old Reuben" from Mabel Cawthorn. It was first recorded on commercial records by a Georgian, Fiddlin' John Carson, in 1924 (Okeh 40196, reissued on Rounder 1003), and later by Riley Puckett in 1930 (Paramount 3237). Hedy West learned "Five Hundred Miles" in north Georgia, and her concert performances led to *recordings by Peter, Paul, and Mary, which made it known nationwide; Hedy West sings it on Vanguard 9124. For by far the most extensive discussion and bibliography and discography of the Reuben's Train / Train 45 / Nine Hundred Miles songs, see Cohen, Long Steel Rail, pp. 503–17. George Childers occasionally calls this song "Railroad Bill," but it has nothing in common with the usual pieces so titled.*

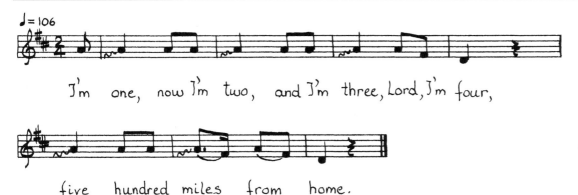

♩ = 106

I'm one, now I'm two, and I'm three, Lord, I'm four,

five hundred miles from home.

1. I'm one, now I'm two, and I'm three, Lord I'm four,
   I'm five hundred miles from home.

2. If this old train runs right, I'll be home tomorrow night,
   I'll sidetrack my engine and go home.

3. *Repeat 1.*

4. My shoes they are worn and my clothes they are torn;
   I can't see my mamma thisaway.

5. Got on the track, hear the rails a-crack,
   Hear the whistle blow a hundred miles.

6. *Repeat 1.*

7. Poor gal's on that track, and I hear the rails crack,
   I hear the whistle blow a hundred miles.

8. If this old train runs right I'll be home by Saturday night,
   I'll sidetrack my engine and go home.

Slippin' and A-Slidin'
with My New Shoes On

Sung by George Childers with five-string banjo; Jasper, Pickens County, June 20, 1980. A variant of this song of the rough and rowdy banjo picker was recorded by Uncle Dave Macon and the McGee Brothers; this recording was the source of the version most widely known today, Doc Watson's "Way Downtown." George learned the present piece from the old friend described above: "I guess that song is eighty years old. I've knowed [the man] since I was ten years old, and I'm sixty-four now. . . . He was playin' it, first time ever I seen him, one britches leg rolled up, drunk as he could be, on a $9.95 Sears Roebuck banjo, out in the rain." Somewhere along the line this song has become fused with "In the Pines."

1. Oh, I'm slippin' and a-slidin' with my
      new shoes on,
   Honey, where'd you stay last night?
   Well I stayed in the pines where the sun
      never shines,
   Shiver when the cold wind blows,
      Shiver when the cold wind blows.

2. Where were you one Saturday night,
   Where were you, my love?
   Layin' in the arms of another man,
   Nowhere to be my love.

3. *Repeat 1.*

"Five Hundred Miles." Harve Childers and His Brother George. Charcoal, 22" × 30", 1980.)

Goin' Down This Road
Feelin' Bad

Sung by George Childers with five-string banjo; Jasper, Pickens County, June 23, 1980. This may well be the folk song most widely known among southern folk musicians, white and black. We have recorded it from Gordon Tanner and Lawrence Eller; Jake Staggers *knows an early version where one line is repeated and the "ain't gonna be treated thisaway" tag is not present. George says he heard it as a child, and the fourth verse in his text evokes the black origin of the song.*

1. Goin' down this road feelin' bad, Lord,
      Lord,
   Now I'm goin' down this road feelin' bad,
   Oh, I'm goin' down this road feelin' bad,
      Lord,
      Now I ain't gonna be treated thisaway.

2. I'm goin' if I never do come back,
      (three times)
      Now I ain't gonna be treated thisaway.

3. They feed me on corn bread and peas,
      (three times)
      Now I ain't gonna be treated thisaway.

4. Black gal, them eyes sure do shine,
      (three times)
      And I ain't a-gonna be treated thisaway.

5. I'm goin' down this road feelin' bad,
      (three times)
      And I ain't gonna be treated thisaway.

6. I'm goin' where the chilly winds don't
      blow, *(three times)*
      And I ain't gonna be treated thisaway.

Audience at Bluegrass Festival. (Lavonia, Franklin County, 1977.)

The Dying Girl

Sung by Mabel Cawthorn with five-string banjo; Carnesville, Franklin County, February 12, 1983. Usually called "The Dying Girl's Message," this is a rather literary nineteenth-century parlor piece that has entered oral tradition. Mabel Cawthorn's strong, poker-faced performance to a driving banjo accompaniment keeps the song safely removed from the maudlin, much as the Carter Family's unsentimental renditions of similar songs imbued them with feeling and dignity. Belden, p. 217, gives a version collected in Boone County, Missouri, in 1906, and says the song, first published in Wehman's Ballad Prints *(1885), may derive from Tennyson's "May Queen."*

Raise that window higher, mother_____, air_____ will ne-ver harm me now_____; let the breeze blow in up-on me____ _____, it____ will cool my fevered brow_____.

3. Mother, there is one, you know him,
   Though I cannot call his name.
   You remember how he sought me,
   How with loving words he came.

4. Life has many weary burdens,
   Sin goes down to the deepest woe.
   Wipe the teardrops from my forehead,
   They are death marks, well you know.

5. Take this ring from off my finger
   Where he placed it years ago,
   Give it to him as I told him
   That in dying I bestow.

6. Now my grave is ready, mother,
   Now my people round me stand.
   I'll be taken to some pleasant,
   To some pleasant churchyard land.

1. Raise the window higher, mother,
   Air will never harm me now;
   Let the breeze blow in upon me,
   It will cool my fevered brow.

2. Soon my troubles will be over,
   Soon will still this aching heart;
   But I have a dying message
   I must give before we part.

Leavin' Here, Don't Know Where I'm Goin'

NEAL PATTMAN, CLIFF SHEATS, WILLIE HILL, JOE RAKESTRAW: BLUESMEN AND SONGSTERS OF THE PIEDMONT

ARLIER IN THIS CENTURY the blues emerged as a distinct and enormously popular Afro-American musical form, defined and proliferated by the compositions of W. C. Handy and the recordings of innumerable blues men and women, rural and urban. The Piedmont of the South, stretching from Atlanta through South Carolina to Durham, North Carolina, produced its own style of blues, recorded commercially by such singer-guitarists as Blind Boy Fuller and Buddy Moss (see Bruce Bastin's *Crying for the Carolines* for a study of the Piedmont blues). We have met four very different blues musicians in the Athens area who play and sing the quick, raggy blues of the region. Beyond that they perform the various kinds of black secular music that blues developed from: country frolic songs, ballads about heroes like John Henry and bad "rounders" like Railroad Bill, ragtime pieces, and railroad songs. The blues served for expression of any feelings other than religious and were also used as dance music at country dances and fish fries, along with the older breakdowns and reels. Movement, emotion, and poetic statement flowed through all these types of folk song, and the four musicians whose stories and songs we give here might better be called by the old term "songsters" rather than the more limiting modern expression "bluesmen."

OF THESE MUSICIANS, Neal Pattman has certainly been the most visible and popular in Athens and beyond, and his voice and (mouth) harp have been heard at country parties and town nightclubs and at folk festivals from Atlanta to Washington. He has "blown" alone or with various blues guitarists, blues bands, and even rock bands. On stage he is a striking figure, a compact and powerfully built man in his middle fifties, wearing a brilliantly flowered silk shirt, projecting both intensity and confidence. He lost an arm in a childhood illness, but his mouth and one good hand can bend the notes of his harp as well as any two-handed player. His repertoire ranges from old-time country pieces like "Lost John" through blues of the thirties like "Keys to the Highway" to his own modern composition, "Lightnin' Twist," and the proudly aggressive modern blues by Muddy Waters, "I'm a Man."

Born in Madison County north of Athens, Neal was given his first harp one Christmas when he was a boy, by his father, who was dressed up as Santa Claus. His first teacher, he recalls, was a man in the community "come around, Oliver Holt, he could blow good, and I jus' kept on learnin' from that, and I kep' on goin'. . . . He played 'Lost John,' 'John Henry,' 'Mamma's Little Baby Loves Shortnin' Bread,' 'Sittin' on Top of the World.' "

Neal's regular job is in the kitchen of the Georgia Center on the University of Georgia campus, and we were talking on the back loading dock of the building. He told about playing at country dances as soon as he became proficient on the harp, and I asked him if he had ever thought there was something wrong in playing the blues.

"No. Love the blues."

"Why do you think some folks don't approve of the blues?"

"Lots of 'em don't know the blues."

"What *are* the blues?" I asked. "What would you say?"

"Well, I'd say the blues sometime start from when you feelin' bad, girlfriend, somethin', done lef' you, you get to feelin' sad, feelin' blue, you get to singin' the blues."

"What do you try to get out of your harp?"

"I try to get the spirit, be bes' part I can out of it. I jus' feel good blowin' it." Neal thought for a time that the old type of music was fading away, but "now it's bloomin' back out. . . . [People who hear him] like it better than the new music."

I asked him if he had ever thought, when he was young, that "there'd be white guys, wanting to play the blues."

He laughed. "No, I didn't, then. There been lots of 'em coming over here, I been teachin' 'em how to play—harp." He has also been teaching a younger black man his style of music, and he "plays with me every weekend.

"I'll be playin' tonight, for people to dance to, out in the country. Every weekend I play at people's houses. They enjoy it, ask me to come back."

A few months after this conversation, I began to hear reports that Neal had quit playing the blues. I dropped by to see him, and he confirmed that this was so. After forty-seven years of playing secular music, he had "changed over to gospel. I got baptized, got sanctified with the Holy Ghost at the Healing Temple Church," he explained. His love for music was undiminished, and he told me he intended to "go over and practice gospel numbers with Doc [Barnes]. I could get with a lot of their numbers, take turns on the harp and guitar."

CLIFF SHEATS was surrounded by a crowd of children and grandchildren as he sat at his old upright piano in his low-ceilinged living room. He played an old spiritual, then sang a blues to a primitive, rhythmic piano accompaniment. As he paused between numbers, I asked him when he got started.

"I started when I was five years old! I started with this song:

Diddle, diddle dumplin', my son John,
Went to bed with his stockings on,
One shoe off and one shoe on,
Diddle diddle dumplin', my son John.

The song was familiar enough, but the bouncing bluesy piano gave it a new energy. Cliff recalled, "I enjoyed that! My children, they's happy. I played "Diddle Diddle." I had an old-fashioned piano in the house, and wasn't nobody but Frankie and, no, not Frank, it was Roy C. and Fannie B. My oldest children, right here! Where they were

born. I been right here a long time, where they were born, they asked [for that song]—and Roy's dead, but Fannie she kep' on livin', she lives over here. Roy's dead. All my children built themselves a nice home, they had beautiful homes, I enjoyed them havin' beautiful homes, my home ain' beautiful, but I'm gonna get my home fixed up, this ol' ragged house, cost a lot to get it fixed."

Cliff swung into "Long-Legged Lula's Back in Town." When he had finished, he said, "Lula's a terrible woman! I can't get it all— there's a whole lot about Lula!"

"A piece like that, where did you learn that? Did someone teach it to you?"

"I was teached to it—I got a little taste of it, I kep' on till I added a little mo' to it."

"Do you remember who you learned it from?"

"My brother. My brother, he was a musician! He was playin' at the university before you were born." Fred Sheats and his dogs that would dance to his guitar playing are a legend in Athens, and Cliff continued, "My brother played, dogs would dance on the street. He'd play guitar, dogs dance on Broad Street. Lot of things used to happen on Broad Street. That was my brother done that. He was liked."

I asked Cliff if he played for dances and parties.

"I did then, when my brother was operatin' good. When he was playin', I'd catch him, and get along with that stuff. I's not no 'fessional player, I'd catch up with him and *hit* it. He was a musician, knew how to tune his guitar, and the piano, when it was flat, out of place, he knew how to do that. He had that much experience 'long with me. He was slow, sometimes, we'd play down at Charlie Williams's place, and I want to get goin'! And he's a little slow, tunin' up too much! And I wanted to hit it, and he's tunin' that guitar, and I wanted to hit it! And they loaded me up with whiskey, and the . . . ladies all over me. I was playin' somethin', I went home with seventy-five, eighty dollars. Heap of money, 'cause I was playin' somethin' that *suit* them folks, and I was enjoyin' myself, too. I had a girlfriend with me, I had a wife, the wife I got then, she wasn't jealous of me then. Pretty girls all over me then. I don't care nothin' about no girls now—don't affect me no kind of way now. I like to have fun. I was quite indifferent then."

Cliff turned back to the piano, and started playing and singing, "Stop That Woman from Ticklin' Me Under My Chin."

Willie Hill, Bluesman of East Athens. (Charcoal, 22" × 30", 1978. Collection of Béla Foltin, Jr.)

Doc Barnes had told me that Willie Hill was one of the few old-style players around Athens; when we met the slight, elderly man at his house in east Athens, I found it hard to believe that he would be able to get any music out of his bony and arthritic fingers; but when he got his electric guitar and tiny amplifier set up, he began to play an interesting assortment of bottleneck blues, finger-picking rags, and song accompaniments, and to sing in a fine old-fashioned style.

When I went to see him last, in the late winter of 1982, he had been in the hospital and had not been playing much, but he was happy to talk about his life and music. I asked him how he started playing.

"How I come out playin'? My first cousin learned me how to play what little I know. John Robert Everhart." This was around Maxeys, in Oglethorpe County. Everhart was seven or eight years older than Willie, and he died back in 1948. "I wish I coulda played like him! Played like I do, but hardly ever with a bottleneck."

Willie was fourteen when he started, and he learned on his cousin's guitar. It was to be some time before he owned his own. In 1928 he got one from Sears Roebuck, for $4.98.

I asked if his cousin played for frolics.

"Sho' did."

"What would they be like?"

"Be eight to the set, fo' men, fo' women, each have a partner, get in a ring, one dance thisaway, come back and swing his partner." These dances were in houses, and the host would give the guitar player all the barbecue he could eat, and maybe a dollar. "We had some swell times."

"You had to work pretty hard?"

"Oooohooo! Good Godamighty! Be so tired when you get home at night, go play at the sawmill, play on Saturday night . . . sometimes all night."

I asked if he would get up Sunday to go to church.

"Sometimes I would, sometimes I wouldn't."

Willie remembers the very day he moved to Athens from the country. "1934. Fifth Sunday in September, I'll never forget it." He worked at landscaping and digging basements, but found time to play music "around home," and with local musicians. "Minor Lumpkin, his brother played violin, he played guitar, at a place called the Rabbit Eye, on the Atlanta highway. George Lumpkin played violin.

Minor played guitar like I did. They'd play jus' any old thing we could make up and play. Listen at a record, play it *my* way." Willie remembers listening to records by Blind Boy Fuller, Buddy Moss, and Blind Lemon Jefferson.

I asked about the old recitations, the toasts.

"Used to tell 'em when I could drink. Dirty toasts! The one about the Titanic

The year eighteen and ninety-nine
The great Titanic sailin' out,
Called Shine from his station low,
Captain said this fixin' to overflow.

There was one about the 'game of skin.' I forget how that goes. There was a party here befo' Christmas, we asked the women to go in the other room, I was tellin' about the ol' Titanic then!" (See Abrahams, *Deep Down in the Jungle*.)

"One thing I never did, never had no fights. Get there when a fight started, I'd walk home. I never had no trouble out of any [white]. I stay in my place. They'd say things I wouldn't like, cuss me, goddam nigger, somethin' like that, I wouldn't say nothin'.''

"Wouldn't the law come down harder on a black person?"

"They would. They was scared to take up against them."

"That wasn't right."

"Not at all. . . . I don't know if things are better or not. I treat people like I want to be treated."

Willie knew Fred Sheats years ago. "If we'd be down to the store, he'd play, and I'd be dancin', buck dance, different breaks, 'kick the dog,' 'shine the shoes.' Some days I'd put in breaks, I'd see somebody else do it, didn't know whether it had a name or not. I'd try it till I'd learn it too." Of course Willie remembered Fred's dog: "Fred had a dog, dance all around, cute, and that dog had a lot of sense, too. He'd make good money, nickels, dimes, dog would dance. I'll never forget one Sunday, Fred went to church, or went off somewhere, and I was tryin' to make that dog dance, I couldn't make him dance for nothin'. I told Fred about it when he got back. I said, 'Fred, I was tryin' to get yo' dog to dance, he wouldn't.' I was sorry I told Fred. He whupped that dog, said I ruint him! I was sorry I told Fred about it." He laughed. "A little ol' fice-lookin' dog about that high. I don't remember what that dog's name was."

IT WOULD BE HARD TO OVERSTATE the importance of the black fiddler, and of the black string band, in the story of the music of the South. In pre-Emancipation days the slave fiddler played for dances at the big house, and for his own people back in the cabins; his music was a blend of British American fiddle tunes, black indigenous "reels," and minstrel-type hybrids. In the late nineteenth century black fiddlers and string bands continued to be prominent at community entertainments and had great influence on what we now consider to be typically white southern fiddle and ensemble styles. Black string bands lost ground to the developing popularity of the solo guitar and, in some localities, jug bands, early in the century, and very little of this kind of music was recorded commercially when the "race" recording industry flourished in the twenties and thirties.

Before World War I there was an active black string band, the three Rakestraw brothers, in the tiny Jackson County community of Arcade. Their repertoire included breakdowns, transitional pieces, and early blues. Their younger half brother absorbed all this and started playing it for himself in the twenties. Today, Joe Rakestraw is a dignified, cultivated man who can perform this now rare old music with authority and sensitivity on both fiddle and guitar.

The Rakestraws owned a cotton farm of a hundred acres when Joe was born in 1910; it had been handed down in the family from a grandfather who had been a bootmaker as a slave and eventually bought his freedom and land. Joe recalls that "music was the chief form of recreation. And . . . in my early days, my older brothers, it was three of them, people would come in buggies and pick them up to play for them, and they would be gone practically all night. They played for square dances and the old-time fiddlin' tunes is what they played. That was Anderson, Dupree, and Delmer. . . . They played bass violin, violin . . . and guitar. There was another man in the community . . . he played . . . five-string banjo. A small banjo, didn't have no ornament around the edge, just a banjo." Joe says that "that was the beginning of my music, just listening to them. And after they went off to the war, World War I. 'Course, they came back and played for a little while, before they left. . . . They went to Detroit, worked at Ford Motor Company, and done pretty good."

"Did they keep playing after they went up there?" I asked.

"One of them sent back and got the violin, that was my oldest brother, Anderson. I heard that he played for some church before he died. He died in Detroit."

"So then you started playing, you had younger brothers that started along with you?"

"I had brothers that came along with me. I had two sets. The older brothers were my half brothers." The boys "picked up what was available. The bass violin and guitar was there." The band patterned itself after the older brothers' group, but "it wasn't from instruction—memory was all the instruction we had."

Joe remembers one other musician in the community. "There was a fella, he was the chorister in the church choir. He could play a [mouth] harp to teach the choir to sing, because there wasn't nothin' like a organ, like they have today, or a piano. They just mostly sung without music, and they could *sing*, I'm gonna tell the truth. Sung the notes, do, mi, sol, do [shape notes], like that! Out of the book. They got the song out of that, then they sung the verses of the song."

The older brothers talked about learning from a man named Broke Rakestraw, who had mastered all the instruments, including piano, and also led a brass band; this band gave concerts in front of the one store and the railroad depot that constituted downtown Arcade.

After the younger Rakestraws had organized their string band, they played at country dances, and also at school commencements. "At school closin' time I was very busy goin' from one vicinity to another. They would have plays and speeches, and I was very popular, 'cause it wasn't but very few that made music." One of the pieces they played for commencement processions was, of all things, "Railroad Bill," because they discovered that their version had a good march tempo.

I asked if it had ever been a problem for him to play the worldly music that was scorned by the strict church members. He laughed. "Never was. I like church music and I like that. Never did make no difference with me, but I tried to conform with the community. I didn't play them on Sunday. Music was music, regardless of what kind it was. My father was very strict, yet and still, he liked both kinds, but I remember my brothers, if they were playin' church songs, he didn't want them to pat their foot, he'd come up behind them [and put his foot on theirs]." Joe never listened much to records. "I learned mostly from listenin' to the people—what the people was singing, is what I learned."

Cliff Sheats and His Family. (Athens, 1982.)

"What would you say if somebody asked you about the blues, what the blues express, what the blues are?"

"I would say," Joe answered, "that was the expression that the people had, of lettin' people know how they felt in them times, such as:

Farmer went to the merchant, ask for meat and meal,
He say, "Go way, po' farmer, you got boll weevils in yo' fiel'."

Such as them was the blues. Just a way of expressing their lonesome feelings, even with their love affairs, they would rhyme up something, express that. That's what I call the blues."

Another old song he sings with fiddle has the lines

Water round here tastes like turpentine,
Goin' where the water tastes like cherry wine,
Leavin' here, don't know where I'm goin'.

His older brothers sang that, and I asked Joe if it expressed their situation when they left for the North.

"Yeah. The biggest time of emigrating was from '21 till '30. People just losin' out. Boll weevils—actually changed the South. Cotton was king, but it didn't last. I can remember when on every hill, almost, was a gin-house, where people ginned cotton, and during the height of the cotton-picking season, the yard was full of wagons waitin' for their turn at the gin, but now it's dwindled down to just one in two counties. . . . I used to—I thought I was a man, then, maybe seventeen, eighteen years old, my dad'd get me in a car to go down the road, get a load of men to pick cotton, and I was the one to weigh the cotton, and I'd give him the figures, and he'd figure out what they'd get paid. I had to pick, too, but weighin' time, it'd give me a superiority," he laughed, "to weigh the cotton. [When the weevil hit], when people was accustomed to making twenty bales a year, maybe it cut 'em down to five or six, and the man they was rentin' from couldn't pay 'em anything, they was catchin' the train, or walkin', leavin' any way they could. I remember my dad lent people some money . . . and in a few years brought us down to where we was barely existin'. Come time for us to go off to school—in 1924 my dad bought a new Ford, purpose for us to come down to Athens and

come to school. We's just fourteen miles out of Athens. And somethin' happened, we didn't get to in 1924, and when '25 come around, we didn't make enough, so for the boys, we just had to forget it. My sister went to school. In Jackson County, there wasn't no high school for colored people in the whole county. The boys kep' workin' on the farm, the girl went to school." His sister became a schoolteacher.

Though he had little formal schooling, Joe considers himself to be "self-educated. I would say that my trip to Europe [in the army in World War II] was worth a college education. . . . Before I went in the army I had done quite a bit of readin', and the museums and things, I had read about them—so when I got over there, when the other soldiers would get a pass, go out chasin' women, I would go out chasin' down these places. And the cathedral there at Rome (St. Peter's) made the most lasting impression. They had in the ceiling of one room, looked like two angels, and as you walked by the door, looked like they would turn their head and follow you. Then, there were steps inside the dome goin' around and around to the top, you can look over the Vatican City. Such things as these, by me havin' just a minute inkling of what it was, made me, whenever I go into a city, that's what I would be looking for."

Joe had moved down to Athens, where he worked first as an insurance agent, then as a carpenter. He also played in a "little orchestra" that entertained at University of Georgia fraternities and sororities; he picked up some popular tunes during this time. He married an Athens woman, Alberta. Joe recalls that Athens thought of itself as "up to date! They didn't know much about this old-time music. [Alberta] was in a [civic] club, she's still a member. . . . It was her time to entertain, so I said, 'Let's carry them up home.' And my brothers were there, and we made music, and they enjoyed it. I think they enjoyed that better than the little modern orchestras they had around Athens, because that was somethin' new to them." The women still remember eating hot biscuits and sausages, and dancing.

Though Joe still owns the homeplace, it has changed. In some ways "it's better. Most all of them seem to have a little bit of education. . . . Also, they are not farming. They get in the car and drive four miles to the mill, a thread mill in Jefferson. The land is in timber, the house is not occupied and fallin' down. And it used to be a showplace between Athens and Jefferson. But it's not like that now."

In his back yard Joe Rakestraw has built an outbuilding in the old log construction style, to remind him of what things were like in the old times, out in the country. For him the old songs have a similar function: "They have a value, a meaning. If you could go back to the author and search his life, you would readily feel, see what he's tryin' to express."

Rakestraw's Dream

JOE RAKESTRAW looked at Howard Finster's painting of a disastrous storm, and it reminded him of a dream he had, in late 1981. He laughed at the memory of it.

"Alberta said she woke me up! She said I's eruuuuh [singing strange notes]. And she woke me up. And she asked me what I was doing. I said, I was singing! She said, you was a-makin' a mighty poor of it. I said, yes, I was singing. We had had a disaster. This is what I dreamed. I dreamed a storm come. Knockin' trees over, blowin' over, it done blew houses down, looked like mos' of them was leanin' mo' or less the same way. And people was, you know, was diggin' in, tryin' to get their possessions, sad, and cryin'. And I crossed the ditch. And this ditch was runnin' clear water. I looked up the stream, a *guitar* come floatin' down. And I picked the guitar up, and the people all around there looked like they had the expression—there's Rakestraw, he's gonna make music at a time like this! . . . But I didn't pay . . . any attention. I picked the guitar up and started to playin'. It felt kinda wet, the first time I went down. Then I started to singing. And I ain't never wrote a poem, I never composed a poem in my life. But I remember the words, I don't never have to rehearse them, just think about that dream, and I can say it:

Look what we have done to this old world,
Look what we have done to this old world,
You ought've been our brothers' keepers,
Never would have been so many weepers.

And about that time, everybody looked around at me singin'. Bein' the ham I was, I got louder. I said:

This water is to cleanse your soul,
Do that, and then go try another role,
Just look what we have done to this old world.

And then I said:

Reach out, give somebody a hand,
And let it stretch all over this land,
What you do, do the best you can,
It will make you a better man,
'Cause this what we done to this old world.

And Alberta woke me up. And I told her, you ought not to woke me up. I might have said somethin' worthwhile down the road."

John Henry

(Laws I1)

Sung by Neal Pattman with harmonica; Oglethorpe County, December 30, 1977. The exploits of John Henry, the black railroad worker who pitted his strength and twelve-pound hammer against the newly invented steam drill in the Big Bend Tunnel being constructed by the C & O in West Virginia in the early 1870s, have been celebrated in America's most important indigenous ballad. Two early book-length studies (Chappell's John Henry: A Folk-Lore Study [1933], and Guy B. Johnson's John Henry: Tracking Down a Negro Legend [1929]) provide research on what is known of John Henry—it is reasonably

John Henry was a little brown boy, sittin' on his mama's knee; says he picked up a hammer and a li'l piece of steel, "Drive this steel like a man," say, "Gonna drive this steel like a man."

likely that he lived and the contest did take place—and many examples of the John Henry ballad and work songs. Cohen, in Long Steel Rail *(1981), pp. 61–89, updates the study and gives the most complete bibliography and discography to date; he cites several scholars who suggest that the ballad may have been of* *white authorship, and that it clearly has many elements of classic British balladry. Certainly the song has been almost universally known by southern singers, black and white. The first commercial recording was by a white Georgian, Fiddlin' John Carson (Okeh 7004, 1924, text and tune in Cohen, p. 61). We have recorded it from Lawrence Eller (Flyright 546), Willie* *Hill, W. Guy Bruce, Joe Rakestraw, and others. Neal Pattman learned his version from Oliver Holt in Madison County. See also Courlander, p. 32; Cox I, p. 505; Henry, p. 321; Laws II, p. 246; Brown, 2:623; Jackson, p. 233; Lomax I, p. 258; Sandburg, p. 24; White, p. 260; Work, p. 242.*

1. John Henry was a little brown boy,
   Sittin' on his mamma's knee;
   Says he picked up a hammer and a li'l
      piece of steel,
   "Drive this steel like a man,"
      Say, "Gonna drive this steel like
      a man."

2. "Who gonna buy my slipper'?
   Who gonna cut my hair?
   Who gonna kiss my rosy cheeks," said,
   "I sho' don' need no man,
      I sho' don' need no man."

3. Say, "My mamma's gonna buy my
      slipper'
   Sister gonna cut my hair,
   Said, "My wife's gonna kiss my rosy
      cheeks,
   I sho' don' need no man,
      Sho' don' need no man."

4. John Henry tol' his captain,
   "Captain, if you go to town,
   Bring John Henry back a twelve-pound
      hammer,
   I'm gonna drive them steels on down,
      I'm gonna drive them steels on down."

5. John Henry tol' his captain,
   "A man ain' nothin' but a man,
   And befo' I let that steel gang down,
   I'm gonna die with my hammer in my
      han',
      I'm gonna die with my hammer in my
      han'."

6. John Henry went up on the mountain,
   Mountain caught on fire,
   Last word I heard po' John Henry say,
   Said, "A cool drink of water fo' I die,
      Cool drink of water fo' I die."

Neal Pattman. (Atlanta, 1977.)

Low-Down Blues

Sung by Neal Pattman with harp (harmonica); Winterville, Clarke County, December 30, 1977. This rambling blues monologue consists of sung phrases, punctuated by harp intervals; it is essentially a two-line blues, an older form than the later standard three-line, twelve-bar format, though it is one that was revived by the Chicago postwar blues bands. It needs no more introduction than Neal's spoken one on the tape: "This gonna be low-down blues, cut deep, way late in the wee, wee hour of the night—you know what I'm talkin' about."

1. Well, I tell all you workin' men, please
    take this advice from me;
   Save yo' money, buy you some good
    clothes, let these crooked women go.

2. Yeah, they'll meet you at the beer gar-
    den, they will drink up yo' last dime;
   Say a thing about it, "Whoa, boy, I'll
    see you some other time!"

Spoken:
Done got yo' money and gone, that's what
  they'll do you.

3. My baby blowed me away this mornin',
    here I didn't have nowhere to go.
   I just stood on the road and cried;
   Baby I didn't have no blues, baby I jus'
    couldn't be satisfied.

4. Yeah, you know it's a lonesome feeling,
    when you by yourself;
   Sometime, make you have fun feelin',
    y'all know what I'm talkin' about.

5. Say, I'm goin' to my baby's house jus'
    one more time,
   This is what I'm gonna tell her:
   "If I can't sleep on yo' bed, mamma,
    please let me sleep on the floor.
   If I don't treat you now better, you can
    call me all dirty names."

6. Babe, you got to have yo' dollar,
   I'm talkin' 'bout a dollar bill;
   Say, you know my money comin', baby,
   Oh, it ain't gonna be no yell.

7. Now when I have plenty money, baby,
    I have plenty friends,
   Now my money gone, baby,
   Woah, I'm standin' all alone.

"Long-Legged Lula's Back in Town." Cliff Sheats at the Piano. *(Charcoal, 22" × 30", 1983.)*

Long-Legged Lula's Back in Town

Sung by Cliff Sheats with piano; Athens, Clarke County, September 23, 1979. Descended from the pop song "Lulu's Back in Town," this song was reworked by Cliff and his late brother, the guitarist Fred Sheats, as Cliff describes above. The transcription of the first verse gives an idea of Cliff's approach, and the rest of the irregular text can be adapted, ad lib, to the basic melodic material.

♩ = 132

Oh Lu-la, oh Lu-la, oh Lu-

la, oh Lu-la, you know

long legged Lula thought she's back in town.

Oh Lula, oh Lula,
Oh Lula, oh Lula,
You know, long-legged Lula thought she's
   back in town!

Oh Lula had a fallin' out,
It was all about another man's wife,
Oh Lula, Lula,
Lula, my baby's back in town.

Oh Lula, Lula, tell me, Lula,
Please tell me Lula, where you stayed last
   night.

One leg up, one leg down,
One leg almost touchin' the ground,
I'm talkin' about Lula,
I'm talkin' about you, Lula,
You know, where you stayed last night.

Tell me Lula, tell me Lula,
Tell me, Lula, honey where you stayed last
   night.

Shake it east, shake it wes',
When I saw Lula, you shake it bes',
Oh Lula, oh Lula,
Tell me, pretty Lula, where you stayed las'
   night.

Oh Lula, Lula, nice and clean,
But ol' Lula was pretty mean,
Oh Lula, oh Lula,
Now tell me, Lula, oh!

She could shake it eas', shake it wes',
Down South, Lulu shake it bes',
Oh Lula, you know Lula,
You know, Lula was a sweet ol' thing.

Ooooo, ooooh, please tell me, Lula, where
   you stayed las' night.
Me'n Lula had a fallin' out, all about another
   man's wife,
Oh Lula, oh Lula, just tell me Lula, where
   you stayed las' night.

Railroad Bill I

(Laws I13)

Sung by Willie Hill with guitar; Athens, Clarke County, December 9, 1978. Willie Hill's masterful performance, with its delicate and halting melodic line, is an important addition to the recorded versions of this blues ballad, to use D. K. Wilgus's term, despite the fragmentary text. The song was based on the exploits of a black train robber by the name of Morris Slater, alias Railroad Bill, who eluded southern lawmen for several years before he was finally shot and killed in Alabama in 1897. See Cohen, Long Steel Rail, *pp.*

Railroad Bill, oughtta been killed, he never worked, an' he

ne—ver will, ridin' after Rail—road Bill. You better let ol' Rail—road

Bill a—lone, you better let ol' Railroad Bill a—lone.

122–31, for a lengthy discussion of the song and the man, including early reports that he had supernatural powers. The song has been well known in Georgia, and the first commercial recording was made at Gid Tanner and Riley Puckett's first recording session in New York in 1924; Gordon Tanner played and sang a version close to his father's and Riley's. Two months later Roba Stanley, also of Dacula, recorded the song for Okeh. Gordon, incidentally, sang the verse that Willie sings here, beginning "Went up on the mountain." Hobart Smith's influential finger-picking performance can be heard on Asch AA4. See also Laws II, p. 252; Lomax I, p. 118; Sandburg, p. 384; Scarborough, p. 251; and Work, p. 240.

1. Railroad Bill, oughtta been killed,
   He never worked, an' he never will,
   Ridin' after Railroad Bill.
      You better let ol' Railroad Bill alone,
      You better let ol' Railroad Bill alone.
   Railroad Bill, Railroad Bill, let ol'
      Railroad Bill alone.

2. Wen' up on the mountain, didn't know
      my route,
   Put me in coffee pot and blow me out
      the spout,
      Ridin' after Railroad Bill.

Jesse James

(Laws E1)

Sung by Willie Hill with guitar; Athens, Clarke County, December 8, 1978. This widely known ballad about the Missouri outlaw has been collected in the South from blacks as well as whites: see Odum and Johnson, p. 209, *and Sandburg, p. 274, for examples. Willie Hill learned this version in Oglethorpe County from his cousin John Robert Everhart, and though the text may be somewhat garbled, the spirit of the song, expressing great admiration*

Oh, Jesse James he was a man who traveled through the lan', pis-

tol and a sword by his side. Robert

Ford caught his eye, and he shot him on the sly, and he

laid po' Jesse James in his grave. Oh,

for the dashing bandit, is clear. The refrain, set to the melody of "John Brown's Body," seems to have enjoyed popularity in northeast Georgia. The white singer Jim Wills told us that the refrain was sung, "Southern people, ain't you sorry?" and explained that Jesse stole from the rich and gave to the poor, and helped the poor southern people. Bascom Lamar Lunsford of North Carolina sang a version beginning, "Down at the depot," and similar North Carolina versions are given in Brown, 2:557 (B and G). See also Belden, p. 401; Cox II, p. 215; Finger, p. 58; Henry, p. 321; Laws II, p. 170; Lomax II, p. 351 (Lunsford version); Riddle, p. 12.

1. Oh, Jesse James was a man who traveled
      through the lan',
   Pistol and a sword by his side.
   Robert Ford caught his eye, and he shot
      him on the sly,
   And he laid po' Jesse James in his grave.

   Chorus:
   Oh people, people, ain't you sorry,
   People, people, ain't you sorry,
   People, people, ain't you sorry,
   When they laid po' Jesse James in his grave?

2. Jesse James told his wife, "I been in
      trouble all my life,
   Some things I heard that was strange—
   My money or my wife, my pistol or my
      life,"
   So they laid old Jesse James in his grave.

3. Jesse James went to the depot, jus'
      some few days ago,
   Some things he never did befo':
   Fell upon his knees and delivered up
      the keys,
   Fo' the train he robbed, years ago.

I'm Goin' Back to Good Ol' Birmingham

Sung by Willie Hill with guitar; Athens, Clarke County, December 8, 1980. If we trace the development of the country blues on their meandering evolution from work songs, railroad songs, and dance pieces through transitional pieces like Joe Rakestraw's "Leavin' Here, Don't Know Where I'm Goin'," we come to an early blues like this. The floating verse, "Went to the depot . . ." made the journey from Rakestraw's fiddle song to Willie Hill's early blues, freer in form than the later twelve-bar blues, set to a bottleneck slide guitar accompaniment.

Refrain:
I'm goin' back to good old Birmingham.

1. I went to the depot, I looked up on the bo'd,   *(three times)*
It's good times here but it was better way up the road.

2. Asked the depot agent, What train must I ride?   *(three times)*
Makes no difference, jus' so you're satisfied.

3. I'm goin' back to Florida where it's warm,   *(three times)*
And lay there on the green grass and look up at the sun.

♩ = 80

I'm go-in' back to good old Bir-ming-ham.　I'm

go-in' back to good old Birmingham.　I

went to the depot _____,　I looked up on the bo'd　went

to the de-pot _____,　I looked up　on the　bo'd,

I went to the depot, I looked up　on the bo'd,

it's good times here but it　was better　way　up the road.

Railroad Bill II

(Laws I13)

Sung by Joe Rakestraw with guitar; Athens, Clarke County, February 11, 1979. This is sung to a finger-picking guitar style in which the melody is carried on the treble strings; the transcription in tablature and music notation gives a typical guitar interlude. Rakestraw's song is closer to "Right On, Desperado Bill" in Odum and Johnson, p. 202, than it is to the usual "Railroad Bill."

1. Railroad Bill was a desperado sport,
   Shot tin buttons off policeman's coat,
   And laid this body nowhere.

2. Railroad Bill, he's so mean,
   Stayed nowhere but down in New
   Orleans.

3. Some of the boys got sixty days, some
   got forty-nine,
   When they passed around the ball and
   chain, honey,
   I got mine.

Joe Rakestraw of Allenville. (Charcoal, 22" × 30", 1980.)

Leavin' Here, Don't Know Where I'm Goin'

Sung and played on fiddle by Joe Rakestraw; Athens, Clarke County, February 1980. Joe Rakestraw learned this song from his older brothers, who played it before World War I.

He sometimes varies the second, third, and fourth verses by repeating the first line and omitting the third. The song is part of an extensive family of lyric songs of the late nineteenth and early twentieth centuries, songs of uprooted wanderers, which continue to be popular in the forms of "Goin' Down This Road Feelin' Bad," (see George Childers's song in this collection, p. 176) and the instrumental "Lonesome Road Blues." Rake-

straw's older song is related to Samantha Bumgarner's "Georgia Blues" and "Worried Blues," Riley Puckett's "Kansas City Railroad," and the Memphis Jug Band's "K. C. Moan"; it is, however, a distinct and excellent song. The "Went to the depot" lines found their way into the later blues. See Cohen's Long Steel Rail, *pp. 406–12, for a discussion of this group of songs.*

1. Leavin' here, don't know where I'm goin',
   Lord, I'm leavin' here, don't know
        where I'm goin',
   I'm leavin' here, don't know where
        I'm goin'.

2. Went to the depot, looked up on the bo'd,
   Says, it's good times here, but better
        down the road,
   I'm leavin' here, don't know where I'm
        goin'.

3. The water round here tastes like tur-
        pentine,
   I'm goin' where the water tastes like
        cherry wine.
   I'm leavin' here, don't know where I'm
        goin'.

4. People round here treat me like a dirty
        dog,
   They make me sleep down in a holler
        log,
   Leavin' here, don't know where I'm
        goin'.

5. *Repeat 1.*

Joe Rakestraw. (Athens, 1980.)

Market Street Blues

Sung by Joe Rakestraw with guitar; Athens, Clarke County, May 7, 1983. Joe Rakestraw heard his oldest brother, Anderson, sing this early blues before World War I, and reconstructed the vocal and guitar parts from memory when he was learning to play in the 1920s. He explains that "the story of this song was about a man who carried his girlfriend down on Market Street, in New Orleans, to get their fortunes told, and some of the gipsies taken a liking to her and stole her away from him, and he was sad. . . . He said his feet was sore, but really his heart was sore." Later Joe went to New Orleans. "Market Street was like I pictured it; it made me realize what my brothers was trying to relate in their song. It had fortune tellers and a Spanish-like, gipsy air to it." This song is something of an abbreviated blues counterpart to the British ballad "The Gipsy Laddie" (Child, no. 200), where a lord's wife is enticed away by a gipsy—in American versions, Black-Jack David.

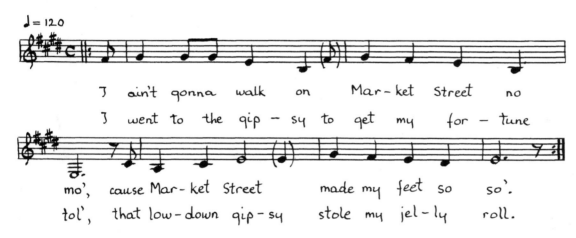

Refrain:
I ain't gonna walk on Market Street
    no mo',
'Cause Market Street made my feet
    so so'.

1. Went to the gipsy to get my
    fortune tol','
That low-down gipsy stole my jelly
    roll. *(Refrain)*

2. Sittin' here worried, a bucket won' hold
    my tears,
Sittin' here worried, a bucket won' hold
    my tears. *(Refrain)*

He Could Fiddle His Way Out of Jail

RAY KNIGHT OF DAHLONEGA

RAY KNIGHT, singer and guitar picker of the old gold-mining town of Dahlonega, is just turning forty; yet he is proud to classify himself an old-timer. He will ask you if you know what an old-timer is and toss back the answer: "In between an antique and a living legend." Full of jokes, stories, and songs, he can talk for hours about his "idol," the late L. D. Snipes, the peripatetic Georgia fiddler who could play the fiddle twenty-one different ways, and was "the only man I knew who could fiddle his way out of jail."

I had heard the story before but knew Ray was ready to tell it again. "Fiddle his way out of jail? You saw him?" I asked.

"I saw him."

"How did that go?"

"Went pretty big, Art. There's a big crowd in town."

"What do you mean fiddling his way out of jail? How did he get in jail in the first place?"

"Well," Ray answered, "he's drunk, in a few cases, y'know. He wrote the song 'Dawsonville Jail' with Shorty [Lunsford] over in Dawson County about thirty odd years ago. There was the high sheriff Glen Wallace raisin' chickens on the chicken farm." Snipes and Lunsford had been living out on the farm, working for Wallace. "These boys go uptown, get too much to drink, and Toy, the chief deputy, lived at the jail, put 'em in jail. They'd get that fiddle and guitar and you never seen such a crowd in front of the jailhouse, to see their idol. I ain't no different; I was one of his idols too, I idolized him."

Snipes had worked with such noted musicians as Gid Tanner and Earl Johnson, and the homemade tapes he left to his friends show him to have been a masterful player of the old-time long-bow Georgia fiddle style, and a first-rate singer. He was difficult to line up for commercial recording sessions, so his fame was spread through radio appearances, theater shows, and spontaneous visits to taverns, homes, and farmers' markets, where he was always ready with a quip and a tune. Ray was a boy when he first heard him, and remembers that later Snipes "come to our house in Gainesville, in 1960, and said that he would teach me the Riley Puckett style [on guitar] in a couple of years. He said he'd teach me the L. D. Snipes lick on the fiddle in three years, if we could be together. And, my God, I never see'd the man 't could equal him yet. Twenty-one different ways, can you imagine that? Trick fiddle—I've seen him take that thing over his head, play it behind his back, lay down on the floor, put it between his legs, take his shoes off, put the bow in his toes, play one." Ray added that, while others pick an easy tune like "Pop Goes the Weasel" for this kind of stunt, Snipes "picked one that was sure enough difficult, 'Johnny Get Your Gun.' He could also play a banjer, a guitar, the saw, trained every wife he had [to play back-up guitar]—he'd been married three or four times."

L. D. Snipes was an "excellent cabinet maker," according to Ray. "Another weird thing that he done, the way he set up a fiddle with a split bridge, I don't know what he done that for. Put a gut string on, tune it a fret below. And he'd clean and polish the fiddle with oxblood shoe polish."

"Now you say Snipes was a great entertainer."

"Lord, I went to visit him at Cumming, when he run the mill house. I said, 'L. D., I ain't hear'd none of that good fiddlin' since I was a kid, could you play me some?' Said, 'I'll play y' a tape, Stella's been in the hospital, and things have been rough around here, I been doin' the cookin', I dropped a biscuit on my toe, it's good for throwin' at the neighbors if you ain't gettin' along, but it ain't eatable.' I remember one time in '52, '53, when Unicoi was on [prisoners were building the Unicoi State Park in the mountains north of Helen]. He was servin' a sentence there, he stopped in a car, he was one of the trusties. He said, 'Stop the car.' I said, 'What is it, L. D.?' He said, 'Don't you see my mansion over there?' Looked like a shack about ready to fall in. He said, 'When I get my liberty I'm gonna rent it.' I said, 'What in the world would a man want with that?' He said, 'To raise lightnin' bugs.' He was colorful," Ray added.

"I'm like him, I improvise. I learned it from him. On stage, he'd make 'Old Joe Clark' come to life—'Let's go over the road, boys, and see old Joe.' You know, he was hard to tell about, you'd hear him do 'Old Joe Clark' this way today, and tomorrow it'd be another variation. He was a living actor on stage. He was unusual."

Ray Knight is part Cherokee Indian, though he says, "I fool lot of 'em, with the brown hair and blue eyes, think I ain't got it. Back in I and L. D. Snipes's day, when I had two sheets in the wind, and had a temper with it, they could tell it. When I had a grudge . . ." He grew up in an area called Knucklesville, where "it wasn't unusual for shootouts—we had a lot goin' on. We lived close to the Gainesville Midland Railroad, used to vibrate the houses." Ray was raised by a great-uncle who "was a good dancer—I learnt to buck-dance from that old man. He used to do that double-clutchin' [dance step] imitatin' the Gainesville Midland pickin' up steam. He had a pretty good ear, just countin' the licks:

GOin' to Augusta, GOin' to Augusta, GOin' to Augusta,
Clickity-click, pickin' up steam.

Ray's father, Homer Knight, had moved to Gainesville from Gwinnett County to work in the textile mills. Ray went on to tell some more of his family history: "My grandmother was Minnie Smith Knight. Her old man was part Cherokee Indian. Her mother was half Cherokee, her daddy was full Cherokee, Bill Williamson, died in a coal mine here in Dahlonega. . . . 'Course my daddy-in-law, Robert Jenkins, he goes back into the mining territory of Dahlonega. His father owned six hundred acres at one time, of gold mine. My great-uncle, his mother was a Davis, that goes back into the Indian ground there. Their uncle, Bill Davis, hit gold . . . at the edge of a peach orchard, and toted the pans a quarter of a mile to a water spout to pan it. . . . Bill was a fiddler, him and L. D. fiddled together. Uncle

Drew had some moonshine hid out over there. Back in them days it wasn't unusual to cut one another."

Although his stories of the past are peppered with shootouts, fights, and drinking, Ray always comes back to his first love, music. He has a fervent desire to keep old-time music alive. "I relate my music like I feel it," he says. He supports his family by working in a chair factory but plays in public whenever he can. For several years he performed with the Dahlonega Hillbillies, with Charlie Payne, an old mountaineer from Union County, on banjo, and Professor Gene Wiggins of North Georgia College on fiddle. More recently he formed a duo with another old-time banjo picker, Ed Teague from Rabun County. Ray plays guitar and spoons, does his great-uncle's double-clutch train step, and improvises jokes. "Comedy is an amazin' thing. I learned music from idolizin' Snipes, and I learned a lot of showmanship. We had some of the greatest entertainers here in Georgia." Among those active in recent years Ray will name Cotton Carrier and Harpo Kidwell, as well as Gordon Tanner. "You know, I idolize Gordon Tanner. I never met Gid Tanner, but I heard a lot of him from Snipes, he idolized him pretty much. When we had those Grass Roots programs in Atlanta, there was an old banjo picker [who was like] a lot of people [who] got to play with Gid Tanner, they thought of theirselves originally as Skillet Lickers. Gordon took the time to talk to that man, and that made that man's day." Ray feels that some country and bluegrass performers have been spoiled by success. "I know some people in bluegrass today—I won't name any names—if it hadn't been [for the influence of old-timers like Gordon Tanner] they wouldn't be drivin' Cadillacs, [they'd be] diggin' a ditch out there. That's the way I feel about it."

Ray Knight is a folk entertainer who refuses to modernize his music, true to the example of his "idols," first among them, Snipes. Ray remembers L. D. at a gathering in the fifties, dedicating a piece to "the old-timers like myself":

Do the highland fling, cut the pigeon wing—
To the funeral . . .

"In other words," Ray explained, "I think he was sayin' goodbye to me."

Several years later Ray "was huntin' L. D. for some show. I heard sketches that he might be gone." When it was confirmed that Snipes indeed had died, "I just squalled. I couldn't believe it."

Dawsonville Jail

Sung by Ray Knight with guitar, banjo by Ed Teague; Dahlonega, Lumpkin County, February 21, 1982. This is the song that L. D. Snipes and Clyde "Shorty" Lunsford

composed to commemorate their stay in the Dawson County jail in Dawsonville, in the fifties. Rather than use the well-worn "hard

Well, I got up Sair-day, walkin' 'round, comin' for to carry me home, and I

heard Glen say you're little too full, comin' for to carry me home.

times in jail" format, they hit upon the idea of using the spiritual "Swing Low, Sweet Chariot" as the framework for their tongue-in-cheek piece of mild protest and contrition; they had been working on the sheriff's chicken farm and were friends with his deputy, Toy, so the whole episode was not taken too seriously. Perhaps this would not have been the case if Snipes had not been such a well-liked and winning fiddler and singer who could attract appreciative crowds to the jail to hear him play.

1. Well, I got up Sa'rday, walkin' around,
    Comin' for to carry me home,
    And I heard Glen say you're a little too
        full,
    Comin' for to carry me home.

2. But I took off to town, Lord, anyhow,
    Comin' for to carry me home,
    Looked over Dawsonville and what did
        I see,
    Comin' for to carry me home,
    Glen and Toy they's comin' after me,
    Comin' for to carry me home.

3. Toy jumped out and kicked me in the
        seat and busted my whiskey,
    Comin' for to carry me home,
    I asked him kindly would he turn me
        loose, he said,
    "Heck no, L. D., you gonna sleep in
        a cell,"
    Comin' for to carry me home.

4. Then along come Shorty to go my bail,
    Comin' for to carry me home,
    They said, "Get in, 'cause you drunk,
        too,"
    Comin' for to carry me home.

5. First thing I saw when I got to jail,
    Comin' for to carry me home,
    Was a blame mess of peas they had the
        night before,
    Comin' for to carry me home.

6. The peas was green and the meat was
        fat,
    Comin' for to carry me home,
    Oh, my Lord, I can't stand that,
    Comin' for to carry me home.

7. When we got to the jailhouse we fell to
        our knees,
    Comin' for to carry me home,
    And we swore to our God we'd drink no
        more,
    Comin' for to carry me home.

8. And then on Monday here come Toy,
    Comin' for to carry me home,
    Said, "Glen's downstairs and he's
        lookin' for his boys,"
    Comin' for to carry me home,
    I heard the key rattle when he opened
        the door,
    Comin' for to carry me home.

9. My advice to you young men that take
        a little snort,
    Comin' for to carry me home,
    Before we take a drink we'd better look
        twice,
    Comin' for to carry me home.

Spoken:
You've heard of free labor and Prince Albert and workin' raisin' chickens for the sheriff? We'uz it!

Sung:
Comin' for to carry me home.

Sally Goodin

Sung by Ray Knight with spoons, banjo by Ed Teague; Dahlonega, Lumpkin County, February 21, 1982. Almost universally known as a fiddle tune in the South, the verses are not sung today as frequently as they were in earlier times. Some typical words are given in Ford, p. 64 and 419. Ray adapted his version from that of L. D. Snipes.

1. Had five dollars, now I've got none,
   Give it all away to see Sally Goodin.
   Hey, ho, old Sally Goodin,
   Hey, ho, old Sally Goodin.

2. Raspberry pie, blackberry puddin',
   Give it all away to kiss Sally Goodin.
   Hey, ho, old Sally Goodin,
   Hey, ho, old Sally Goodin.

The Crazy Mountain Boys. Roy Adams, Ed Teague, and Ray Knight at the Georgia Folklife Festival. (Atlanta, 1982.)

Do 'Round My Lindy

Sung by Ray Knight; Dahlonega, Lumpkin County, March 1982. Originally a minstrel-show song, this offshoot was recorded by the great Fannin County, Georgia, singer Fiddlin' John Carson (OK 45032, New York, 1925, reissued on Rounder 10003). Ray Knight learned it from L. D. Snipes, who got it directly from Carson. In his notes to the Rounder reissue, Mark Wilson points out that Lindy should be "fat" to rhyme (somewhat) with "lap," though Carson sings "hat!" Ray has her sitting on his "hand," but this is a nonsense song, after all. Ray has modified the melody as well.

Chorus:
Do 'round my Lindy, do 'round my Jane,
Gonna run away with a pretty little girl,
Coming home again.

1. My Lindy, she's handsome, my Lindy
   she's stout,
   Broke my new suspenders down and sat
   down on my hand. *(Chorus)*

2. Wisht I was an alligator, I'd go away to
   swim,
   Open up my mouth as wide as I could
   and scoot little Lindy in. *(Chorus)*

Do 'round my Lindy, do 'round my Jane, gonna run away with a pretty little girl, comin home a — gain.

Gold Strike

Sung by Ray Knight with guitar; Dahlonega, Lumpkin County, February 21, 1982. This original song by Ray Knight celebrates his town's colorful history as a gold-mining and coin-minting center, going back to the discovery of gold there over twenty years before the gold rush to California. Though mining is no longer a major activity in and around Dahlonega, it figures importantly in local lore and in the image the area projects to tourists. Ray's father-in-law, Robert Jenkins, was a gold miner, and his uncle, a fiddler named Carl Weaver, took part in the 1958 wagon-train expedition from Dahlonega to Atlanta to bring gold for the regilding of the state capitol's dome. Ray is annoyed when people assume that he based his song on Bill Monroe's instrumental "Gold Rush." His piece has a very different melody, and a catchy one; eventually it may enter into oral circulation as a regional folk song rather than an individualistic folklike composition.

Chorus:
There's gold in the hills, gold in the streams,
I'm goin' down to Dahlonega, honey lamb,
The great gold rush is on!

1. In 1828 Benjamin Parks stumped his toe,
    Lord, he looked down at his feet and saw a shiny nugget,
    And the great gold rush was on.
    (Chorus)

2. Just saw Tom and Luke and Robert Jenkins today,
    Heading over yonder to the Jenkins Holler,
    Just panning out them nuggets.
    (Chorus)

3. They got a mighty factory called the Consolidated Mill,
    With a hundred and twenty stamps,
    She stands proudly on that hill.
    (Chorus)

4. They got a mint in Dahlonega town,
    Makin' so much money, honey,
    Just minting out them coins.   *(Chorus)*

Written by Ray Knight.© 1983, Ray Knight.

Little Old Log Cabin in the Lane

Sung by Ray Knight with guitar; Dahlonega, Lumpkin County, February 21, 1982. This is the reworking by L. D. Snipes of the old favorite song, well known to Georgia's old-time musicians. Ray feels that Snipes intended this to be a fiddler's farewell tune. Originally written by the nineteenth-century composer Will B. Hays, it had many offshoots, such as the western homesteader's "Little Sod Shanty on My Claim." It became the song that launched the country-music recording industry when Fiddlin' John Carson recorded it and "The Old Hen Cackled, and the Rooster's Going to Crow" in Atlanta in June 1923 (Okeh 4890, reissued on Rounder 1003). The story has often been told: the Atlanta Okeh distributor and furniture dealer Polk C. Brockman brought the "local talent" John Carson, a native of Fannin County, to the attention of Okeh's Ralph Peer, who skeptically recorded the rough-hewn vocal and solo fiddle; the record's impressive sales in the area convinced Peer that there was a strong market for such music. (Fiddler Eck Robertson and guitarist Henry Whitter were already on wax, but it was unquestionably Carson's recording that marked the beginning of successful marketing of old-time or "hillbilly" music on records.) The song was later recorded by Riley Puckett and by Arthur Tanner, among others.*

1. I'm gettin' old and feeble, my sight is
      growing dim,
   I hang up the fiddle on the wall,
   How they did that highland fling, how
      they cut that pigeon wing,
   To the tune of the fiddle and the bow.

2. Old master's gone on, gone on before,
   And my lovin' kindred so dear,
   How they did that highland fling, how
      they cut that pigeon wing,
   In the good old, long, long ago,
      To the tune of the fiddle and the bow.

3. Now the only friend I've got is that little
      old dog of mine,
   In the little old log cabin in the lane,
   How they had those good old times,
      long, long ago
   To the tune of the fiddle and the bow.

Ray Knight with the Crazy Mountain Boys and Photograph of L. D. Snipes and Shorty Lunsford. (Charcoal, 22" × 30", 1983.)

I Got a Woman
on Sourwood Mountain

Sung by Ray Knight with guitar, five-string banjo by Ed Teague; Dahlonega, Lumpkin County, February 21, 1982. Like "Little Old Log Cabin in the Lane," this is an early north Georgia recording artist's reworking of an older song. The fiddler Earl Johnson took the old mountain hoedown "Sourwood Mountain," added some new couplets, and replaced the usual "hey-de-ing-dang diddle ally-day" sort of refrain with the "What in the world" line.

He recorded it in the late 1920s with his string band, the Clodhoppers (reissued on County 544, Georgia Fiddle Bands, volume 2). Ray—who learned it from L. D. Snipes, who in turn learned it from Johnson—performs it at a moderate pace, in contrast to the fast tempo of Johnson's original. For versions of the older "Sourwood Mountain," see Combs, p. 228; Fuson, p. 170; Lomax II, p. 76; Randolph, 3:417; Sandburg, p. 170; Sharp, 2:305.

Well, I got a woman on Sourwood Mountain, what in the world can I do?

had so many children I couldn't count 'em, what in the world can I do?

1. Well, I got a woman on Sourwood
   Mountain,
     What in the world can I do?
   Had so many children I couldn't
     count 'em,
     What in the world can I do?

2. Now the old grey goose she swim that
     river,
     What in the world can I do?
   She ran off, my gander with her,
     What in the world can I do?

3. I got a wife, I think she's crazy,
     What in the world can I do?
   She won't work and I'm too lazy,
     What in the world can I do?

4. I got a woman thinks she's a quaker,
     What in the world can I do?
   She won't work, I can't make her,
     What in the world can I do?

5. *Repeat 1.*

Man of Visions

PREACHER HOWARD FINSTER OF PENNVILLE

A LONG HORIZONTAL PAINTING in tractor enamel from Howard Finster's Paradise Garden shows a landscape of flood and devastation: trees uprooted, boats sinking, and cars overturned, their tiny human occupants reaching for help; and out of this rises a great head of Albert Einstein, labeled "Einstein painted from a postage stamp," his eyes plaintively turned up toward heaven. A crudely lettered poem reads:

The storm has swept my golden shores and took
My friends away. The youth has rose and know me not
I am a stranger on my way. My treasures lie beyond
This land my Gold is in the skye; I'll find my friends
    once again,
I'll meet them by and by.

Finster is projecting part of his own complicated view of the world through the great physicist; he has described his own brain as "beyond the light of sun." He calls himself "Man of Visions" and a stranger in this world. His garden extends over two acres behind his simple home to a church he recently bought on the next street, which is to become the "world's first Folk Art Church." In the garden Howard has laid out walkways, lagoons, and bridges; a thirty-foot-high tower of bicycle parts carries roses toward the sky; there are paintings of George Washington and of himself on the pavement, and there is a wire rabbit hutch in the shape of a locomotive, and hundreds of concrete walls, sculptures, and structures with pottery shards and mirror fragments set in them. A plywood angel flies above a house of mirrors, and another house is built of blue Phillips Milk of Magnesia bottles ("That house is unfinished," Howard

explains, "I run low on that blue glass, they're about played out, and people brings them to me"). There are paintings of Elvis Presley and Henry Ford as children, and overhead trellises with flowers, bean vines, and as close to "every man-made item" as Howard could find, clinging to them. Until about 1975 few people outside the Chattooga County community of Pennville had seen any of this; at that time a woman from Summerville alerted a TV news team, which, as Howard says, "started the publicity part of it." Now the fame of the preacher, singer, banjo picker, writer, and painter who created the garden has spread over the nation. "It's been sort of like a dream," Howard told us on one of our visits to the garden, in 1981. "If a man had told me ten years ago that I'd be invited to speak in an art class in these big universities, I wouldn't have b'lieved him, I'd a-laughed at him. And if someone had told me some day you'll go to California, it'll cost $491 to get you there and back, and you'll go to Colorado and you'll speak at a university, and see Pike's Peak, and go to California, speak at two universities, and you'll be cared for, you live in a museum when you're there, won't cost you nothin', and you'll come home with a little pick-up money, I wouldn't have believed that. I give God credit for all these things. That's what the garden is all about." The art students who meet Howard Finster on his lecture tours encounter a small man with slicked-back hair, wearing a rumpled double-breasted suit; his eyes squint and shine out of his lined face, and he pours out a seemingly endless stream of reminiscences, parables, songs, poems, and advice on how to make art out of such things as salmon cans. Visitors to the garden find him working or lying at repose on an insistently decorated walkway or under a bower, dressed in his paint-spattered "hobo" clothes, as if he were in some hobo jungle of the thirties. A sign facing the street announces, I TOOK THE PIECES YOU THREW AWAY AND PUT THEM TOGETHER BY NIGHT AND DAY. WASHED BY RAIN, DRIED BY SUN, A MILLION PIECES, ALL IN ONE.

In 1976 Howard began to produce paintings to be exhibited outside the garden, and he has numbered each one since that time; to date he has painted over two thousand and has had one-man shows in New York, Chicago, and San Francisco. His paintings were first exhibited in 1977 at the Atlanta Historical Society's comprehensive show of Georgia folk art, "Missing Pieces." He was invited to the gala opening. "I'd never been to no art show," he recalls. "They talked me into goin'. They wanted me to play the banjo—well, when I got down there I told them I'd rather make a little talk. . . . The floor announcer had a little stage, the governor's wife was there; when I first went in there they put me in this show room, I said, now I'm seein' my garden, and butterflies, and they was sellin' a book for five dollars with my work in it, and they had a life-size post card of me on the wall. My wife and daughter was surprised . . . and [Herbert] Hemphill of New York had some paintings he'd bought from me, and we just sorta felt at home. And when I went in there to make that talk, everybody was standin' around laughin', eatin', and drinkin', just a-roarin' there, the dome was like sixty feet. And I never had been in a buildin' that big before, and he come around and said, 'Mr. Finster, I don't b'lieve I'll ever get 'em quieted down so you can talk'; and I said, 'I know it, I realize.' Twenty or thirty minutes went on, he come back a second or third time, said, 'I can't get 'em to quieten down for you to talk.' I said, 'I know it.' And this Indian [folk artist, dressed like an Indian, Eddie] Martin, sittin' in a chair, I knelt down, played the French harp (harmonica) for him, and this feelin' come to me to holler just as loud as I could holler, like I did when I was fox huntin'. I 'cided to myself, they'd probably put me in jail . . . and I got to studyin' about it, I said what do I care to go to jail—I'd as soon be in jail as anywhere else if they want me there. And I decided to do it, and I just raised off my feet and I pointed right up to the center of that dome, and I hollered just as loud as I could holler, my wife said I hollered so loud my daughter jumped, kindly. It just shocked ever'body, and everything quieten down like a pin. Everybody's lookin' right at me, and I said, 'Folks, I'm gonna have to leave here, and I want to say a word or two 'fore I go.' Well I meant I's gonna have to go home, and they thought I's havin' a heart attack, I reckon, and they's a-waitin' for me to die, y'know, and I said, 'You folks come here, and one of the wonderfulest and beautifulest things, you brought out the hidden man in yourself,' I said, 'you've put your work out, dis-played yourself, the internal part of y'. . . . Just like Columbus when he discovered America, he discovered all our modern conveniences, it all had to come out of the earth. It was hidden in there.' I said, 'Y'all discovered it, and got it on dis-play here.' Well, I made my little talk, and got it over so quick, y'see, I seen I had the attention long enough to do what I's gonna do."

Though Howard Finster willingly accepts the designation "folk artist," there are some who question whether a self-taught visual artist without a body of material tradition and personally transmitted instruction and example should be so designated. But there is no doubt that the man does spring from the hardscrabble mountain folk culture of north Georgia and Alabama: his speech is that of a country preacher and evangelist, his thinking is steeped in the apocalyptic visions of frontier fundamentalism; he grew up singing fa-sol-la shape-note hymns out of the *Sacred Harp,* attending and leading brush-arbor revivals, picking the five-string banjo at Saturday-night parties, and learning to make do on what the land and his own ingenuity could provide. His folk-culture background defines part of the man and the artist; the rest is determined by the strange and usually lonely path he chose to take in his middle years.

Music is an essential part of Howard Finster's experience and expression. He can remember the old camp-meeting songs and play-party, banjo, and fiddle songs, the yodel and hobo songs of his youth. Sometimes he will sing these in a free-form medley, stringing ten or twenty song fragments together in the sung counterpart to some of his assemblages of found objects, clippings, photos, and artifacts. He has composed hundreds of his own songs that reflect his visions of other worlds, his notions of morality and conduct in this world, and comment on his own experiences.

He plays the piano, harmonica, and guitar, but his favorite instrument is the banjo, and he carries a nondescript old instrument along to art openings and to his talks on college campuses. He has been playing since he was "ten or fifteen. . . . I love a banjo," he says. "The old banjos were no good. My brother learned on a screen door.

Just patted his foot and drug his hand across the screen door, played music. . . . We used to have people come to our house when I was little, play fiddles and banjos, on Saturday nights. And play till late in the night. And when everybody was gone, I'd get an old banjo out, and I learned to play alone. I didn't want nobody around when I was trainin'." His first tune was "Cripple Creek":

Goin' up Cripple Creek, goin' in a run,
Goin' up Cripple Creek to get my gun.

I slipped into mamma's bed,
She put a shovel aside my head!

Of course he never used the banjo in his ministry. "Baptist people don't believe in banjers or music, you know. Some of them got to where they use a guitar, but back when I was a boy, if you take a banjer in a church, they run y' out." It was felt that the instrument in church would be "an abomination." I asked if he played at home after he became a preacher.

"Oh, I played the banjo at home. Some people claim they don't do nothin' at home they don't do at church, but they're just lyin', you know."

Born in Valley Head, Alabama, in 1915, Howard has farmed and been a small-engine and bicycle repairman as well as preacher and evangelist. A vision of a face he saw in a spot of paint on his finger as he was touching up a bicycle's paint was the sign of his calling to do "sacred art." He said, "As a retired minister, a feelin' come over me that there was still somethin' for me to do. And I always enjoyed talkin' and preachin', and seemed like God spoke to me, said you can preach all over the world and never get out of yo' yard. So I couldn't understand that . . . cause I knew how much it cost to get on TV . . . to publish a newspaper. And when a voice came to me said you could preach all over the world and stay inside your fence, that's exactly what I wanted to do, but didn't see no way. Well time went on, and these interviewers started comin' in here, takin' thousands of slides, and my message is goin' ever'where. They're makin' movies. They'll come in here and take all these sermons and poems, by the thousands, and they'll finally multiply into millions."

I asked Howard how the garden started.

"I had a garden at Trion, I done a little of it, and moved down here, well, this thing come a second time. I had a feelin' I had to build a garden, that the world started with a garden, and the world should end with a garden. . . . And I didn't have nothin' to build it out of 'cep' the county dump. I had a church, 'bout fifteen miles from here, had a beautiful hillside and big pine trees and a well—I wanted to build a garden on church property . . . for church work. I refused to get any backing from the church officials . . . never did bring it up before the church, they wasn't interested enough in it. . . . So I come home and sit down here in this swamp, lookin' around, and so I just give the church up, I went back to resign. I was goin' to build a garden, but I didn't know what the garden was about . . . and a thousand things come along: What fer? Who needs a garden? Where'll I get the money to build a garden? Ever'thing was against me from every pointer that comes in about buildin' a garden, except that Howard has to build a garden. When the first call come, in the late forties when I built this little museum, and the second call come when I come here. That's that same way when I was called to preach, I said, I cain't do it, I don't have a suit of clothes, I don't have an education, and I just told God plainly I couldn't do it—and I told Him put it off a year. I thought that was the last of it. And the second call I got really shook me. That's the way it is about the garden: the first time, I built a little old garden, maybe a few things in it. Well that give me an idea. When I come here and found this abandoned lake where doctors used to come here on rowboats and kill ducks, I found this woman begged me to buy it, it was a wasteland . . . for a thousand dollars. Two acres of it. . . . Well I got down here and found all these spring branches and thought it's the very place for a garden. The only thing was, it needed a lot of fillin' in, and they couldn't get in here with a bulldozer, and I couldn't hire one, at twelve dollars an hour, so I just took a wheelbarrow from under the basement, and started fillin' this in, just for exercise each day, and in about seven years I had it filled in where I could start on the garden. When I first started, I wasn't thinkin' about havin' an overhead trellis. I had no idea of even puttin' Bible verse in it. It's just like follerin' a blueprint they give you, one page at a time. That's the way this whole set-up is. If it all flashed on my mind [at once] it might of shot a fuse, you know! I got the garden started, and it come to me to build this trellis overhead. And I said, What for? For one thing, it'd camouflage it from the air, in case of a war. And another

Howard Finster in His Paradise Garden. (Pennville, 1980.)

thing, in the wintertime it takes care of your small seeds and things, from the frost." He showed us a rose bush, and explained: "The trunk of this rose bush, when you get anything to grow in the shade, it grows farther growin' up . . . twice as fast. Art, it runs up there, and when it gets up there, sunshine kisses, and it takes care of its roots, and you see how beautiful."

Howard wants others to use his garden, to share its solitude and its message. "What I call retirin' is you forget about the calendar and watch, put a fence around your garden, and when you're in there, you're free, you don't have no sheriff, no lawyer, no president, you don't have nobody. You're just loose, as far as your mind's concerned. Lock all your gates, start workin' on your flowers, you're in the Garden of Eden for a little while. I like other people to feel the same way when they're here. So I put high fences up, put bob wire over 'em, and when people come here they're isolated from the public, and if I had some guest rooms for 'em, they could live in the garden a night or two. And walk . . . through two acres in the moonlight. And I marry right smart of people, and they come here and pick a spot to get married. If I had some nice guest rooms—lot of 'em go to a motel for the first night, I said, if you want to come here and spend the night in Paradise Garden, on your honeymoon, it'd be a lot nicer than a motel, you could walk around in the roses of a night—I have pole lights in here. I told my wife, I don't need a garden this big, I's makin' it for the people, I feel dedicated to the people. I'd've like t've boated, and I like to fish, I like to hunt, but I don't do nothin' like that. I stay right here in my project that I'm in here for. Accordin' to the statistic, a man don't have just so long to do what he does in the world. See, there's three periods of Eternity—one of 'em from the time you're born till you die, that's the mornin'—second period is while you're restin' in the grave, third period's when you wake up to your destin'. . . . So that's the way it is when a man's in the first period of life from the cradle to the grave, he starts dyin' the moment he's born, dies daily till the last day that he's here. . . . Death is not such a tragedy—it's just a changeover."

In the back of the garden, Howard showed us a crumbling, weed-covered mound of concrete. "This tomb you see right here, this Egyptian tomb right here, there was a dental doctor here in Trion, sort of a collector, and he started to build his mansion, when he did, he tore down an old Civil War house, and when they moved this Civil War house, this girl had been shallowly buried under the floor. They took the planks up, and buried her under the house. Well he had an autopsy held, had the bones cleaned, and everything, and 'fore he died, he represented her to me, give her to me, y'know, in my custody. Her teeth was in her skull, she had a hole in the middle of her skull, like a black walnut, looked like a minnie ball had went through her, or a hammer, and they estimated her to be about seventeen years old, and there I was with that. So I just made this tomb, and laid her in there, her backbone and her head. I had a glass over where you could look in and see her teeth and all, and the ice in the winter's got bad, and that glass broke, people got to raisin' it up, and finally I just sealed it up in there, and even my weeds started growin' inside it with that glass . . . there. And I tried to get a minister here to come and hold a funeral over this woman. He said it'd been too long, it wouldn't be no use. Well I didn't feel thataway about it. Time to me—yesterday was when I seen my sister—two years old, is the way that seemed to me." He was talking about the first vision he had, at the age of three, when his dead sister appeared to him, standing on the highest of seven steps in the sky. "My whole life seems like just yesterday," he continued. "I don't look back through my life as a long routine. I look back through it just yesterday. And I'm lookin' for tomorrow, y'know. I have a feelin' I been here a day, and peradventure will be here another day. That's as fur as I get backwards or forwards except for visions. So I just went and had my own sermon and put her away alone. I didn't have nobody here. I didn't figure she'd had any funeral, 'cause she'd been killed right at the end of the Civil War. She might have been raped and killed. No tellin' what happened to the girl. No tellin' how good of a kid she was. So I felt like she deserved a buryin' and a funeral."

Howard does not care what will become of his garden after he goes on to another world. He feels he has been in another world and done a work there, and has been "reincarnated here for this particular purpose. I ain't never felt like an artist. I just felt like somebody the contractor's called to do a job."

As Howard sees it, "[my] brain is a gigantic warehouse of my supplies, and I keep all of my stories in there, and there's so many of them I've never found any tape long enough or any book big enough to hold it all. In fact, I can't even hold it all. I've got it on hundreds of cards, notes—my mind's just about full. When you ask me of my childhood, you see, I open up that cell and go into it like you would a warehouse like you go for parts. Well, you ask me about my ministry work, I shut up that door about the childhood and go into ministry work. I've learned to close doors. When you walk through there and get about ten or fifteen subjects on your mind, it's not good—if you go in a warehouse and get the carburetors mixed up with the fenders and the fenders mixed up with the mufflers, it's a mess. And a man has a lot to do with trainin' his own mind. That's the reason you go to college ten years to be a doctor, you have to go over that same thing until it's indelibly written on your brain cells. . . . That's the reason you have to play a banjo for five years to get to where you can just pick it up and play it any time you want to, it won't never leave you, 'cause you engravin' it so deep. When you write somethin' shaller, it just fades out. . . . Brain is a house of odds and ends—think, gouge, think, gouge, you think and scribble, and you just start puttin' them down like they just comin' off a computer." Howard is certain that you can tell when your brain is working under a "guilty feelin'," or when it is "a-workin' good and divinely inspired."

In 1979 Howard stopped in Virginia on his way to the opening of one of his exhibitions in New York. He took a long walk from his host's home, and went through the campus of a small women's college. He fell into talking with a group of students. They told him about their college, and he in turn told them about his art and his visions of other planets. With the young women he "felt like a young man again," and he lost track of the time. Eventually he was found by a "colored policeman," who said they had been searching everywhere for him. Howard saw the rest of the town from the police car. He made up a pithy little song from the experience, sung to the tune of the last two lines of "Bury Me Not on the Lone Prairie"; it expresses Howard's ironic view of the risks one takes at the edge of "normal" consciousness.

Just a-hanging around in old Virginia land,
All the pretty girls fell into my hand.

Leaned back on my thumb, looked up in their face,
And they asked me did I really come from space?

I have nothing to lose, everything to gain;
If I lose my mind I get a super brain.

In recent years Howard has felt in some ways closer to the community of artists than to many of the conservative people in his locality. Artists from over the country visit his garden, exchange ideas, works, and mementos with him, and correspond with him afterwards. In 1981 two of his paintings were to be included in an exhibition at the Smithsonian's National Museum of American Art of the work coming out of present-day Appalachia; when I was asked if I could provide a name for the show, I called Howard. In a few days I received in the mail three index cards with some ninety of his suggested titles, among them, "In the Valley of the Mountain Artist," "Artist Glow at the Big Show," "Selected Artists Around the Coffee Pot," "Mountain Artist Meets the Gang," "There's an Artist Behind Each Artical," "Painting in the Artist Blood," "The Artist of You Name It," "Do Artists Grow Old If They Keep Drawing Themselves Young," and "Artist Draw Citys Mountains and Hills, Calm and Rejoicing, Quiet and Still." A line from one of his songs, "More than Land or Sky," was finally chosen.

In 1980 Howard was asked to come out of retirement to be the pastor of a church at Silver Hill, a mountain community south of Summerville. This worked out for a time, but eventually he had a falling-out with some of the elders who did not understand his nonconformist views and objected to the publicity brought to their quiet country church by the folk-artist celebrity preacher. We attended what was to be his last service there and recorded his sermon, a blend of old-time preaching and his own strange and compelling visions of this and other worlds.

Howard Finster's Sermon
Silver Hill Baptist Church, September 21, 1980

The choir has just sung "Going Home."

AMEN, THANK Y'ALL VERY MUCH. Now at this time we're comin' to the message here—you'll find our message this mornin', to be found from Second Chronicles, the sixth chapter, and the eighteenth verse—this question was asked of a man in the days of old. He was talkin' to David, and he said . . . : "Now the Oh Lord God of Israel, let Thy Word be verified, which Thou has spoken unto Thy servant David." This David was a great man of God. David done some of the awfulest things in the world that ever find in the history—he done some of the *greatest* things ever find in the history of man. God spoke to David. . . . David pleased God in many ways. But one day David did a very bad thing. And David did a very cruel thing. The cruel thing that brought tears to his eyes. He said, "I have wet my couch with tears all night." And God was a-bringin' judgment to David's house for his sin. . . . Now the judgment came to his house, and that's what we today, young children and men and women all over this world, is to try to escape the judgment of God. And the best thing to do . . . is to stay out of the hands of the po-lice. Stay out of the hands of the patrol. Stay out of court. Stay out of all these things—now how do you do it, live by the laws of the land and participate in things that's right? Howard Finster never had a traffic ticket in his life. It ain't because I haven't made mistakes, it's because I haven't drove wild! It's because I've been careful. . . . Sometimes I'll get out, you know, and the boy's ridin' in the back of the truck, and I'll swerve around and sling 'im around and watch him laugh. Lord, if a patrolman was to catch me, they'd put me in the jailhouse, I guess. But somehow I've escaped and never had a traffic ticket, and I've drove thousands, tens of thousands of miles. . . .

So we need to avoid—the things comin'. He said here, David said here, David asked a question, "Will God in verity dwell with men on the earth?" There's a question mark right there. "Will God indeed dwell with men on earth?" That's not all that it was. He said right here . . . "Behold the heaven." H-e-a-v-e-n. He said, "Behold the heaven and the heaven and the heavens cannot contain thee, how much less unless the house which I have built to contain God," blessed friends. There is more than one heaven. He said, "Here, the heaven—h-e-a-v-e-n—of the heavens—h-e-a-v-e-n-s." There are heavens out there. Paul, the great apostle of Jesus, cried: "He spoke of the third heaven." And I believe in other heavens. David was saying . . . "Behold, no man can weigh God." No man can understand God. He is so great—of an engineer. Now in my visions God didn't only make this earth in six days, I believe He's been makin' earths since this one's here. I believe He'll be makin' earths and heavens after this one is gone, because I have visions of God! He said in the last days old men shall have visions, young men shall dream dreams— then it said one place: "Except they have a vision they will also perish." People got to have a vision! God spoke to the world through the Commandments! God spoke loud to the world through the blood of the Cross! God spoke to people through the Flood. God spoke to people through the Prophets, and in the last days of God's speakin' to people in the ministers of Vision! Hear me, my friends, in the heaven of the heavens. A lot of people, beloved friends, to . . . the people of this planet I'm a stranger. Because people don't understand me! And a lot of what I have to say, they don't understand, and I can't see why, that people can't understand a thing so plain as this is this mornin'. David, back yonder, before our latest scientists— David, back yonder, before the atomic energy—David back yonder before any of these things we've got—he knew that! Or he wouldn't have spoken about the "heaven of the heavens." More than one heaven. . . . In these latter days some people don't even believe in no heaven, just believe in a sky full of things and stars that borned themselves. Believe me, this earth and stars and the moon and all the planets in space, they're carefully blueprinted and made by a great Engineer. And it's a God of all gods. The Lord of Isaac, Abraham, Jacob—engineered this earth and all the other planets and heavens. . . .

Y'know, a man has to have a lot of patience to preach things and make it plain. And I believe one of the writers said, "It's so plain that even if a man be a wayfaring man, or a hobo, or a fool, he shouldn't miss heaven." Heaven's out there, not only heaven, but h-e-a-v-e-n-s, heavens out there. Now a lot of people don't believe in other planets. I've become a stranger in the world, and I'm traveling through! And I will believe what God shows me, I will preach it and I will tell it! If nobody on earth believes it but me, I'll be believin' it . . . when Jesus Christ comes back. And I know of three planets that God spoke of that have life on them right now. Jesus Christ come from a planet! He came from His Father! And His Father lives on a planet where there's eternal life. And while He was down here by the seashores talkin' to the disciples, He said He was goin' back to His Father! And He was on earth's planet . . . that meant He was on a planet and had come from a planet and was goin' back to a planet. And Jesus Christ . . . spoke about the third new heaven and new earth there would be created for the righteous, that would be the third planet we're liable to be on, I mean Howard Finster I think's goin' to be on that third one . . . the holy new city of God, where

Howard Finster Preaching, Silver Hill Baptist Church. (Chattooga County, 1980.)

mansions will be out of gold. Jesus spoke of His Father's house. He said, "In My Father's house there are many mansions." When I was in New York I went in the World Warehouse Building, and it's so high you look down and see the State Empire Building. And God's living room has mansions in it bigger than that. Because Jesus warned us not to be in trouble, Jesus knew that an atomic age would come. Jesus knew that atomic war would come. Jesus knew that perilous times would come, and pest'ence, and all these things, 'cause He told 'em while He's here they's comin'. Howard Finster and Art over there and many others have lived to see come to pass what Jesus said would come to pass here in this world. Oh my God, my friends today, can't you see through the stars, can't you see no higher than the enzone layer that's burnin' out and turnin' the sun in on us, can't you see no higher 'n that? Can't you see more 'n one world? God only made us in His image and His likeness. And mankind won't quit at no kind of creation. Mankind will make a billion and four hundred automobiles—he won't quit. Mankind will make a hundred thirty-two thousand ships, and he won't quit! Mankind will make a hundred thirty-two billion houses, he won't quit. He's only in God's image. . . . One thing is the trouble with people on this planet now, they don't even realize how great God is. With His little finger He can turn the mountains over, and they deny that He exists. Some say He's dead. Some say He's never been at all. . . . We ought to pray for people like that. . . . There's a passage in the Bible, says, "And he that think he knoweth all things, knoweth not anything yet which he ought to know." People know how a baby's formed, they know how a baby's borned, they can see the whole thing completed . . . and nobody understands it, because it's the mystery of God. And then they'll say, "Oh, God didn't do it, there's no God. I didn't come from God. I come from an old long-tailed monkey." I don't contradict that! I don't contradict people that think they come from monkeys, 'cause them people look to me like they did come from a monkey. I'd rather think, my friends, that the monkey come from the people! I am a stranger!

I believe when God made mankind, if there's any possible relation between man and animal, that man got so lazy and so no-count, they got to loafin' in the streets, in the jungles after the Garden of Eden, if there's any difference between animals and man, they got so sloppy and nasty, you know, they sort of drifted off into monkeys. I

don't even believe *that,* but I'd rather believe in that than believe that I come from a monkey. I've looked at myself over good in the mirror . . . and I can't ever even find where I've ever had a sign of a tail bein' on me. . . . Now they's people right around that believes people come from animals, I don't contradict 'em, I love 'em! If they're right, I want them to be sure and teach me when I'm wrong. That's what I told in Sunday school this mornin'. Sometimes we see things different in our Sunday school room. Sometimes we see things different. And I said, "Beloved friends, brothers, though we see things different, please don't have no hard feelin's." There's not even a star in heaven that don't differ. You can take a bushel of black-eyed peas, split every one of 'em open, take a picture of 'em, each one's different. People's different. But God's not different!

Some people justify themself—God's plan didn't work. But . . . we need to listen to the Engineer of earth's planet. You say, Mr. Finster, what you preachin' on planets this mornin', don't you know you ought to be preachin' on Jesus Christ? Jesus Christ is right now buildin' one or already got it done. He said, I want to prepare a place. . . . You say, preacher, He was talkin' to the disciples and apostles. That's exactly the way, Howard Finster's disciple and apostle. That's one reason, brother Art . . . that I got in to do art. That's one reason I like to do art and write letters, because writing— a message in writing stays there day and night, year after year, till Jesus comes! You get up on a TV and preach a message and a lot of people forget it before evening. You get up and teach a class, and they'll forget that. Get on the radio and they forget that—I've been on these places. And beloved brethren, when you write a message and get in a big museum, it's there today, it's there tomorrow, it's there till Jesus comes. It's preachin' night and day if there's anybody there to look at it. And I have three of 'em in New Mexico. One thousand seven hundred and sixty-four somewhere. . . .

David said . . . "And God in verity did dwell with men on earth, behold the heavens of the heavens cannot contain Him." How much less than the house that I've built? I'm buildin' a solar-heat room over there right now. I had a vision of it one night and I seen it in the dark, and I couldn't go to sleep. When I have a vision to do something, ain't but one thing will satisfy me, and that's to get my hammer and get up there and do what I have a vision of. I've got this thing planned where the sun rays . . . shine in the wintertime, built to the specification of the vision I saw. And I'm buildin' it so there's solar heat, and the Lord showed me how to make containers that collect heat, and put it out in the sunshine with rollers on it, the sun'll heat it all day, and you take that unit and roll it in the bathroom, anywhere, heats the house anywhere, be a kind of a headquarters of a heat unit. And of a daytime no matter how cold it is the sun's heatin' it in that room, and they call it solar energy. I'm workin' on that. And Jesus Christ wants preachers to do more 'n just preach the Gospel! He wants them to get out there and tell people how to survive in time of need, how to raise food and how to do things. I think that's one of my callings in the world to tell people how to get ready for an emergency in the time of atomic fallout! . . . Beloved friends, Howard Finster—I can preach with my shirt-tail out, like I have here right now, I don't care if I get through! I'd never have a tape long enough to tape what I'm gonna say. I've never had a visitor here yet who could stay as long as I want to preach—they have obligations! And it's almost twelve o'clock, and I'm quittin' right now! I want the choir director to come up here and direct a song.

Some Have Fathers
Over Yonder

Sung by Howard Finster with five-string banjo; Pennville Community, Summerville, Chattooga County, August 21, 1980. Howard introduces this song by saying that it is the first song he learned, and that "it's not in the book." By this he means that, unlike many of the religious songs he knows, this is not a song that was sung from any of the shape-note hymnals, such as the Original Sacred Harp, or any of the later seven-shape or round-note books; it is purely a word-of-mouth song, and he heard it sung by the old-timers at the revivals of his youngest days. Of a type born in the revival days early in the nineteenth century, it *is a camp-meeting song, emphasizing repetition—such songs were quickly picked up and sung with fervor by worshipers for whom the old lined-out hymns would have been too slow and who were unskilled at reading words or music. A minor modal version of this song, "I've Got a Mother Bound for Glory," was learned by Jean Ritchie as a girl in east Kentucky. See also Lomax, 1:572.*

1. Some have fathers over yonder,
   (three times)
   Over on the other shore.

2. Some bright day we'll go and see
   them, *(three times)*
   Over on the other shore.

3. Some have mothers over yonder,
   (three times)
   Over on the other shore.

4. Some bright day we'll go and see
   them, *(three times)*
   Over on the other shore.

5. Some have brothers over yonder,
   (three times)
   Over on the other shore.

6. Some bright day we'll go and see
   them, *(three times)*
   Over on the other shore.

7. Some have a Savior over yonder,
   (three times)
   Over on the other shore.

8. Some bright day we'll go and see
   Him, *(three times)*
   Over on the other shore.

9. That bright day may be tomorrow,
   (three times)
   Over on the other shore.

Howard Finster, Man of Visions. (Charcoal, 22" × 30", 1979.)

Five to My Five

Sung by Howard Finster with five-string banjo; Pennville Community, Summerville, Chattooga County, August 1, 1980. Howard remembers that the cotton pickers would have "house dances" on Saturday nights after a hard week's work: "We'd march up and down, goin' under one another's hands, and all that." This counting piece is a play-party song, and "they'd all sing it"; however, there were also "fiddles, guitars, and all." "Skip to My Lou" was also played at these dances. Howard sometimes sings the lines "bushel of wheat, bushel of rye, marching up the levee" to this tune, but he thinks it probably belongs in another song.

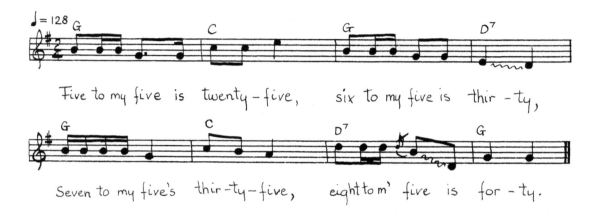

Five to my five is twenty-five, six to my five is thir-ty, Seven to my five's thir-ty-five, eight to m' five is for-ty.

1. Five to my five is twenty-five,
   Six to my five is thirty,
   Seven to my five's thirty-five,
   Eight to m' five is forty.

2. Nine to my five is forty-five,
   Ten to my five is fifty,
   Eleven to my five is fifty-five,
   Twelve to my five is sixty.

Little Mary Phagan

(Laws F20)

Sung by Howard Finster with five-string banjo; Pennville Community, Summerville, Chattooga County, August 1, 1980. This is a fragment of what was certainly the most widely sung ballad to come out of Georgia in this century. We have collected other incomplete versions of the song, suggesting that a vignette of poor Mary Phagan on her way to her murder at the pencil factory where she worked lingered in singers' memories after the rest of the narrative had faded away. The nearly seventy-year-old case made headlines in the March 8, 1982 Atlanta Constitution, and the article reported: "Leo Frank, a Jewish factory superintendent lynched near Marietta after his 1913 conviction for the murder of a fourteen-year-old girl in Atlanta, was innocent, according to an eighty-three-year-old man who was once Frank's office boy." Alonzo Mann, after keeping silent since the trial, swore that a sweeper, Jim Conley, not Frank, killed Mary Phagan in a $1.20 robbery, saying, "At last I am able to get this off my heart." There might have been information about Frank's innocence at the time, as Governor John Marshall Slaton commuted his death sentence, but the backlash of bigotry following this led to Frank's lynching and the end of Slaton's political career. This song was presumably written by Fiddlin' John Carson—at any rate he sold it as a song sheet with his name as author—and he was known to have sung it at the time of the commutation of Frank's sentence. Later his daughter Rosa Lee ("Moonshine Kate") recorded it for Okeh, though her record was released after one by Vernon Dalhart, who must have learned it from her test pressing. While the song was undeniably part of the moral climate of the day, it was very much in the tradition of many melodramatic nineteenth-century murder ballads and did not refer to Frank's religion—it presented a story of pathos. However, there is no hint of sympathy for the accused murderer, as there is, through the use of the first person, in such murder ballads as "Knoxville Girl," "Pretty Polly," and, in this collection, "Poor Ellen Smith." The tune used here is that of "The Roving Gambler." See Eddy, p. 252; Henry, p. 337; Killion, p. 260, and Laws II, p. 196.

1. Little Mary Phagan, she left her home
    one day,
   She went to the pencil fact'ry to get her
    weekly pay.

2. Left her home at seven, she kissed her
    mother goodbye,
   Not one time did the poor child think
    that she was going to die.

Just a Little Tack in the Shingle of Your Roof

Sung by Howard Finster with five-string banjo; Athens, Clarke County, November 1980. This is one of Howard's didactic pieces. He recalls having composed it several years ago *in a private interview, up in Allan Jabbour's office in the Library of Congress." It has the infectious lilt of some of Woody Guthrie's compositions, and it is inevitably requested by audiences at Howard's lecture-concerts. He has also recorded it on a privately issued 45-rpm record which he sells much as the broadside hawkers of earlier times sold their song sheets. "That song is reachin' around," Howard says.* *"That song is goin' over." The fragility and interdependence of the parts of a house are metaphors for the difficulties in sustaining marriage relationships these days. "I tell 'em in a jokin' way," Howard explains, "so many people separate, this [song] gets them back together. If my wife ever left me, maybe I could sing her back home!"*

Just a little tack in the shingle of your roof, just a little tack in the

shingle of your roof, I'm just a little tack in the shingle of your roof to

hold your house to - geth - er.

1. Just a little tack in the shingle of your
      roof, *(three times)*
   To hold your house together.

   Chorus:
   Come on back and stay with me,
   Come on back and let me see,
   Come on back and stay with me,
   Make your little house what it
      ought to be,
   Make your little house what it
      ought to be.

2. Just a little nail in the plank of your
      wall, *(three times)*
   To hold your house together. *(Chorus)*

3. Just a little plank in the wall of your
      house, *(three times)*
   To hold your house together. *(Chorus)*

4. Just a little rock in the pillar of your
      house, *(three times)*
   To hold your house together. *(Chorus)*

Written by Howard Finster. © 1983, Howard Finster.

"Some Have Fathers Over Yonder." Howard Finster. (Chattooga County, 1983.)

Bibliography

ABRAHAMS. Abrahams, Roger. *Deep Down in the Jungle*. Hatboro, Pa.: Folklore Associates, 1964.

ARNOLD. Arnold, Byron. *Folksongs of Alabama*. University: University of Alabama Press, 1950.

BASTIN. Bastin, Bruce. *Crying for the Carolines*. London: Studio Vista, 1971.

BELDEN. Belden, H. M. *Ballads and Songs Collected by the Missouri Folklore Society*. Columbia: University of Missouri Press, 1940.

BOTKIN. Botkin, B. A. *A Treasury of Southern Folklore*. New York: Crown Publishers, 1949.

BREWER. Brewer, G. Mason. *American Negro Folklore*. Chicago: Quadrangle Books, 1968.

BREWSTER. Brewster, Paul G. *Ballads and Songs of Indiana*. Bloomington: Indiana University Press, 1940.

BRONSON. Bronson, Bertrand. *The Traditional Tunes of the Child Ballads*. 4 vols. Princeton, N.J.: Princeton University Press, 1959.

BROWN. *North Carolina Folklore*. Vol. 2, *Folk Ballads from North Carolina,* and vol. 3, *Folk Songs from North Carolina*. Edited by H. M. Belden and A. P. Hudson. Durham, N.C.: Duke University Press, 1952.

CHAPPELL. Chappell, Louis W. *John Henry: A Folk-Lore Study*. Port Washington, N.Y.: Nennikat Press, 1933.

CHILD. Child, Francis James. *The English and Scottish Popular Ballads*. 5 vols. 1882–98. Reprint ed. New York: Dover Publications, 1965.

CHRISTESON. Christeson, R. P. *The Old-Time Fiddler's Repertoire*. Columbia: University of Missouri Press, 1973.

COHEN. Cohen, Norm. *Long Steel Rail: The Railroad in American Folk Song*. Urbana: University of Illinois Press, 1981.

COMBS. Combs, Josiah. *Folk-Songs of Southern United States*. Edited by K. K. Wildus. Austin: University of Texas Press, 1967.

COURLANDER. Courlander, Harold. *Negro Songs from Alabama*. New York: Oak Publications, 1960.

COX I. Cox, John Harrington. *Folk Songs of the South*. 1925. Reprint ed. Hatboro, Pa.: Folklore Associates, 1965.

COX II. ——. *Traditional Ballads and Folk-Songs Mainly from West Virginia*. 1939. Reprint ed. Philadelphia: American Folklore Society, 1964.

DAVIS I. Davis, Arthur Kyle. *Traditional Ballads of Virginia*. Cambridge, Mass.: Harvard University Press, 1929.

DAVIS II. ——. *More Traditional Ballads of Virginia*. Chapel Hill: University of North Carolina Press, 1960.

DUNSON. Dunson, Josh, and Ethel Raim. *Anthology of American Folk Music*. New York: Oak Publications, 1973.

EDDY. Eddy, Mary O. *Ballads and Songs of Ohio*. 1939. Reprint ed. Hatboro, Pa.: Folklore Associates, 1964.

FINGER. Finger, Charles. *Frontier Ballads*. New York: Doubleday, 1927.

FORD. Ford, Ira. *Traditional Music in America*. 1940. Reprint ed. Hatboro, Pa.: Folklore Associates, 1965.

FOXFIRE. Wigginton, Eliot, and Paul F. Gillespie, eds. *Foxfire*. 7 vols. Garden City, N.Y.: Doubleday, Anchor Press, 1972–83.

FUSON. Fuson, Harvey H. *Ballads of the Kentucky Highlands*. London: Mitre Press, 1931.

HENRY. Henry, Mellinger Edward. *Folk-Songs from the Southern Highlands*. New York: J. J. Augustin, 1938.

HURSTON. Hurston, Zora Neale. *Mules and Men*. Philadelphia: Lippincott, 1935.

JACKSON, B. Jackson, Bruce. *Wake Up, Dead Man: Afro-American Work Songs*. Cambridge, Mass.: Harvard University Press, 1972.

JACKSON, G. P., I. Jackson, George Pullen. *White Spirituals of the Southern Uplands*. 1933. Reprint ed. Hatboro, Pa.: Folklore Associates, 1964.

JACKSON, G. P., II. ——. *Spiritual Folk-Songs of Early America*. 1937. Reprint ed. New York: Dover Publications, 1964.

JOHNSON. Johnson, Guy B. *John Henry: Tracking Down a Negro Legend*. Chapel Hill: University of North Carolina Press, 1929.

JONES, B. Jones, Bessie, and Bess Lomax Hawes. *Step It Down: Games, Plays, Songs, and Stories from the Afro-American Heritage*. New York: Harper and Row, 1972.

JONES, L. Jones, Loyal. *Radio's Kentucky Mountain Boy: Bradley Kincaid*. Berea, Ky.: Appalachian Center, 1980.

KEPHART. Kephart, Horace. *Our Southern Highlanders*. New York: McMillan, 1922.

KILLION. Killion, Ronald, and Charles Waller. *A Treasury of Georgia Folklore*. Atlanta: Cherokee Publishers, 1972.

KORSON. Korson, George. *Pennsylvania Songs and Legends*. Philadelphia: University of Pennsylvania Press, 1949.

LAWS I. Laws, G. Malcolm. *American Balladry from British Broadsides*. Philadelphia: American Folklore Society, 1957.

LAWS II. ——. *Native American Balladry*. Philadelphia: American Folklore Society, 1950.

LOMAX I. Lomax, John, and Alan Lomax. *American Ballads and Folk Songs*. New York: Macmillan, 1934.

LOMAX II. ——. *Folk Song, U.S.A.* New York: Duell, Sloan, Pierce, 1947.

LOMAX III. Lomax, Alan. *The Folk Songs of North America*. New York: Doubleday and Company, 1960.

LUNSFORD. Lunsford, Bascom Lamar, and Lamar Stringfield. *Thirty and One Folksongs from the Southern Mountains*. New York: Carl Fischer, 1929.

MORRIS. Morris, Alton C. *Folksongs of Florida*. Gainesville: University of Florida Press, 1950.

NEWELL. Newell, William Wells. *Games and Songs of American Children*. 1903. Reprint ed. New York: Dover, 1963.

NLCR. Cohen, John, and Mike Seeger. *New Lost City Ramblers Song Book*. New York: Oak Publications, 1964.

ODUM AND JOHNSON. Odum, Howard W., and Guy B. Johnson. *The Negro and His Songs*. 1925. Reprint ed. Hatboro, Pa.: Folklore Associates, 1963.

O'NEILL. O'Neill, Francis. *Music of Ireland*. Chicago: Lyon and Healy, 1903.

OSH. *Original Sacred Harp*. 1844. Reprint ed. Sacred Harp, 1966.

PARRISH. Parrish, Lydia. *Slave Songs of the Georgia Sea Islands*. 1942. Reprint ed. Hatboro, Pa.: Folklore Associates, 1965.

PERDUE. Perdue, Charles L., Jr. *"Don't Let the Devil Out Talk You."* WPA Collection of Georgia Folklore and Ex-Slave Interviews, University of Georgia Libraries, Athens.

POUND. Pound, Louise. *American Ballads and Songs*. New York: Scribner's, 1922.

RANDOLPH. Randolph, Vance. *Ozark Folk Songs*. 4 vols. Columbia: University of Missouri Press, 1946–50.

RIDDLE. Riddle, Almeda. *A Singer and Her Songs*. Edited by Roger Abrahams. Baton Rouge: Louisiana State University Press, 1970.

RITCHIE. Ritchie, Jean. *Singing Family of the Cumberlands*. 1955. Reprint ed. New York: Geordie, 1980.

ROBERTS. Roberts, Leonard. *Snag Branch Settlers*. Austin: University of Texas Press, 1974.

SANDBURG. Sandburg, Carl. *The American Songbag*. New York: Harcourt, Brace, 1927.

SCARBOROUGH. Scarborough, Dorothy. *On the Trail of Negro Folk Songs*. 1925. Reprint ed. Hatboro, Pa.: Folklore Associates, 1963.

SCRUGGS. Scruggs, Earl. *Earl Scruggs and the Five-String Banjo*. New York: Peer International, 1968.

SHARP. Sharp, Cecil J. *English Folk Songs of the Southern Appalachians*. 2 vols. London: Oxford University Press, 1932.

SOC. *Social Harp*. 1855. Reprint ed. Athens: University of Georgia Press, 1974.

WHITE. White, Newman I. *American Negro Folk Songs*. Cambridge Mass.: Harvard University Press, 1928.

WORK. Work, John W. *American Negro Songs*. New York: Howell, Soskin, 1940.

A North Georgia Discography

THIS IS A LISTING OF LP records pertinent to the older forms of traditional music presented in this collection. It does not include most non-Georgia material cited in the headnotes. Many are reissues of sides from the wealth of material on early commercial 78s; others were produced from early or more recent field recordings, and from studio recordings of traditional or tradition-oriented artists. Newer forms of blues and gospel, as well as bluegrass and modern country music, have been excluded. Although most of the items are from north Georgia, a few recordings from elsewhere in the state and from neighboring regions have been included when they are of special interest. Some anthologies having one or more good north Georgia selections are listed. Although some of the records are no longer in print, many are available through mail outlets like Elderly Instruments Catalog, 1100 North Washington, P.O. Box 14210, Lansing, Michigan 48901.

Atlanta Blues 1933, John Edwards Memorial Foundation JEMF LP 106. Previously unissued recordings by Blind Willie McTell, Curley Weaver, and Buddy Moss.

Banjo Pickin' Girl: Women in Early Country Music, Rounder 1029. Has Moonshine Kate, and Roba Stanley of Dacula.

Blind Willie McTell, 1927–1935, Yazoo 1037. Reissue of commercial sides.

Blind Willie McTell, 1940, Melodeon MLP 7323. Noted bluesman and twelve-string-guitar player's Library of Congress recordings, with field notes by John A. Lomax.

Blind Willie McTell Last Session, Prestige 7809.

A Corn Licker Still in Georgia, by Gid Tanner and His Skillet Lickers, Voyager VRLP 303. Reissue of comedy skits with music.

Darby and Tarlton, Old-Timey LP 112. Reissue of influential white musicians with blues elements.

A Day in the Mountains, 1928, County 512. Reissue of comedy and music from old records, with Gid Tanner, Lowe Stokes, Bert Layne, and others.

Down Yonder: Old-Time String Band Music from Georgia, with Gordon Tanner, Smoky Joe Miller, and Uncle John Patterson, Folkways FTS 31089. Recorded and annotated by Art Rosenbaum.

Earl Johnson and His Clodhoppers: Red Hot Breakdown, County 543. Reissues of one of the best Georgia fiddle bands.

Early Country Music, Historical HLP 8002. Includes John Dilleshaw.

A Fiddlers' Convention in the Mountains of Tennessee, County 525. Two John Carson sides.

Fort Valley Blues, Flyright SDM 250. Library of Congress field recordings of central Georgia performers at the Fort Valley Festival, 1941–43. Edited by Tony Russell.

Georgia Blues Today, Flyright FFY 576. Excellent collection, with William Robertson, John Lee Ziegler, Jimmy Lee Williams, and James Davis. Recorded by George Mitchell, 1976–79.

Georgia Fiddle Bands, vol. 2, County 544. Important reissues, a sequel to County 514, with informative notes by Gene Wiggins.

Georgia Grassroots Music Festival, Georgia Folklore Society. Anthology of artists appearing at 1976 and 1977 festivals.

The Georgia Mountain Fair: Country Music in the Mountains, HS 0001. Recent recordings by Fiddling Howard Cunningham and others of Hiawassee.

Georgia Sea Islands, vols. 1 and 2, Prestige International 25001 and 25002. Features Bessie Jones and John Davis. Recorded and annotated by Alan Lomax.

Gid Tanner and His Skillet Lickers: Hear These New Southern Fiddle and Guitar Records, Rounder 10005.

Gid Tanner and His Skillet Lickers: The Kickapoo Medicine Show, Rounder 1023. Contrasts Skillet Lickers' traditional and popular aspects.

God's Great Love: Jim Southern and the Southern Sounds, Atteiram API-L-1596. Mountain gospel from Towns County with Ross Brown on fiddle.

Goin' to Georgia: Mountain Music—The Eller Brothers and Ross Brown, Flyright LP 546. Recorded and annotated by Art Rosenbaum.

Hedy West, Vanguard VRS-9124. Versions of "Shady Grove," "Sweet Jane," and "Lord Thomas," also found in the present collection, are sung by Hedy West as she learned them in Gilmer and Pickens counties.

Hell Broke Loose in Georgia, County 514. Reissue of string-band sides, with "Soldiers' Joy" from Skillet Lickers' 1934 session.

In Celebration of a Legacy: Traditional Music of the Chattahoochee River Valley, Columbus (Georgia) Museum of Arts and Sciences. Documentary recordings by George Mitchell of the black and white traditions.

Mountain Banjo Songs and Tunes, County 516. One Land Norris side.

Mountain Blues, County 511. A good Lowe Stokes side.

Mountain Fiddle Music, vol. 2, County 503. A good Earl Johnson cut.

Mountain Songs, County 504. Includes Lowe Stokes's "Wish I Stayed in the Wagon Yard."

North Georgia Mountains, Foxfire 101. New songs in old-time and gospel style.

The Old Hen Cackled and the Rooster's Going to Crow: Fiddlin' John Carson, Rounder 1003. Important reissue of recordings by pioneer Georgia fiddler and singer.

Old-Time Fiddle Classics, County 507. Includes a Lowe Stokes and Riley Puckett side, "Billy in the Low Ground."

Old-Time Fiddling Favorites: Jack Weeks, LP DSP 465-274. Private issue by modern fiddle champion from Dalton.

Old-Time Greats, vol. 1, *Riley Puckett,* Old Homestead OHCS 114.

Old Times and Hard Times: Hedy West, Folk-Legacy 32. A talented singer from north Georgia performs songs and ballads from local and family tradition.

Old-Time Southern Dance Music: The String Bands, vol. 2, Old-Timey LP 101. Includes Earl Johnson, Scottsdale String Band, Riley Puckett, The Three Stripped Gears.

Paramount Old-Time Tunes: A Sampler from the Paramount Label, JEMF 103. Has "Rabun Gap" by Chumbler, Coker, and Rice.

Riley Puckett, GNP 102. Reissues of the Skillet Lickers' great singer and guitar picker.

Riley Puckett: Waitin' for the Evening Mail, County 411. More classic sides by Puckett.

Sacred Harp Singing at the Old Country Church, Sacred Harp Publishing Company 103 (Box 185, Bremen, Georgia 30110). The important four-note shape-note singing tradition, edited by Hugh McGraw.

Sacred Harp Singing with Dinner on the Ground, Sacred Harp Publishing Company 104.

The Skillet Lickers: Old-Time Fiddle Tunes and Songs from North Georgia, vol. 2, County 507.

Smoky Joe Miller and His Georgia Pals, Newman Young and Lawrence Humphries, Sing Old American Heart Throbs, Folkways FTS 31093. 1982 recordings of sentimental favorites in Blue Sky Boys style.

Smoky Mountain Ballads, RCA LVP-507. Reissue anthology, including Skillet Licker and Tanner-Puckett sides.

The Social Harp: Early American Shape-Note Songs, Rounder 0094. Sacred and secular pieces from the 1855 northeast Georgia fa-sol-la book, sung in 1978 by Hugh McGraw and others, with notes by Dan Patterson.

Songs of the Railroad, Vetco LP 103. Has Skillet Lickers' "Casey Jones" and John Carson's "I'm Nine Hundred Miles from Home."

The Sound of Howard Finster. 1979 recordings, some with church choir, available from Howard Finster, Route 2, Box 155, Summerville, Georgia 30747.

Uncle John Patterson: Plains, Georgia, Rock, Arhoolie 5018. Banjo instrumentals and piano by important musician, produced and annotated 1976–77 by George Mitchell.

William Robertson: South Georgia Blues, Southland Records SLP-5. Great country blues, recorded in 1976 by George Mitchell.

Willie Guy Rainey, Southland Records SLP-7. Alabama-born elder bluesman, now of Atlanta.

Yonder Come Day: Note Singing and Spirituals from South Georgia, Front Porch Records 79-001. Recorded in the late 1970s by Carl Fleischauer, Dennis Coelho, and others.

Index of Titles and First Lines of Songs